OCCASIONAL PAPER 253

The Macroeconomics of Scaling Up Aid
Lessons from Recent Experience

Andrew Berg, Shekhar Aiyar, Mumtaz Hussain,
Shaun Roache, Tokhir Mirzoev, and Amber Mahone

INTERNATIONAL MONETARY FUND
Washington DC
2007

© 2007 International Monetary Fund

Production: IMF Multimedia Services Division
Cover design: Choon Lee
Typesetting: Bob Lunsford

Cataloging-in-Publication Data

The macroeconomics of scaling up aid : lessons from recent experience
/ Andrew Berg ... [et al.] — Washington, DC : International Monetary
Fund, 2007.

    p. cm.—(Occasional paper (International Monetary Fund) ; 253)

Includes bibliographical references.
ISBN 978-1-58906-591-8

    1. Absorptive capacity (Economics) — Africa — Case studies.
2. Government spending policy — Africa — Case studies.
3. Economic assistance — Africa — Case studies. I. Berg, Andrew.
II. International Monetary Fund. III. Series: Occasional paper
(International Monetary Fund) ; 253

HC800 .M337 2007

Price: US$30
(US$28 to full-time faculty members and
students at universities and colleges)

Please send orders to:
International Monetary Fund, Publication Services
700 19th Street, N.W., Washington, D.C. 20431, U.S.A.
Tel: (202) 623-7430 • Telefax: (202) 623-7201
E-mail: publications@imf.org
Internet: http://www/imf.org

Contents

Figures

The following conventions are used in this publication:

• In tables, a blank cell indicates "not applicable," ellipsis points (. . .) indicate "not available," and 0 or 0.0 indicates "zero" or "negligible." Minor discrepancies between sums of constituent figures and totals are due to rounding.

• An en dash (–) between years or months (for example, 2005–06 or January–June) indicates the years or months covered, including the beginning and ending years or months; a slash or virgule (/) between years or months (for example, 2005/06) indicates a fiscal or financial year, as does the abbreviation FY (for example, FY2006).

• "Billion" means a thousand million; "trillion" means a thousand billion.

• "Basis points" refer to hundredths of 1 percentage point (for example, 25 basis points are equivalent to ¼ of 1 percentage point).

As used in this publication, the term "country" does not in all cases refer to a territorial entity that is a state as understood by international law and practice. As used here, the term also covers some territorial entities that are not states but for which statistical data are maintained on a separate and independent basis.

Preface

The international community has recently focused on scaling up aid in support of the Millennium Development Goals. Using aid effectively is thus a key priority for economic policymakers in low-income countries. This paper analyzes key macroeconomic issues in managing large increases in aid. It develops an analytical framework that emphasizes the different roles of monetary and fiscal policy and draws lessons from the recent experiences of five countries: Ethiopia, Ghana, Mozambique, Tanzania, and Uganda. An earlier draft of this paper was prepared as background for the IMF Executive Board discussion of the 2005 review of program design of the Poverty Reduction and Growth Facility.

This paper was prepared by a staff team under the general guidance of Mark Allen, Director of the Policy Development and Review Department (PDR), and under the supervision of Mark Plant, Senior Advisor in PDR. The authors are grateful to numerous reviewers both within and outside the IMF for providing valuable input to the paper. Without implicating them in the analysis and views expressed in the paper, we would like to especially thank G. Russell Kincaid, Peter Heller, Leslie Lipschitz, Peter Isard, Arvind Subramanian, David Bevan, Christopher Adam, Catherine Pattillo, and participants at a Centre for Studies and Research in International Development seminar in Clermont-Ferrand, France, at an IMF Institute–sponsored conference in Maputo, and at the World Institute for Development Economics Research Conference in Helsinki. The authors are indebted to Emmanuel Hife for excellent research assistance, to Pille Snydstrup and Trevlyn Cubitt for providing outstanding administrative and organizational support, and to David Einhorn of the External Relations Department for editorial assistance and production of the publication.

The opinions expressed in this paper are solely those of its authors and do not necessarily reflect the views of the International Monetary Fund, its Executive Directors, or country authorities.

Executive Summary

Central to managing a surge in aid inflows is the coordination of fiscal policy with exchange rate and monetary policy. To highlight this interaction, the analytical framework in this paper focuses on two distinct but related concepts: absorption and spending. Absorption is defined as the widening of the current account deficit (excluding aid) due to incremental aid. It measures the extent to which aid engenders a real resource transfer through higher imports or through a reduction in the domestic resources devoted to producing exports. Spending is defined as the widening of the fiscal deficit (excluding aid) accompanying an increment in aid.

Spending depends on fiscal policy. For a given fiscal policy, absorption depends on exchange rate policy and monetary policy. If the government receives aid in kind, or uses aid directly to finance imports, spending and absorption are equivalent. More typically, the government sells aid dollars to the central bank, and uses the local counterpart currency to finance spending on domestic goods.

In this case, absorption depends on the response of the central bank, with foreign exchange sales influencing the exchange rate and interest rate policy shaping aggregate demand, including for imports. The combination of absorption and spending chosen by the authorities defines the macroeconomic response to aid.

To absorb and spend is the textbook response to aid— the government increases investment, and aid finances the resulting rise in net imports. Even if the government spending is on domestic goods, the aid allows the resulting higher aggregate demand and spending to spill over into net imports without creating a balance of payments problem. Some real exchange rate appreciation may be necessary to enable this reallocation of resources.

In a sample of five countries studied in this paper, however, a full absorb-and-spend response was found to be surprisingly rare. Typically, there was a reluctance to absorb—and face a consequent real appreciation—due, at least in part, to concerns about competitiveness.

To save incremental aid—that is, to neither absorb nor spend—may be a good way to build up international reserves from a precariously low level or to smooth volatile aid flows.

In two of the sample countries—Ethiopia and Ghana—absorption and spending were both very low. In Ethiopia, reserves were accumulated to bolster the exchange rate peg against the dollar. In Ghana, a buffer against extremely volatile aid inflows was built.

To absorb but not spend substitutes aid for domestic financing of the government deficit. Where the initial level of domestically-financed deficit spending is too high, this can help stabilize the economy. Alternatively, this approach to aid can also be used to reduce the level of public debt outstanding, crowding in the private sector. When debt reaches low levels, however, there are typically limits to the extent to which the financial system can effectively channel additional resources to the private sector. Further attempts to absorb without spending may amount to "pushing on a string," increasing excess liquidity or even causing capital outflows rather than increased domestic activity.

To spend and not absorb was a common but problematic response, often reflecting inadequate coordination of monetary and fiscal policies. This response is similar to a fiscal stimulus in the absence of aid. The aid goes to reserves, so the increase in government spending must be financed by printing money or by government borrowing from the domestic private sector. There is no real resource transfer, given the absence of an increase in net imports. In effect, this is ultimately a futile attempt to use the same aid dollar twice, once to build reserves and once to finance government expenditure. The cases reviewed in this paper suggest that trying to do so may reduce the effectiveness of aid.

In Mozambique, Tanzania, and Uganda, spending exceeded absorption, creating a surge in domestic liquidity. In Mozambique, this led to high inflation. In Uganda and (initially) Tanzania, treasury bill sales were used to contain inflationary pressure, leading to a rise in interest rates and the domestic debt burden.

Spending and not absorbing can, over time, lead to a spend-and-absorb outcome, if monetary and exchange rate policies are supportive. The fiscal stimulus potentially increases import demand and hence admits the possibility of greater absorption in a later period. This delayed absorption could then be financed by the accumulated aid. In order for this mechanism to operate, however, some real appreciation may be necessary, including through inflation if the exchange rate is pegged. Curtailing liquidity through treasury bill sterilization could lead to the least desirable result: no absorption of aid, coupled with a crowding out of the private sector.

The experience in these cases sheds little direct light on the medium-term implications of absorbing and spending aid, mostly because this strategy was not consistently pursued in the sample. There is no evidence of aid-related Dutch disease in the sample countries, with the real effective exchange rate remaining stable or depreciating. This is due in large part to the policy decision to accumulate reserves rather than fully absorb aid—a policy typically inspired by concerns about competitiveness and the level of the nominal exchange rate.

In general, targets in programs supported by the International Monetary Fund's Poverty Reduction and Growth Facility appear to be compatible with an absorb-and-spend response. But the consistency of monetary and exchange rate policy with fiscal policy needs greater attention in cases where the authorities deviate from this approach. Fiscal targets accommodate

surges in aid, and reserve targets are consistent with an (aid-financed) increase in the current account deficit. However, where countries are unwilling to follow this strategy—perhaps in order to guard competitiveness—more care needs to be taken to achieve an appropriate second-best outcome. In particular, when recommending treasury bill sterilization to reduce aid-related money growth, concerns about inflation must be balanced against the dangers of failing to absorb the aid and crowding out the private sector.

The key long-run strategic choice is whether to use the aid—by absorbing and spending—or not, in which case the aid should be neither absorbed nor spent. The latter choice, in the long run, is equivalent to forgoing aid, unlike the short run, where it can be used to smooth aid volatility. Thus, it is only appropriate when competitiveness concerns dominate the returns from productive aid-financed investment. In this case, attention should be focused on how, and how fast, to scale up aid so as to minimize competitiveness problems, such as by focusing on ways to use aid to increase productivity.

I Introduction

Andrew Berg, Shekhar Aiyar, and Mumtaz Hussain

Aid facilitates a transfer of resources from donor to recipient countries that enables the recipients to increase consumption and investment. It thus presents an opportunity to reduce poverty, increase the standard of living, and generate sustained growth. However, the effective use of increased aid also presents challenges. Good projects must be found and managed, and conditions for budgetary support must be agreed upon and implemented. The imperative to use the funds well can strain the administrative capacity of recipient governments. In addition, aid flows can weaken country ownership of economic and social policies.

Related to, but distinct from, these microeconomic and institutional issues are the macroeconomic challenges of managing aid. High levels of aid inflows can cause upward pressure on the real exchange rate, to the detriment of the exporting industries that may be critical to long-run growth. This is fundamentally rooted in the real effects of aid and hence is a microeconomic issue in nature. But in the short run, macroeconomic policies can determine how aid is absorbed in the domestic economy. Aid inflows can also create problems of fiscal management and debt sustainability, particularly when they are volatile and when they come in the form of debt.

Aid to low-income countries has increased somewhat over the past 10 years. In a few relatively well-performing low-income countries, aid inflows have increased substantially from what were already significant levels. Larger and more widespread increases in aid inflows are seen as critical to achieving the Millennium Development Goals (MDGs).[1] A scaling up of aid will amplify the macroeconomic policy challenges arising from the management of aid inflows. In its capacity as a key macroeconomic policy advisor, the International Monetary Fund (IMF) needs to help low-income countries confront these challenges squarely. Helping countries effectively manage the macroeconomic impact of increased aid inflows would be one of the IMF's main contributions toward the achievement of the MDGs.

This study attempts to identify and analyze some of the key macroeconomic issues that arise in connection with high levels of aid inflows. The focus is first on developing a framework that will aid economists—both from within and outside the IMF—in studying the policy questions that arise from the scaling up of aid. The framework is then applied to five countries that experienced large inflows in recent times. The questions addressed include the following:

- Do recipients of aid surges encounter macroeconomic absorptive capacity constraints?
- Is Dutch disease a real concern? That is, do aid surges lead to real exchange rate appreciations that are harmful to the export sector and hence economic growth?
- How should fiscal policy be adapted to aid surges?
- Are aid inflows inflationary, and what is the appropriate monetary and exchange rate policy response? Is there a role for sterilization?
- Have programs supported by the IMF's Poverty Reduction and Growth Facility (PRGF) adequately managed the macroeconomic impact of surges in aid inflows?

This study complements existing work in two ways. First, it develops a framework to examine nuts-and-bolts policy questions of direct relevance to the design of IMF-supported programs, and more generally, to macroeconomic policymakers. Second, it systematically analyzes cases in which countries experienced large aid surges, thereby complementing existing research, which is based mainly on cross-country and panel regressions.[2]

The case study approach has several advantages. Critical variables are hard to measure in a broad sample. The regression framework handles only with great difficulty the possibility of complex interactions, such

---

[1]A key recommendation of the UN Millennium Project Task Force is to increase official development assistance rapidly for at least a dozen or so fast-track countries in order to support the MDGs. World Bank and IMF (2005) also advocate a substantial increase in aid to low-income countries.

[2]An earlier version of this study was presented to the IMF Executive Board (IMF, 2005a). The analytical framework and empirical evidence in this earlier paper are supplemented here by the presentation of the five case studies that informed that paper. In addition, this study formalizes the analytical framework using a New Keynesian open economy model.

as those between terms-of-trade shocks, quality of policies, and the macroeconomic effects of aid inflows. Case studies allow the examination of countries that are not in a "steady state," but that also face a challenging and dynamic macroeconomic environment. Finally, only a few cases exist (generally those covered in this study) of countries that received macroeconomically significant increases in aid—several percentage points of GDP—in the context of reasonably strong policies and governance.

Of course, a case study approach carries its own limitations. The small sample size makes it more difficult to generalize the results to all aid recipients. In addition, it becomes hard to control quantitatively (as opposed to qualitatively) for exogenous changes in the economic environment during the period of increased aid inflows. Some of the countries studied here experienced various shocks—such as large terms-of-trade movements and natural disasters—that could independently affect macroeconomic outcomes. Finally, the study is limited to a short- to medium-term policy horizon of three to four years following the initial surge in aid. While this allows for examining in much greater detail the macroeconomic policy response—particularly monetary policy, which can change with high frequency—long-run effects may be hard to trace.

Surprising Results

Initial expectations were that this study would grapple with a particular set of issues that tend to dominate the macroeconomic literature on aid inflows: the real exchange rate and Dutch disease. That is, when aid surges by several percentage points of GDP over a number of years, this may be accompanied by real exchange rate appreciation and threaten the competitiveness of exports.

In fact, the case studies revealed no significant real appreciation accompanying the surge in aid in any of the sample countries; indeed, in the majority there was substantial real depreciation over the period. This may have been partly due to simultaneous terms-of-trade shocks in some countries, but in general the magnitude of the increase in aid dominated the terms-of-trade movements, suggesting that a puzzle remained.

An obvious possibility was that the aid led directly to increased imports, so that it placed no pressure on the real exchange rate. Another was that the aid led to supply responses that kept the price of nontraded goods from rising. More detailed analysis revealed an alternative explanation, rooted in the macroeconomic policy response, which in turn formed the basis for the analytical framework developed here. All the countries in the sample were reluctant to fully absorb the increments in aid through a corresponding rise in net imports. In other words, a considerable part of the aid

was used to build international reserves, rather than to transfer resources from donor to recipient country.

Why were central banks reluctant to sell the foreign exchange associated with aid inflows to accommodate a rise in net imports? The analysis here suggests that a primary concern was competitiveness, manifested in a reluctance to accept real appreciation of the exchange rate. Thus, the study finds no evidence of actual Dutch disease, but there is ample evidence that the fear of real exchange rate appreciation played an important part in the policy reaction to aid.

While the central banks held a substantial part of the aid in reserves, the fiscal authorities often increased expenditures on domestic goods and services, using the local currency obtained from selling the aid to the central bank. In effect, this is an attempt to use the same aid dollar twice, once to build reserves and once to finance government expenditure. Such a policy is very similar to a domestically-financed fiscal expansion (with the difference that reserves are now larger). It leads to identical outcomes, such as a surge in the money supply, and a consequent need to decide between inflation, on the one hand, and crowding out the private sector through the sale of treasury bills, on the other.

Thus, the country studies suggest that it is crucial for fiscal and monetary authorities to coordinate their responses to an aid surge. An uncoordinated response—typically arising because the fiscal authority wants to spend aid while the monetary authority wants to avoid exchange rate appreciation—can have unintended negative macroeconomic consequences. Hence, this study develops an analytical framework that emphasizes the interaction between the policy choices faced by fiscal and monetary authorities. This framework, in turn, helps make sense of the broad patterns observed in the individual country cases.

Work Program

With the recent focus on scaling up aid to low-income countries and various debt relief initiatives, the IMF has been deeply involved in examining the policy issues from both a theoretical and empirical perspective. Apart from this study, concurrent work has been undertaken in various area and functional departments. Rajan and Subramanian (2005a, 2005b) have conducted an extensive empirical investigation to identify the reasons why aid has historically had such a weak link with growth. They conclude that real appreciation of the exchange rate resulting from aid is likely to be a key impediment to sustained growth in recipient countries, thus emphasizing an issue that country authorities already take seriously, as documented in our case studies. Gupta, Powell, and Yang (2005) survey the extensive economic literature on the macroeconomic challenge of scaling up aid to Africa in order to provide practical guidance to policymakers. In addition to a discussion of monetary and fiscal policy, which draws on the framework presented here, they cover a number of critical issues only touched on here, including debt sustainability, governance, and the impact of aid on revenue performance. Heller (2005) discusses the impact of higher aid inflows on the competitiveness of aid recipients, the delivery of public services, the management of fiscal and monetary policy, behavioral incentives, and the growth rate of the economy.[3]

The absorb-and-spend framework developed in IMF (2005a) and in this paper has been used in a number of subsequent analyses, including Adam and others (2006), Chowdhury and McKinley (2006), Foster and Killick (2006), Mohanty and Turner (2006), and United Nations (2006). The model presented in Chapter VIII, which formalizes this framework, abstracts from several features that are key to the policy implications of scaled-up aid, such as private capital mobility and

sterilization through treasury bills. Ongoing research focuses on extending the model to capture the key trade-offs faced by fiscal and monetary authorities. The model could then be calibrated to a country in which the management of aid is a central macroeconomic challenge, in order to analyze more systematically the macroeconomic policy implications of aid volatility and scaling up. A next step would be to simplify the model into a practical tool for ongoing forecasting and policy analysis in aid-dependent, low-income countries.[4]

Preliminary work on this more complete model has already highlighted that private capital flows may respond to aid flows in various potentially important ways. This realization, and more broadly the growing importance of private capital flows even to some of the poorest countries, suggest that the role of private capital flows to low-income countries looks to be a fruitful topic for further analysis.

---

[3]There is, of course, ample research from outside the IMF. Isard and others (2006) bring together a wide-ranging set of recent papers on the macroeconomic management of aid.

[4]An example of such a tool is the model presented in Berg, Karam, and Laxton (2006), which has been used by IMF economists to analyze several developed and emerging market economies. Research is needed, however, to develop a similarly simple model appropriate to aid-dependent, low-income countries.

II Conceptual Framework and Its Application to Five Countries

Andrew Berg, Shekhar Aiyar, and Mumtaz Hussain

This chapter develops an analytical framework for examining policy responses to a surge in aid inflows, summarizes the evidence from a sample of five low-income countries, and seeks out general lessons that may be of relevance to other countries expecting scaled-up aid. The complete country studies are contained in subsequent chapters. The sample of countries focuses on strong performers in terms of institutions and economic policies. This permits the drawing of lessons relevant for situations in which, broadly speaking, policymaking is not dominated by macroeconomic disarray, misgovernance, or post-conflict reconstruction. The goal is to learn how to help those countries that are well-positioned, institutionally and in terms of the policy framework, to absorb large quantities of aid. An important number of such countries have emerged in the past decade or so, including in Africa (World Bank and IMF, 2005). The selected low-income countries satisfy two criteria: first, each (except Ethiopia) ranks relatively high on the World Bank's indicator of quality of economic institutions and policies—the Country Policy and Institutional Assessment (CPIA)—and second, each received large amounts of aid in the late 1990s and early 2000s, including a surge in aid inflows at some point over the period. The countries covered are Ethiopia, Ghana, Mozambique, Tanzania, and Uganda.[1]

Macroeconomic Framework for Analysis of Increases in Aid Inflows

The macroeconomic impact of aid depends critically on the policy response to aid. In particular, it is the interaction of fiscal policy with monetary and exchange rate policy that is important. In order to highlight this interaction, it is useful to introduce two related but distinct concepts: absorption and spending.

Absorption is defined in this study as the extent to which the non-aid current account deficit widens in response to an increase in aid inflows.[2] This measure captures the quantity of net imports financed by an increment in aid, which represents the real transfer of resources enabled by aid. Absorption captures both the direct and indirect increase in imports financed by aid, i.e., direct purchases of imports by the government, as well as second-round increases in net imports resulting from aid-driven increases in government or private expenditures. Absorption reflects the aggregate impact of the macroeconomic policy response to higher aid inflows, encompassing monetary, exchange rate, and fiscal policies.

Absorption can be defined and understood in terms of the balance of payments identity:

$$\text{Current account} + \text{Capital account} = \Delta\text{Reserves}.$$

Breaking the current and capital accounts into their aid and non-aid components and rearranging items yields the following identity:

$$\text{Aid inflows} = \Delta\text{Reserves} - (\text{Non-aid current account} + \text{Non-aid capital account}).[3]$$

Thus, an increase in aid can serve some combination of three purposes: an increase in the rate of reserve accumulation; an increase in non-aid capital outflows; and an increase in the non-aid current account deficit. The rate of absorption of an increase in aid is then defined as the change in the non-aid current account deficit as a share of the change in aid inflows:[4]

$$\text{Absorption} = \frac{\Delta(\text{Non-aid current account deficit})}{\Delta\text{Aid}}.$$

For a given fiscal policy, absorption is controlled by the central bank, through its decision about how much of the foreign exchange associated with aid to sell, and

---

[1]Appendix 2.1 discusses sample selection in more detail.

[2]This usage of absorption should not be confused with the related concept of "absorptive capacity," which, in addition, involves questions about the rate of return on investments financed by aid.

[3]The non-aid current account balance is the current account balance excluding official grants and interest on external public debt, while the non-aid capital account balance is the capital account net of aid-related capital flows, such as loan disbursements and amortization.

[4]With this definition, aid that finances capital outflows is not absorbed. This makes sense insofar as aid that flows back out of the country does not transfer real resources to the country.

through its interest rate policy, which influences the demand for private imports via aggregate demand.[5] The mechanism will depend on the exchange rate regime, but under any regime, the monetary authority can choose to accumulate reserves or to make them available for importers. In the extreme case where the central bank uses the full increment in aid to bolster international reserves and does not increase net sales of foreign exchange, none of the extra aid will be absorbed.

Spending is defined as the widening in the government fiscal deficit net of aid that accompanies an increment in aid:[6]

$$\text{Spending} = \frac{\Delta(G - T)}{\Delta\text{Aid}}.$$

Spending captures the extent to which the government uses aid to finance an increase in expenditures or a reduction in taxation. Even if the aid comes tied to particular expenditures, governments can choose whether or not to increase the overall fiscal deficit as aid increases. The aid-related increases in expenditures could be on imports or domestically-produced goods and services. Analyzing spending is important because of the natural focus on the budget as a policy variable, and also because of the importance of tensions between the fiscal policy response to aid and broader macroeconomic objectives with respect to the exchange rate and inflation. These definitions of absorption and spending take into account, by construction, the fungibility of aid.[7]

Absorption and spending are distinct, though related, concepts and policy choices.[8] If aid comes in kind,

or if the government spends aid dollars directly on imports, spending and absorption are equivalent, and there is no impact on macroeconomic variables like the exchange rate, price level, and interest rate.[9] This paper, however, concentrates on the more difficult and empirically relevant case where aid dollars are given to the government, which immediately sells them to the central bank. Subsequently, the government decides how much of the local currency counterpart to spend on domestic projects, while the central bank decides how much of the aid-related foreign exchange to sell on the market; and, in general, spending differs from absorption.[10]

Different combinations of absorption and spending define the policy response to a surge in aid inflows. The four basic combinations of absorption and spending are described below, together with a discussion of the macroeconomic implications of each. Box 2.1 provides a numerical example showing how the central bank and fiscal accounting work in each of these four cases.

Aid Absorbed and Spent

This is the situation assumed (explicitly or implicitly) in most discussions of the macroeconomic implications of aid inflows (Bevan, 2005). The government spends the aid increment and foreign exchange is sold by the central bank and absorbed by the economy via a widening of the current account deficit. The fiscal deficit is larger, but financed by higher aid. Spending and absorption of aid allows an increase in government spending by redeploying resources that had been devoted to the traded goods sector. In terms of the familiar national income identity $Y = C + I + G + (X - M)$, for a given output, a fall in $(X - M)$ allows a rise in G. The aid dollars fill the foreign exchange gap that would otherwise result.

Of course, output may not be fixed. Government expenditures may well increase output, both in the short run through the effects of increased spending on aggregate demand and in the long run through the increase in the capital stock. To the extent that output can be increased through a fiscal expansion without leading to a deterioration in the current account, however,

---

[5]Aid that is directly used to finance imports by the government (e.g., a grant in kind, a grant of foreign exchange that the government immediately uses to purchase imports, or aid that goes directly to nongovernmental organizations to finance imports) effectively bypasses the central bank and would lead directly to absorption. Technical assistance is also directly absorbed.

[6]The deficit net of aid is equal to total expenditures (G) less domestic revenue (T), and is financed by a combination of net aid (including both external loans and grants) and domestic financing: $G - T$ = Fiscal deficit net of aid = Net aid + Domestic financing.

[7]For example, if the government allocates a new grant to financing a domestic project that was earlier financed from different sources, this does not constitute an increase in spending, because the non-aid fiscal deficit remains unchanged. Similarly, if the foreign exchange associated with a particular grant is sold by the central bank, but overall net sales of foreign exchange do not increase, this does not constitute an increase in absorption, because no extra foreign exchange is available to finance an increase in net imports.

[8]The distinction between absorption and spending, in the terminology used in this paper, is one of the central issues associated with the "transfer problem" discussed in Keynes (1929). Keynes was concerned with Germany's problems in generating current account surpluses to pay reparations after World War I. He argued that for the fiscal authorities to accumulate the local currency counterpart to the required transfers was only part of the transfer problem—the other part being generating the net exports and therefore the required for-

eign exchange. See Milesi-Ferretti and Lane (2004) for a recent general discussion of the transfer problem and the real exchange rate.

[9]Strictly speaking, this is true only if the gifted or directly imported good is one for which there was no existing effective demand. If the good transferred was already demanded domestically, then increasing the good's supply would depress the price of tradables relative to nontradables, leading to real appreciation.

[10]Prati and Tressel (2005) find that monetary policy can control the timing of absorption. Aid could also go to the private sector directly. Here, too, if the private sector uses the dollars to directly finance imports, there is unlikely to be much macroeconomic impact. Where the private sector sells the dollars to the central bank and uses the local currency proceeds to finance domestic expenditures, similar issues will arise as in the case of government spending.

Box 2.1. Absorption, Spending, and Central Bank and Fiscal Accounting

In this numerical example, the government sells the aid dollars to the central bank and receives a local currency deposit at the central bank in return. Net international reserves (NIR) increase by 100 and net domestic assets (NDA) of the central bank fall by 100 (because government deposits with the central bank are a negative NDA item). This places the economy in the lower-right box of the matrix. What happens next depends on whether the central bank sells the foreign exchange and on whether the government increases the deficit. Each case is discussed in the main text. The example below assumes a floating exchange rate regime. With a peg, the accounting story would be the same, but the numbers and details would be different.

Central Bank and Fiscal Accounts: Example With Aid Inflow of 100

	Spend				Don't Spend			
Absorb	Central Bank Balance Sheet				Central Bank Balance Sheet			
	NIR	0	RM	0	NIR	0	RM	−100
	NDA	0			NDA	−100		
	Fiscal Accounts				Fiscal Accounts			
	External financing[1]	+100	Deficit	+100	External financing[1]	+100	Deficit	0
	Domestic financing[2]	0			Domestic financing[2]	−100		
Don't absorb	Central Bank Balance Sheet				Central Bank Balance Sheet			
	NIR	+100	RM	+100	NIR	+100	RM	0
	NDA	0			NDA	−100		
	Fiscal Accounts				Fiscal Accounts			
	External financing[1]	+100	Deficit	+100	External financing[1]	+100	Deficit	0
	Domestic financing[2]	0			Domestic financing[2]	−100		

Note: NIR = net international reserves; NDA = net domestic assets; RM = reserve money.
[1]Refers to external financing of the deficit.
[2]Refers to domestic financing of the deficit.

these increases in aggregate demand and investment could have been undertaken without the aid flows. Aid absorption refers to the use of aid to finance changes in the current account deficit associated with aid-related increases in aggregate demand, investment, and output in general.

Some real exchange rate appreciation may be necessary and indeed appropriate in response to a sustained higher level of aid. This is because some combination of exchange rate appreciation and (if there is excess capacity) increased aggregate demand is necessary to generate the increased net imports that aid allows.[11]

The degree of exchange rate appreciation required to absorb the aid will depend, in general, on the structural response of the economy and the extent to which aid directly finances imports. For example, real appreciation would be higher to the extent that aid inflows finance expenditures on nontradable goods rather than directly financing imports.[12] On the other hand, if higher incomes feed strongly into higher import demand, and if the supply of nontraded goods responds

---

[11]The real exchange rate is generally understood in this paper to refer to the relative price of nontraded to traded goods, as a conceptual matter. When it comes to measurement, however, data availability usually dictates the choice of real exchange rate concept.

The case studies here follow the common practice of measuring the real exchange rate as a function of the nominal exchange rate and changes in consumer price indices. It turns out for the cases under consideration that this is unlikely to make a major difference, but further work on the correct measurement of the real exchange rate would appear justified.

[12]One category of nontradable goods that might be important in this process is skilled labor; if aid raises the wages of skilled professionals, this could translate into real appreciation.

strongly to the increase in their relative price, the real appreciation would be limited. In economies with significant unemployment and the potential for a quick supply response, the additional demand for nontradable goods could induce additional employment and production, with little increase in the price level and limited real appreciation. In the longer run, investments that increase productivity in the nontradable sector could also reduce or even eliminate the real exchange rate appreciation.[13]

The mechanism for real appreciation would vary depending on the exchange rate regime. In a pure float, the central bank would sell the foreign exchange associated with the aid, causing a nominal (and real) exchange rate appreciation. In a peg, the real appreciation would take place through a period of inflation, with the increase in government expenditure accommodated by the central bank. The increase in aggregate demand and real appreciation would again increase net import demand, leading the central bank to sell foreign exchange in defense of the peg.

Aid Neither Absorbed Nor Spent

The authorities could choose to respond to the aid inflow by building international reserves, and neither increasing government expenditures nor lowering taxes. In this case there is no expansionary impact on aggregate demand, and no pressure on the exchange rate or prices.[14]

Not spending the aid may be infeasible over a longer time period, as donors need to account for how their assistance has been used. Of course, money is fungible, so that in principle not spending aid dollars is compatible with undertaking the projects favored by donors, while cutting back on other budgetary expenditures. In practice, the extent to which this is possible would depend on the room available—both fiscally and politically—to cut expenditures in other areas.

Aid Absorbed but Not Spent

Increased aid inflows can be used to reduce inflation in those countries that have not yet achieved stabilization. In such a case, the authorities can sell the foreign exchange associated with increased aid inflows to sterilize the monetary impact of domestically-financed fiscal deficits. The result would typically be slower monetary growth, a more appreciated real exchange rate, and lower inflation. Aggregate demand may increase as the inflation tax declines, with a corresponding increase in private consumption and investment. The deterioration

of the trade balance that often accompanies such a stabilization program is financed by the aid inflow.[15]

In countries that have already achieved inflation stabilization but have large domestic public debt, the government could use the proceeds from aid to reduce the stock of local currency government bonds outstanding. This would tend to result in increased private consumption and investment, which would raise net imports through the indirect effect of higher private after-tax income on import demand. The extra foreign exchange sold by the central bank would finance this increased demand for net imports. Again, some real exchange rate appreciation is likely to be necessary to mediate the increase in net imports.

Whether a strategy of retiring public debt through absorbing but not spending aid is appropriate in a particular situation depends partly on whether lower interest rates would translate into higher domestic investment and/or consumption. If there are no good private investment opportunities, for example, an increase in credit to the private sector could result in private capital outflows or a buildup of excess commercial bank reserves at the central bank.[16] In addition, as with the neither-absorb-nor-spend strategy, donors' needs to account for the use of their assistance may make it difficult to sustain a no-spending approach.

Aid Spent but Not Absorbed

A fourth possibility is that the fiscal deficit, net of aid, increases with the jump in aid, but the authorities do not sell the foreign exchange required to finance additional net imports. The macroeconomic effects of this fiscal expansion are similar to increasing government expenditures in the absence of aid, except that international reserves are higher. The increased deficits inject money into the economy.

In this case, the aid does not serve to support the fiscal expansion. This point is central and deserves elaboration. A transfer of real resources to the recipient country occurs only if aid finances additional net imports. Aid also serves as a way for the government to finance its domestic expenditures, as an alternative to domestic tax revenue or borrowing, either from the public or from the central bank. It may seem, therefore, that the financing of domestic expenditures, such as the hiring of nurses, is an alternative use for aid, in addition to imports. But this approach to the function of aid is misleading; after all, the government could always simply borrow from the central bank (i.e., print

---

[13]Many of these channels are explored in Chapter VIII.

[14]There may be second-order effects, e.g., expectations may change as a result of the central bank's higher international reserve position.

[15]This is the case emphasized by Buffie and others (2004).

[16]The IMF Independent Evaluation Office (2004) argues that program assumptions of the Poverty Reduction and Growth Facility that crowding-in will ensue from an increase in availability of credit to the private sector are often left unexamined and also often do not turn out to be correct.

money) to finance increased domestic expenditures. Rather, the purpose of the aid is to provide the foreign exchange required to satisfy the increased demand for foreign currency resulting from higher import demand.[17]

Consider a thought experiment in which, for a given level of aid, the government first decides on the appropriate level of government expenditure and its financing. This set of decisions, in principle, takes into account the scope for seigniorage, the supply response to increased fiscal expenditures, the productivity of the resulting public investment and the generation of higher exports that may result, and other such factors. Then, aid increases. What has changed is not that the government could now productively hire, say, more nurses to fight HIV/AIDS. It could have done that before. The difference is that, whereas before such additional expenditures would have caused too much inflation or a nonfinancable deterioration of the current account through second-round increases in import demand, now the incremental aid increases international reserves, which could be sold to pay for the higher imports. But this is the definition of aid absorption; aid that is not absorbed cannot fulfill this function.[18]

There are several monetary policy responses to a situation in which aid is being spent by the government but not absorbed in the economy. Absent foreign exchange sales to mop up the additional liquidity, the monetary policy options are the same as in the case of any domestically-financed fiscal expansion. One option is to allow the money supply to increase. This is essentially monetizing the fiscal expansion and would tend to be inflationary. Without foreign exchange sales, the nominal exchange rate will tend to depreciate as well, with a larger supply of domestic currency pushing up the price of foreign exchange. The resulting inflation

tax helps contain absorption by transferring resources from the private sector. If, alternatively, the authorities resist nominal exchange rate depreciations, then the resulting inflation would generate a real appreciation, the demand for imports would eventually increase, and the supply of exports would decrease. Provided that foreign exchange was eventually sold to satisfy this demand for net imports, the foreign exchange sales would have a sterilizing impact and dampen inflation. With some delay, then, the aid would be used and absorbed. Although this strategy has the advantage that aid is eventually absorbed, the period of inflation may carry costs of its own, especially in countries with a history of high inflation.[19]

Another response is to sterilize the fiscally-driven monetary expansion through the issuance of treasury bills. This strategy would tend to raise interest rates and crowd out private investment. In effect, there is a switch from private investment to government consumption or investment.[20] This strategy is likely to be particularly difficult and costly in countries with thin financial markets.[21]

There are opposing effects on the real exchange rate in the spend-but-don't-absorb case. In a given situation, the net effect will depend on specific factors, including the strength of contrasting policy choices and other influences, such as the terms of trade. The fiscal expansion tends to raise demand for nontraded goods, causing an appreciation; on the other hand, it increases import demand and lowers export supply, pushing the exchange rate toward depreciation. The net effect depends, inter alia, on the price and income elasticity of the country's export supply and import demand. In addition, the central bank's resistance to absorption creates pressures for real depreciation. In a float, aid-related liquidity injections will tend to depreciate the nominal and, in the short run, the real exchange rate. Over time, higher inflation and the associated inflation tax will reduce private demand and lower the real exchange rate and absorption. Alternatively, sterilization through the sale of treasury bills will also depress private demand and hence the real exchange rate and absorption. In a peg, only the sterilization channel operates.

---

[17]Related to this point is an accounting issue: "domestic financing" as usually defined in the budgetary accounts is misleading as an indicator of aid usage. It may be useful to consider the following example. Suppose aid is saved entirely in the form of gross international reserves, the government builds up deposits at the central bank, and the fiscal deficit excluding aid remains unchanged. By construction, the fiscal accounts will show a shift in financing from domestic financing (which will fall due to a reduction in net central bank credit to the government) to external financing. But the aid has no macroeconomic effects in this don't-absorb-and-don't-spend case—the money supply, fiscal stance, and interest rates are unaffected (except insofar as interest earnings of the central bank are higher). More generally, aid that is not absorbed does not contribute to financing of the government deficit in an economic sense. Thus, it would be misleading to conclude from a perusal of below-the-line financing items in the budget that aid inflows were actually financing the deficit to a greater extent than before.

[18]It is possible that optimal domestically-financed spending would be greater with higher reserves, perhaps because the higher reserves lower the risk premium the country must pay. This is likely to be a small effect, however. Moreover, borrowing domestically while building reserves would imply losses on the spread between the cost of borrowing and the return on reserves.

[19]Inflation can dampen private sector confidence and hinder financial deepening, in addition to disproportionately hurting the poor.

[20]Private investment and government expenditure could have different import intensities, which would modify the details of the argument but not alter the main point. Similarly, the fiscal expansion may increase aggregate output, so it is not the case that there need be a one-for-one trade-off between government spending and private investment. But such an aggregate output expansion could have been engineered without the aid.

[21]Depending on how open capital markets are, such a strategy can also be self-defeating. That is, sales of treasury bills, by raising the domestic interest rate, may attract international capital flows and appreciate the currency.

Choosing an Absorption and Spending Combination

Which of these combinations is best in the face of extra aid depends on many factors, including the level of official reserves, the existing debt burden, the current level of inflation, and the degree of aid volatility. For specific situations, some responses are more promising than others:

- *To absorb and spend* the aid would appear to be the most appropriate response under "normal" circumstances. In this case there is a real resource transfer through an aid-financed increase in net imports, and a corresponding increase in public expenditures.
- *To neither absorb nor spend* may be an appropriate short-run strategy where aid inflows are volatile or international reserves are precariously low.[22] Accumulating international reserves while avoiding an injection of domestic liquidity through fiscal expansion could help smooth the path of the real exchange rate if aid inflows are temporarily high but expected to fall. However, it is not an appropriate response to a permanent increase in the level of aid, unless Dutch disease concerns fully outweigh the benefits from the absorption of aid inflows (Appendix 2.2).
- *To absorb but not spend* the aid might be an appropriate response if inflation is too high (possibly owing to a very expansionary fiscal policy), resources are scarce for private investment, or the rate of return on public expenditure is relatively low. Sustained nonspending of aid may not be feasible, however, given donor objectives.
- *To spend and not absorb* would appear to be the least attractive option. The use of aid to build reserves while financing the increased deficit domestically is generally unwise. Inflation can only finance a small amount of expenditure; attempts to go further tend to raise little finance while damaging the economy (Selassie and others, 2006). The use of domestic sterilization is also unlikely to be a sensible medium-run strategy, as it tends to shift resources from the private to the public sector and does not allow the country to benefit from a real transfer of resources financed by aid.

Findings from Country Studies

Pattern of Aid Inflows

Table 2.1 shows the pattern of aid inflows for all the countries in the sample. Gross aid inflows are the sum of grants and loans, including both program and project financing. Net aid inflows are gross inflows plus debt relief, net of amortization, interest payments on public debt, and arrears clearance.[23] This is the headline measure of aid inflows, since it best captures the actual inflows of foreign exchange and hence the scale of the macroeconomic challenge. All the countries in the sample received debt relief over the period, which, in turn, permitted the clearance of external arrears in some cases and increased net aid inflows in others.

All five countries experienced a surge in net aid during the study period. The net aid increment ranged from an average of 2 percent of GDP in Tanzania to an average of 8 percent of GDP in Ethiopia. The level of net aid was also high in all countries, ranging from 7 to 20 percent of GDP. In Ghana, there were two different episodes of surging aid inflows, with a sharp increase in 2001 followed by a slump the next year, followed by another surge in 2003. In all other countries, the surge in aid was persistent, in that after the initial jump, aid inflows remained substantially higher than in the pre-surge period.

Net Budgetary Aid

Net budgetary aid is the sum of budget grants and loans (including debt relief), net of public debt service and arrears clearance. Net budgetary aid usually differs from net aid inflows to the economy, for example, because some aid is channeled directly to the private sector and spent on projects outside the government budget. In this sample, however, the two aid measures behave similarly, in broad terms. On average, net budget aid has increased in recent years in all five countries. This is illustrated in Figure 2.1, where $t = 0$ denotes the country-specific year in which aid increased substantially. While the aid surge was gradual and steady in Tanzania, it was more volatile in the other cases.

There is a clear shift from project aid to program assistance (Figure 2.2). Since the inception of the Poverty Reduction and Growth Facility (PRGF) approach in

---

[22]Recent cross-country evidence (e.g., Bulí̕ and Hamann, forthcoming) indicates that aid continues to be volatile, that aid commitments consistently exceed disbursements, and that aid disbursements are generally procyclical—thereby increasing volatility of public expenditures rather than lowering it. Prati and Tressel (2005) construct a theoretical model to consider the optimal pattern of absorption. Implicitly, they compare absorbing and spending to neither absorbing nor spending, in the terminology used here.

[23]Net aid inflows = Gross aid inflows + Debt relief (including relief under the Heavily Indebted Poor Countries Initiative) – Debt service + Arrears accumulation; with a clearance of arrears taking a negative sign. This paper uses aid data from IMF country reports. This is generally based on recipient country reporting and may differ significantly from donor data, such as those reported by the Organization for Economic Cooperation and Development's Development Assistance Committee (OECD/DAC), for a number of reasons, including the timing of aid delivery, and donor reporting of technical assistance delivered outside the recipient country as aid.

Table 2.1. Patterns of Aid Inflows
(In percent of GDP)

	1998	1999	2000	2001	2002	2003
Ethiopia[1]						
Net aid inflows	...	4.7	6.0	**8.8**	**16.1**	**15.0**
Gross aid inflows	...	11.7	8.8	**24.3**	**18.1**	**17.5**
Ghana						
Net aid inflows	3.2	2.8	−0.3	**10.6**	**2.6**	**7.1**
Gross aid inflows	8.7	7.5	8.8	**14.9**	**6.1**	**9.5**
Of which: program aid	1.8	1.9	3.8	**5.6**	**2.6**	**5.1**
Mozambique						
Net Aid Inflows	11.6	11.4	**20.4**	**15.4**	**16.4**	**15.0**
Gross aid inflows	13.4	13.4	**20.0**	**16.7**	**18.5**	**17.4**
Of which: program aid	6.3	6.3	**5.3**	**7.0**	**7.9**	**6.6**
Tanzania[1]						
Net aid inflows	4.6	6.6	**7.5**	**7.9**	**6.6**	**7.6**
Gross aid inflows	13.3	12.7	**12.8**	**12.5**	**10.5**	**10.5**
Of which: program aid	2.0	1.8	**2.3**	**2.7**	**3.8**	**5.1**
Uganda[1,2]						
Net aid inflows	...	8.4	9.4	**14.2**	**13.7**	**12.9**
Gross aid inflows	...	9.8	10.3	**13.9**	**13.8**	**12.9**
Of which: program aid	...	3.0	3.5	**6.8**	**8.3**	**8.2**

Note: Figures in bold represent periods of aid surges.
[1]Data are for the fiscal year. For example, July 1998 to June 1999 is reported as 1999.
[2]Uganda data revised for net, gross, and program aid. Compiling a consistent series for recent aid inflows in Uganda is complicated by extensive revisions to data. For fiscal year 2000/01, the data in the table include about $80 million per annum of off-budget aid, which is not accounted for in previous years. Excluding this amount would somewhat reduce the size of the aid surge, without changing the analysis in any significant way.

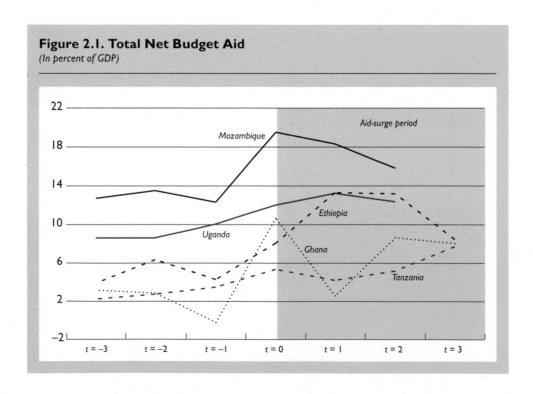

Figure 2.1. Total Net Budget Aid
(In percent of GDP)

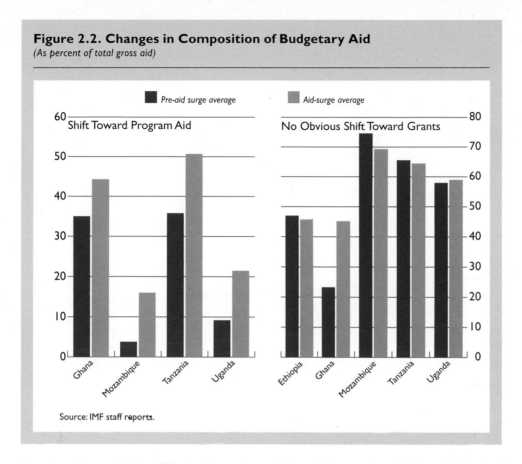

Figure 2.2. Changes in Composition of Budgetary Aid
(As percent of total gross aid)

Source: IMF staff reports.

1999, donors have been increasingly willing to channel their assistance to the recipient country's general budget. This eases administrative and institutional constraints in recipient economies, and gives recipient countries more flexibility in spending the aid.[24] However, there is no obvious shift from loans to grants, except in Ghana (Figure 2.2). This distinction is potentially important because loans add to debt service costs in the 0.future and therefore have implications for debt sustainability, while grants do not. On the other hand, there is some evidence that grants may have an adverse impact on the government's revenue collection, while loans may have a positive impact (Gupta and others, 2003).

Macroeconomic Context, Real Exchange Rate, and Dutch Disease

Growth was generally robust in most countries both before and during the aid-surge period, although exogenous shocks set growth back in some years (Table 2.2).[25]

Three of the sample countries—Ethiopia, Tanzania, and Uganda—kept a tight curb on inflation, both before and during the aid-surge period. In Mozambique, however, the aid surge coincided with a sharp increase in inflation. Ghana's inflation was high and volatile before and during the aid-surge period. The private investment-to-GDP ratio was mostly stable in the sample. In Ethiopia and Tanzania, average private investment during the surge period declined slightly relative to the pre-surge average. In Uganda, it increased in the surge period. In most countries, the average public-investment-to-GDP ratio was higher during the aid-surge period.

There was no sign of Dutch disease in the sense that real exchange rates in the sample did not appreciate during the aid surges (Table 2.3).[26] During the years in which aid inflows surged, there was typically a depreciation of the real effective exchange rate, ranging from 1.5 percent (Mozambique in 2000) to 6.5 percent (Uganda in 2001).[27] Ghana, however, observed a

---

[24]For example, in 2001, more than 1,200 donor-funded projects were being implemented in Tanzania. Managing and coordinating such a large number of projects was a challenge for the authorities.

[25]Devastating floods reduced Mozambique's growth rate in 2000, a drought reduced Tanzania's growth rate in 1999, and a severe drought caused a two-year contraction in Ethiopia.

[26]See Appendix 2.2 for a discussion of the theoretical and empirical literature on Dutch disease.

[27]These real effective exchange rate (REER) indices are based on nominal exchange rates and consumer price index (CPI) inflation in the target country and its trade partners. Lack of data prevents supplementing these indices with the REER measured by unit labor costs, or the REER measured as the price ratio between nontradables and tradables.

Table 2.2. GDP Growth, Inflation, and Private Investment
(In percent)

	Pre-Aid Surge Average[1]	Aid-Surge Average[1]	Difference
Ethiopia			
GDP growth	5.7	1.8	−3.9
Inflation	4.7	2.6	−2.1
Investment/GDP	16.4	19.6	3.2
Private	9.8	9.4	−0.4
Public	6.6	10.1	3.5
Ghana			
GDP growth	4.1	4.6	0.6
Inflation	85.2	20.5	−64.6
Investment/GDP	23.6	23.2	−0.4
Private	14.1	13.8	−0.3
Public	9.5	9.4	−0.1
Mozambique[2]			
GDP growth	9.7	7.3	−2.4
Inflation	1.8	12.8	11.1
Investment/GDP	30.4	40.9	10.5
Tanzania			
GDP growth	2.8	5.4	2.6
Inflation	9.9	4.9	−4.9
Investment/GDP	15.5	17.8	2.2
Private	12.4	11.5	−0.8
Public	3.2	6.2	3.1
Uganda			
GDP growth	6.6	5.6	−1.0
Inflation	3.0	2.7	−0.3
Investment/GDP	19.6	21.0	1.4
Private	11.2	13.9	2.8
Public	8.5	7.1	−1.3

[1]For Ethiopia, Ghana, and Uganda, 1999–2000 is the pre-surge period and 2001–03 is the aid-surge period. For Mozambique, 1998–99 is the pre-aid-surge period and 2000–02 is the aid-surge period. For Tanzania, the corresponding periods are 1998–99 and 2000–04.

[2]Mozambique lacks reliable data on private investment.

small real appreciation over both episodes of surging aid inflows (Figure 2.3).

A real depreciation in the face of surging aid inflows may indicate (1) structural features of the economy such as a rapid supply response to aid expenditures or high import propensities, though this would tend to mitigate the appreciation rather than cause a depreciation; (2) a fiscal and monetary policy stance that leans against real appreciation; or (3) other exogenous events, notably a negative terms-of-trade shock. Subsequent sections consider the first two explanations. With respect to the latter, two countries in the sample, Ethiopia and Uganda, were hit by significant negative terms-of-trade shocks during the aid-surge period. However, as shown in Box 2.2, even in these cases the incremental aid flows were much larger than the scale of the terms-of-trade shocks. There is also no case where a significant change in private inflows counteracts the pattern of aid inflows.

Consistent with real depreciation, export performance was strong in most of the sample, especially in Mozambique and Tanzania. In Ghana as well, export performance was strong despite a stable real exchange rate. In both countries that were affected by the decline in coffee prices, real depreciation helped export performance. In particular, nontraditional exports grew strongly, and increased as a proportion of total exports, enabling robust export growth in Ethiopia and moderating the decline in exports in Uganda.

Was Incremental Aid Absorbed?

In general, country authorities were reluctant to fully absorb the incremental aid. Following the framework introduced earlier in this chapter, Table 2.4 decomposes the increment in aid in each country into the change in the non-aid current account, the change in the rate of

Table 2.3. Real Effective Exchange Rate
(Percent change over previous year, unless otherwise specified)

	Pre-Aid Surge Average[1]	Aid-Surge Average[1]	Difference
Ethiopia			
REER (depreciation −)	−2.0	−2.1	−0.1
NEER (depreciation −)	−5.0	−1.5	3.5
RER (bilateral with dollar)	−5.7	−1.9	3.8
Terms of trade	−18.3	−4.1	14.2
Exports	−9.6	−0.1	9.5
Nontraditional exports/ exports (percent ratio)	44.0	63.5	19.5
Ghana			
REER	−17.5	0.5	18.0
NEER	−27.8	−17.8	10.0
RER (bilateral with dollar)	−12.0	−6.6	5.4
Terms of trade	−12.7	9.7	22.3
Exports	−3.8	8.9	12.7
Nontraditional exports/ exports (percent)	30.2	33.0	2.8
Mozambique			
REER	−0.0	−6.4	−6.4
NEER	1.6	−14.1	−15.7
RER (bilateral with dollar)	−5.0	−11.1	−6.1
Terms of trade	−8.8	1.2	10.0
Exports	11.2	39.5	28.3
Tanzania			
REER	−2.3	−9.8	−7.5
NEER	6.3	−8.7	−15.1
RER (bilateral with dollar)	3.5	−6.1	−9.6
Terms of trade	3.3	−4.1	−7.3
Exports	−17.3	16.1	33.4
Nontraditional exports/ exports (percent)	41.3	74.7	33.4
Uganda			
REER	−6.6	−6.3	0.3
NEER	−8.6	−5.8	2.8
RER (bilateral with dollar)	−12.0	−6.6	5.4
Terms of trade	−14.0	−3.6	10.4
Exports	1.1	4.0	2.9
Nontraditional exports/ exports (percent)	51.4	78.9	27.5

Note: NEER = nominal effective exchange rate; REER = real effective exchange rate; RER = real exchange rate.
[1]For Ethiopia, Ghana, and Uganda, 1999–2000 is the pre-surge period and 2001–03 is the aid-surge period. For Mozambique, 1998–99 is the pre-aid-surge period and 2000–02 is the aid-surge period. For Tanzania, the corresponding periods are 1998–99 and 2000–04.

reserve accumulation, and the change in the non-aid capital account.

In three countries, the aid led to some increase of the non-aid current account deficit, but this increase was typically modest, except in Mozambique, which absorbed over half the incremental aid inflow. In Tanzania and Ghana, the non-aid current account deficit actually shrunk by 2 and 10 percentage points of GDP, respectively, implying that the incremental aid was not absorbed. In all countries, the aid surge increased the rate of reserve accumulation. This pattern is consistent with the failure of the real exchange rate to appreciate in line with the surge in aid inflows.

In all countries, part of the aid increment was lost through reductions in the rate of capital inflow. In Ghana, the deterioration in the non-aid capital account exceeded the entire increment in the aid inflow. In Tanzania and Uganda, the reduction in the rate of non-aid capital inflows was comparable to the aid surge. Some short-run movements in the non-aid capital account could reflect

Figure 2.3. Real Effective Exchange Rates and Aid Inflows

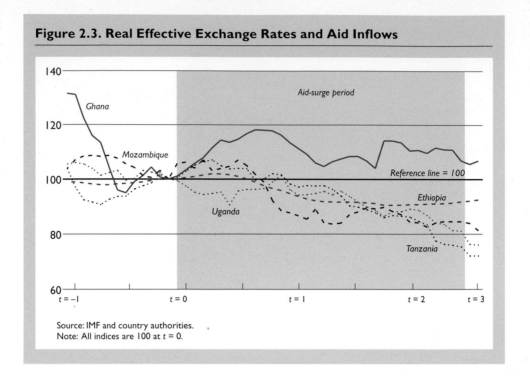

Source: IMF and country authorities.
Note: All indices are 100 at $t = 0$.

lags between foreign exchange being made available for absorption and the actual increase in imports that comprises absorption.[28] However, this would not seem to be an adequate explanation for the more sustained changes observed in the sample.[29] Box 2.3 explores possible links between private capital flows and aid.

Was Incremental Aid Spent?

The governments in Mozambique, Tanzania, and Uganda spent most of the additional foreign assistance (Table 2.5). A variety of factors encouraged these countries to spend the incremental budgetary aid. Because these countries had attained macroeconomic stability in the mid-to-late 1990s before the aid surge, reducing domestic financing of the budget deficit was not a major goal. Neither was retiring domestic public debt a key objective, as these countries had rather low domestic

financing of the deficit as well as domestic debt and debt service prior to the aid surge (Table 2.6). Furthermore, they had strengthened their expenditure management systems, partly because of the Heavily Indebted Poor Countries (HIPC) Initiative, which helped them spend most of the incremental aid that they received as program assistance.[30] To the extent that these countries spent the aid increments, the additional spending was concentrated on capital and poverty-reducing expenditures.

The governments in Ghana and Ethiopia, however, spent very little of the incremental aid. These countries had a relatively weak record of macroeconomic stability, and a low level of international reserves before the aid surge, which limited their ability to spend additional aid. As these countries also had relatively high domestic debt and domestic financing of the budget prior to the aid surge, reducing domestic public debt (and hence domestic debt service) was also a consideration for not spending the additional aid. In Ghana, which experienced highly volatile aid inflows, aid volatility appears to have been a major factor in saving incremental aid in 2003. In Ethiopia, limited administrative capacity and weak institutions following the conflict with Eritrea may have been additional factors.

The government can also spend aid indirectly by lowering taxes and transferring aid to the private sector.

---

[28]For example, consider a case in which government expenditures raise wages for a set of workers. This increases their demand for imports. However, when they purchase dollars from the central bank, they do not immediately spend them on imports, but in the first instance, deposit them in dollar accounts held with domestic commercial banks. This would count as a deterioration in the non-aid capital account (due to an increase in commercial banks' net foreign assets). Subsequently, when they spend the dollars on imports, there would be a corresponding improvement in the non-aid capital account.

[29]In some countries, large errors and omissions in the balance of payments accounts could be partly responsible for measured fluctuations in the capital account.

[30]Mozambique, Tanzania, and Uganda reached their decision point under the HIPC Initiative before mid-2000. Improving expenditure management and tracking was part of the fiscal conditionality in all three countries.

Box 2.2. Terms-of-Trade Shocks and Aid Inflows

The table below attempts to disentangle the terms-of-trade effect from the aid-inflows effect for the two countries in the sample that were affected by a significant terms-of-trade shock during the aid-surge period: Ethiopia and Uganda. In both countries, the main export commodity is coffee. A sharp and prolonged decline in world coffee prices caused a deterioration in the terms of trade for both countries, and in each case this deterioration coincided with surging aid inflows.

The table contains estimates of the loss in dollar inflows through net exports resulting from the terms-of-trade shock, and compares it with the increase in dollar inflows due to the surge in aid. In this calculation, year t prices of exports and imports are fixed at the level of year $t-1$. This yields a counterfactual series for exports and imports; the difference between this series and the actual data on exports and imports is taken as the terms-of-trade effect.

In both cases, in the first year the incremental aid inflow dominated the negative effect from the terms-of-trade shock. This is also true of the average over the aid-surge period. Nonetheless, in both cases there was a nominal and real depreciation.

Terms-of-Trade Shocks
(In millions of U.S. dollars, unless otherwise specified)

	1999	2000	2001	2002	2003
Ethiopia					
1. Terms-of-trade effect on net exports[1]	−54	−484	**−13**	**−36**	−59
2. Change in aid inflows	−15	24	**235**	**417**	21
3. Net effect (1 + 2)	−69	−460	**222**	**381**	−38
NEER (percent change)	−8.4	−1.6	**5.9**	**−1.6**	−9.0
REER (percent change)	−5.1	1.1	**−3.5**	**−4.9**	2.2
Uganda					
1. Terms-of-trade effect on net exports[1]	−53	−106	**−52**	**11**	60.1
2. Change in aid inflows	−82	54	**246**	**−2**	10
3. Net effect (1 + 2)	−135	−52	**194**	**9**	70
NEER (percent change)	−14.0	−3.2	**−6.9**	**2.3**	−12.7
REER (percent change)	−13.0	−0.2	**−6.5**	**−1.7**	−10.6

Note: Figures in bold represent periods of aid surges. NEER = nominal effective exchange rate; REER = real effective exchange rate.
[1]Calculated as the difference between actual net exports and net exports, keeping unit export and import prices unchanged.

Contrary to theoretical considerations of moral hazard and some evidence from other countries,[31] the revenue-to-GDP ratio either improved (in Ethiopia, Ghana, and Mozambique) or remained largely unchanged (in Tanzania and Uganda). For the latter cases, additional fiscal aid might have reduced the incentives for aid recipients to strengthen revenue efforts, as total revenues stagnated below 15 percent of GDP.[32]

In neither Ghana nor Ethiopia were program targets in IMF-supported programs generally responsible for the underspending of the aid increments. In most cases, programs supported by the PRGF allowed aid-recipient countries to spend the aid inflows. These programs accommodated expected increases in aid flows with a comparable expansion in targets for the fiscal deficit excluding aid (Figure 2.4).

However, in a few exceptional cases, the IMF-supported programs envisaged only a partial spending of additional aid. One significant case is Ethiopia in the

---

[31]Gupta and others (2003) find evidence that aid lowers revenue effort in a large sample of developing countries, though the effect is modest except in countries with relatively high levels of corruption. McGillivray and Morrissey (2001) reported a significant negative incremental impact of aid on domestic revenue for Pakistan and Côte d'Ivoire.

[32]Of course, in the absence of a counterfactual, it is difficult to gauge whether revenue effort was harmed by aid. One indicator, however, is provided by PRGF revenue targets. In general these were met by most countries in the sample for most periods. The exceptions were Ethiopia and Mozambique, which missed several quar-

terly targets on government revenue. However, these episodes did not appear to be the result of moral hazard arising from increased aid inflows. In Ethiopia, the 2004 ex-post assessment argues that the revenue targets were overly ambitious given the pace of structural adjustment in the country. In Mozambique, these episodes were more attributable to a drop in excise and import taxes arising from an increase in world oil prices.

Table 2.4. Balance of Payments Identity
(Annual averages in percent of GDP)

	Pre-Aid Surge Average[1]	Aid-Surge Average[1]	Difference	Incremental Aid Absorbed?[2]
Ethiopia				
Net aid inflows	5.3	13.3	8.0	
Non-aid current account balance	−9.2	−10.8	−1.6	Partly absorbed
Non-aid capital account balance	2.0	1.3	−0.7	20%
Change in reserves (increase −)	1.9	−3.8	−5.7	
Ghana				
Net aid inflows	1.3	6.8	5.5	
Non-aid current account balance	−13.4	−3.4	10.0	Not absorbed
Non-aid capital account balance	9.9	2.1	−7.8	0%
Change in reserves (increase −)	2.2	−5.4	−7.6	
Mozambique				
Net aid inflows	11.5	17.4	5.9	
Non-aid current account balance	−19.7	−23.6	−3.9	Mostly absorbed
Non-aid capital account balance	8.7	8.3	−0.4	66%
Change in reserves (increase −)	−0.5	−2.1	−1.7	
Tanzania				
Net aid inflows	5.6	7.8	2.2	
Non-aid ccurent account balance	−9.2	−6.8	2.3	Not absorbed
Non-aid capital account balance	4.1	1.7	−2.4	0%
Change in reserves (increase −)	−0.6	−2.7	−2.2	
Uganda				
Net aid inflows	8.9	13.6	4.7	
Non-aid current account balance	−10.1	−11.4	−1.3	Partly absorbed
Non-aid capital account balance	1.6	−1.1	−2.8	27%
Change in reserves (increase −)	−0.4	−1.1	−0.7	

Source: IMF staff reports.

Note: Errors and omissions are included in the capital account.

[1]For Ethiopia, Ghana, and Uganda, 1999–2000 is the pre-surge period and 2001–03 is the aid-surge period. For Mozambique, 1998–99 is the pre-aid-surge period and 2000–02 is the aid-surge period. For Tanzania, the corresponding periods are 1998–99 and 2000–04.

[2]Non-aid current account deterioration as a percent of incremental aid inflow is truncated at 0 and 100.

2001/02 fiscal year, when a budgetary aid surge of about 5 percent of GDP was envisaged but the PRGF-supported program did not accommodate this expected increase in aid with a commensurate increase in public spending. In this instance, the program was aiming to reduce inflation driven by an excessive deficit and associated monetary financing during the war period of 1997–2000.[33] In Ghana, the IMF-supported programs anticipated only partly spending the aid increments because the goal was to use part of the incremental aid to reduce domestic financing and thus lower domestic interest rates and the government's interest bill. In the event, probably in part because of the high aid volatil-

ity, even these targets for spending were not binding, particularly in 2003.

Aid volatility also contributed to some governments' choice of not spending the aid increments. There are two broad fiscal responses to aid volatility: adjust expenditures in line with the aid fluctuations, or smooth spending by building up reserves (and government deposits) when aid is up and drawing down these savings when aid shortfalls occur. For example, in Ghana, overall expenditures were relatively unresponsive to aid volatility, and past aid savings as well as additional domestic financing were used to offset shortfalls in budgetary aid. To some extent, the preference to build up official reserves in Ethiopia and Ghana appears to have contributed to saving the incremental aid, particularly in the second aid surge in Ghana in 2003. In general, the IMF-supported programs allowed for measures to mitigate the impact of volatile aid on public expenditures (Box 2.4).

---

[33]Of course, project aid was expected to be spent; the program targeted overall expenditures and thus implied a reduction in non-aid-financed spending.

Box 2.3. Aid, Absorption, and Capital Flows

Were the reductions in capital inflows in Ghana, Tanzania, and Uganda a result of the aid surge itself? If so, the aid surges did not serve their intended purpose of promoting absorption. Aid inflows that trigger capital outflows weaken the link between central bank sales of foreign exchange and absorption, because a (possibly volatile and unpredictable) part of the foreign exchange may leave the country through private capital account transactions.

The question arises as to how to relate the reduction in capital inflows in many sample countries to the policy response to aid. It is important to identify the direction of causation between the changes in aid and the changes in capital flows, and also to identify the appropriate counterfactual, which is what would have happened in the absence of aid.

Assume that the reductions in capital flows are exogenous to the aid flows. Then, there are two possible counterfactuals. First, the central bank could have sold dollars to accommodate the outflow even in the absence of the aid. Given this counterfactual, the aid allowed the authorities to accumulate reserves and pursue a don't-absorb strategy. Second, in the absence of the aid surge the central bank could have resisted the capital outflow by not making dollars available in the foreign exchange market. This would have caused the domestic currency to depreciate, thus increasing net exports through the price effect. In this case, the aid dollars allowed the authorities to accommodate the capital outflow, increasing absorption relative to the counterfactual. But associated with this capital outflow would have been a reduction in demand for domestic money or assets. Thus, the use of reserves for this purpose would not have enabled financing of domestic spending. Therefore, whichever the counterfactual, it remains the case that the same aid dollar cannot be used twice: if a dollar is used to accommodate an exogenous capital outflow, it cannot simultaneously be used to finance government spending.

In Ghana, for example, the reduction in capital inflows seems to have been associated not with the aid surge but with macroeconomic disarray. Following a negative terms-of-trade shock and with reserves almost depleted, non-aid capital inflows fell sharply in 2000 and 2001. In 2000, the exchange rate weakened sharply and inflation shot up. With an aid surge in 2001, the authorities were able to avoid devaluing the exchange rate. In this case, the aid inflows likely kept absorption higher than it would have been.

Whether to treat changes in capital flows as exogenous to increased aid is, however, an open question. It is possible that an aid surge could encourage private capital inflows. For example, Buffie and others (2004) argue that increased aid, by reducing seigniorage and hence expected inflation, may lead to domestic agents substituting foreign currency assets with domestic currency assets, which would appear in the balance of payments as a capital inflow.

Similarly, an aid surge could trigger a capital outflow in certain circumstances. For example, when the authorities attempt to absorb but not spend aid, channeling incremental aid to the private sector through the financial system by reducing the stock of domestic bonds outstanding, lack of investment opportunities at home as well as portfolio diversification goals could encourage private investors to invest abroad—which will appear as a deterioration of the capital account. However, none of the countries pursued a policy of channeling aid to the private sector through the financial system. It would thus appear unlikely that such a policy resulted in the reduction in capital inflows observed during the aid-surge period.

An aid surge could also cause a capital outflow if it leads the authorities to pursue an excessively loose monetary policy. Aid-related fiscal spending tends to increase the money supply. If the authorities allow this to lead to excessively low interest rates and excess liquidity in the banking system, capital outflows could result. As discussed later in this chapter, aid inflows to Tanzania were associated with periods of relatively loose monetary policy, and this may have contributed to the slowdown in capital inflows. Direct evidence is scarce, however. Identifying the conditions under which aid would lead to a capital outflow or inflow is, therefore, a nontrivial undertaking that for now is left to future work.

Table 2.7 presents a summary of the absorption and fiscal responses discussed above. Surprisingly, a full absorb-and-spend response is not observed in any of the sample countries. Two countries (Ethiopia and Ghana) adopted a neither-absorb-nor-spend response to the aid surge. Both entered the aid-surge period with a precariously low level of reserves and used the additional aid to build those reserves. In Ethiopia, reserves were accumulated to bolster the de facto exchange rate peg against the dollar. In Ghana, a buffer against extremely volatile aid inflows was built. The remaining sample countries (Mozambique, Tanzania, and Uganda) spent the incremental aid without fully absorbing it. In all three countries, concerns about the negative impact of a real appreciation on competitiveness dictated the pattern of aid absorption. In general, aid was much more likely to be spent than to be absorbed.

Monetary Impact of Aid and Policy Response

On the basis of the policy response to aid, two main groups of countries can be discerned: (1) countries where the aid impact was limited because only a small part of it (if any) was either absorbed or spent (Ethiopia, Ghana); and (2) countries where expenditure exceeded absorption, resulting in an injection of domestic liquidity and creating upward pressure on prices (Mozambique, Tanzania, and Uganda).[34] These patterns of absorption

---

[34]This broad grouping of sample countries is based on comparing period averages for pre-aid-surge and aid-surge periods. Since the periods under consideration range from two to four years, the averages mask considerable year-to-year policy variations in many of these countries. The countries' policy responses are discussed further in Chapters III through VII.

Table 2.5. Allocation of Incremental Net Budgetary Aid: Spent or Saved
(In percent of GDP)

	Pre-Aid Surge Average[1]	Aid-Surge Average[1]	Difference	Incremental Aid Spent or Not?[2]
Ghana				
Net fiscal aid inflows	1.3	7.3	6.0	
Revenue (excluding grants)	17.1	19.0	1.9	
Expenditure (excluding external interest)	26.9	29.3	2.3	Not spent
Overall fiscal balance before aid	−9.9	−10.3	−0.4	7%
Ethiopia				
Net fiscal aid inflows	5.3	11.2	5.9	
Revenue (excluding grants)	17.9	19.4	1.5	
Expenditure (excluding external interest)	31.8	32.5	0.7	Not spent
Overall fiscal balance before aid	−13.8	−13.0	0.8	0%
Mozambique				
Net fiscal aid inflows	12.9	17.9	5.0	
Revenue (excluding grants)	12.6	13.9	1.3	
Expenditure (excluding external interest)	26.0	32.7	6.7	Spent
Overall fiscal balance before aid	−13.0	−18.5	−5.5	100%
Tanzania				
Net fiscal aid inflows	4.7	8.6	3.9	
Revenue (excluding grants)	12.1	12.5	0.4	
Expenditure (excluding external interest)	16.7	20.7	4.0	Spent
Overall fiscal balance before aid	−4.8	−8.3	−3.5	91%
Uganda				
Net fiscal aid inflows	9.3	12.5	3.2	
Revenue (excluding grants)	12.6	12.8	0.1	
Expenditure (excluding external interest)	22.2	24.7	2.5	Mostly spent
Overall fiscal balance before aid	−9.6	−12.0	−2.4	74%

[1]For Ethiopia, Ghana, and Uganda, 1999–2000 is the pre-surge period and 2001–03 is the aid-surge period. For Mozambique, 1998–99 is the pre-aid-surge period and 2000–02 is the aid-surge period. For Tanzania, the corresponding periods are 1998–99 and 2000–04.

[2]Non-aid fiscal balance deterioration as a percent of incremental aid inflow is truncated at 0 and 100.

and spending defined the challenge for monetary policy in response to the aid surges.

Cases with Limited Aid Impact

In neither Ethiopia nor Ghana was the aid surge accompanied by an increase in domestic spending in excess of revenue generation. Therefore, over the period as a whole, the aid did not lead to a substantial injection of domestic liquidity.[35]

The monetary policy responses of these two countries were not restricted by the PRGF-supported program

(Figure 2.5). In general, Ethiopia overperformed on monetary and reserve targets under the PRGF-supported program during the aid-surge period.[36] This implies that the authorities' chief concern—accumulating reserves to keep the nominal peg against the dollar—diverged to some extent from the PRGF target path, which envisaged more spending (supported by a higher target for net domestic assets—NDA) coupled with greater sales of foreign exchange (reflected in a lower reserves target).[37]

In Ghana, the strategy of the PRGF-supported program was to absorb and partly spend the expected aid

---

[35]Although both countries avoided substantial real appreciation, this was achieved through different combinations of inflation and nominal exchange rate movements. In Ethiopia, the birr was pegged to the dollar, which necessitated a low rate of inflation to keep the real effective exchange rate on a downward path. Consistent with this objective, reserve money growth remained low during both pre-aid-surge and aid-surge periods. Ghana, on the other hand, experienced a combination of high inflation and nominal depreciation, the net effect of which was a fairly stable REER.

[36]During most of the aid-surge period, net domestic assets remained below their targeted path, while reserves remained above the target path.

[37]It appears that the program may have been too restrictive in its reserve money path. Despite base money exceeding its programmed path during most of the aid-surge period, inflation was contained at a low level. Implicitly, it seems that the increase in money demand accompanying post-war monetization was underestimated. This was inconsequential in practice because the reserve money target was only indicative.

Table 2.6. Domestic Debt and Debt Service Indicators
(In percent)

	Pre-Aid Surge Average[1]	Aid-Surge Average[1]	Difference
Ethiopia			
Domestic debt[2]	37.8	39.1	1.3
Interest payments[3]	7.4	5.6	−1.8
Nominal interest rates on treasury bills[4]	3.4	1.6	−1.8
Real interest rates in treasury bills[4]	−0.8	−2.1	−1.3
Ghana			
Domestic debt[2]	23.0	23.1	0.2
Interest payments[3]	28.0	27.5	−0.5
Nominal interest rates on treasury bills[4]	38.1	26.5	−11.6
Real interest rates in treasury bills[4]	19.3	1.7	−17.6
Mozambique[5]			
Domestic debt	0.3	2.6	2.2
Interest payments[3]	0.2	3.8	3.6
Nominal interest rates on treasury bills[4]	11.8	24.0	12.2
Real interest rates in treasury bills[4]	9.0	11.1	2.2
Tanzania			
Domestic debt[2]	10.1	9.5	−0.6
Interest payments[3]	6.9	7.4	0.6
Nominal interest rates on treasury bills[4]	11.6	8.0	−3.6
Real interest rates in treasury bills[4]	1.3	3.0	1.7
Uganda			
Domestic debt[2]	3.4	8.1	4.7
Interest payments[3]	2.6	6.9	4.3
Nominal interest rates on treasury bills[4]	8.2	10.3	2.2
Real interest rates in treasury bills[4]	3.6	7.2	3.6

[1]For Ethiopia, Ghana, and Uganda, 1999–2000 is the pre-surge period and 2001–03 is the aid-surge period. For Mozambique, 1998–99 is the pre-aid-surge period and 2000–02 is the aid-surge period. For Tanzania, the corresponding periods are 1998–99 and 2000–04.

[2]Domestic public debt as percent of GDP.

[3]Interest payments on domestic public debt in percent of government revenue.

[4]Average interest rates on treasury bills (in percent).

[5]In Mozambique, values for domestic public debt and treasury bill rates are for 1999 only.

increments. During the first aid surge in 2001, the government focused on reducing high inflation from the previous period, including sterilization through the sale of foreign exchange. While NDA and money growth exceeded the program targets, inflation came down over this period. Aid collapsed in 2002. When aid surged again in 2003, the authorities were much more cautious and saved most of the incremental aid inflow through the accumulation of government deposits at the central bank. Consequently, in this period, Ghana overperformed on both monetary and reserve targets under the PRGF-supported program; better adherence to the program path in 2003 would have resulted in more spending of aid combined with sterilization through foreign exchange sales. Presumably influenced by the negative consequences of the aid collapse in the previous period, the authorities opted for the more risk-averse strategy of reserve accumulation.

Cases Where Spending Exceeded Absorption

Given that the fiscal authorities in these countries (Mozambique, Tanzania, and Uganda) spent the aid, but central banks were unwilling to allow full aid absorption, the question arises as to how they handled the increase in money supply associated with this spend-but-don't-absorb response.

Each of the three countries followed a combination of options: either allowing the money supply to increase or sterilizing monetary expansion through treasury bills. In all three countries, concerns about the negative

Figure 2.4. Programmed vs. Actual Levels of Fiscal Deficit (Excluding Aid) and Net Budget Aid
(In percent of GDP)

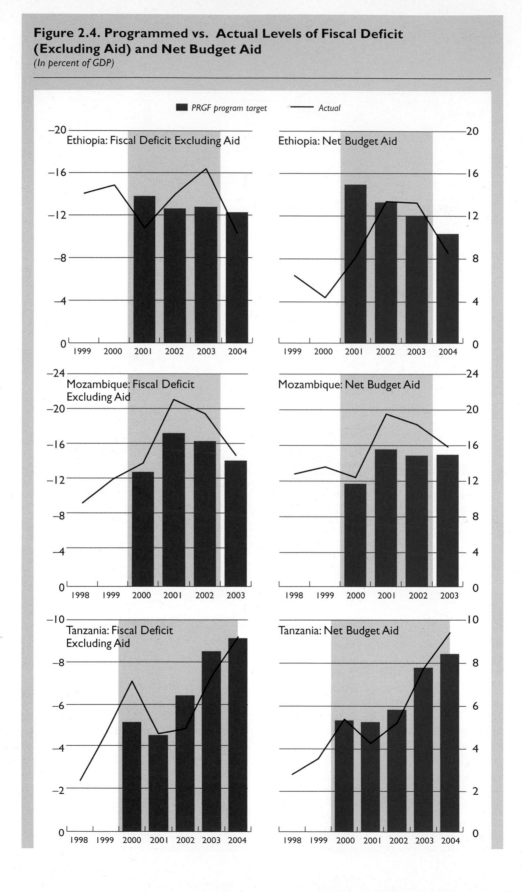

Figure 2.4 (concluded)

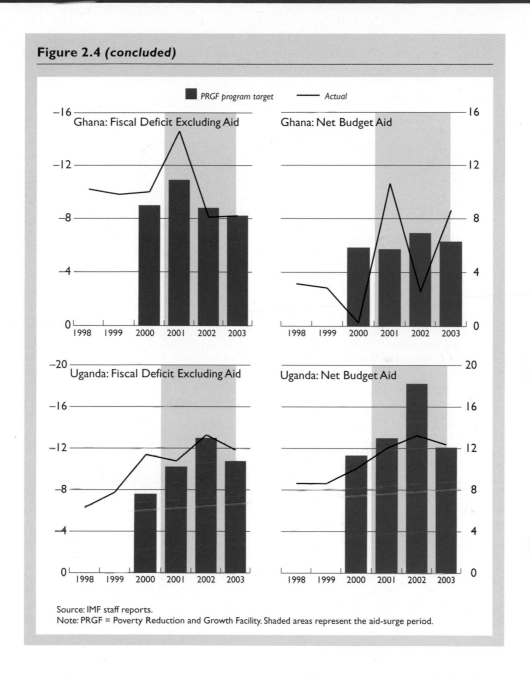

Source: IMF staff reports.
Note: PRGF = Poverty Reduction and Growth Facility. Shaded areas represent the aid-surge period.

impact of a real exchange rate appreciation on competitiveness led the central banks to contain net foreign exchange sales to a level consistent with a depreciating nominal exchange rate.[38] Because the governments in these countries simultaneously increased domestic

expenditures, this injection of liquidity led to inflationary pressures and various episodes of attempted sterilization through treasury bill sales.[39]

In Tanzania and Uganda, the authorities were largely successful in keeping inflation in check, with underlying consumer price index (CPI) inflation never exceeding 10 percent during the aid-surge period. However, in both cases this was achieved at the expense of squeezing private sector investment through the sale of

[38]In Uganda, this concern was magnified by the simultaneous terms-of-trade shock. An appreciating real exchange rate would have further reduced earnings in the coffee sector, with possible adverse consequences for poverty, and may have hindered the expansion of noncoffee exports. In addition, the central bank was concerned that the commercial banks' appetite for foreign exchange would be limited, putting a limit on sterilization through foreign exchange sales.

[39]See Chapters III to VII for more details on varying monetary policy responses to the aid surges.

Box 2.4. Aid Volatility and Programs Supported by the Poverty Reduction and Growth Facility

Aid inflows remain generally volatile and unpredictable, and volatility has potentially serious adverse consequences for the recipients of those aid inflows.[1] For example, Celasun and Walliser (2005) find that periods of excess aid and tax revenue are not used to accelerate domestically-financed investment spending to compensate for previous shortfalls. This implies that the lack of predictability of aid may have permanent costs in terms of lost output. In addition, volatility may complicate systemic liquidity management by injecting large and unpredictable amounts of money into a thinly monetized economy.

In the sample considered here, aid was hard to predict even one year ahead (Figure 2.4). Part of the aid volatility is a welcome response to exogenous shocks—for example, aid inflows to Mozambique increased sharply in response to floods in early 2000, and in Ethiopia in response to drought in 2002. Because low-income countries are disproportionately prone to exogenous shocks such as terms-of-trade declines or natural disasters, aid inflows should ideally be able to cushion at least part of the adverse impact of these shocks (IMF, 2003a; Guillaumont and Chauvet, 2001). Volatility may also reflect aid conditionality and thus is, to some extent, endogenous to the recipient government's actions. It may also reflect the donors' budget cycles.

While prediction errors were common, the International Monetary Fund was not systematically overcautious in projecting net aid inflows for the budgets. In none of the five sample countries considered here was there a consistent pattern of under- (or over-) prediction, except in Mozambique.

In most cases, programs supported by the Poverty Reduction and Growth Facility (PRGF) allowed aid-recipient countries adequate fiscal space to spend anticipated aid inflows. The PRGF-supported programs generally dealt with aid surprises more cautiously than with expected changes in aid. As shown in the table, in the case of positive aid surprises, PRGF-supported programs limited the spending of aid in excess of projections by reducing the ceiling on net domestic financing of the government in three of the five countries. Such an adjustment in the ceiling sets an implicit limit on the fiscal deficit.[2] When actual program aid exceeded the level projected under the program, net domestic financing of government budget was reduced by the full amount of the excess aid.

In the case of negative aid surprises, the PRGF-supported programs implied a limited degree of fiscal adjustment by allowing some increase in net domestic financing of the government and lowering international reserve targets. At one extreme, the PRGF-supported program in Tanzania allowed increases in the net domestic financing target by 100 percent of any aid shortfall; on the other extreme, the program in Mozambique did not allow for any adjustment in net domestic financing. In other cases, the programs allowed for only partial upward adjustment in net domestic financing in response to a negative aid shock.

During the event, only in Ghana were these adjusters binding. The downward adjustment in the ceiling on domestic financing of the government in Ghana limited spending of incremental aid in 2001. In view of the subsequent unexpected collapse in aid, this turned out to be welcome. In other cases there were no significant positive surprises during the period of study or there was no adjuster (Mozambique), allowing surprises to be spent (and requiring a contraction in the case of shortfalls).

---

[1]Bulíř and Hamann (2005) find that aid volatility—measured as the ratio of the variance of aid to the variance of revenue—increased over 2000–03 compared with the level over 1995–98 for all five countries in the sample. Simulations from a calibrated real business cycle model in Arellano and others (2005) suggest that aid volatility may cost poor countries as much as 3 to 4 percent of GDP.

[2]If the aim is to fix spending regardless of aid, then net domestic financing would be adjusted downward by the full amount of unprogrammed aid. If the aim is to allow spending to vary fully with aid, there would be no adjuster on net domestic financing of the government.

---

government paper during some periods. In Tanzania, the treasury bill rate rose from 2.6 percent in September 2002 to 7.6 percent by end-2003, while in Uganda two episodes of treasury bill sterilization pushed rates to over 20 percent in early 2001 and end-2003.[40]

There were considerable year-to-year policy variations in these countries. For example, in Tanzania, an early response focused on sterilizing through treasury bill sales was largely abandoned subsequently in favor of allowing the money supply to increase. This latter policy created excess liquidity in the banking system and eventually led to an increase in inflation. Thereafter, the authorities turned toward

---

[40]In the absence of a counterfactual, it is difficult to ascertain by how much the private sector was squeezed. In Tanzania, private sector investment fell from an average of 12.4 percent of GDP in the pre-surge period to 11.6 percent in the aid-surge period. In Uganda, the private investment ratio improved from 11.2 to 13.9 percent, but given the substantial increase in interest rates during the ster-

ilization episodes, it is possible that more improvement may have occurred in the absence of treasury bill sterilization.

Adjustments in the Net Domestic Financing Target under IMF-Supported Programs in Response to Aid Shocks

	Excess Aid (actual aid is higher than programmed)	Shortfall in Aid (actual aid is lower than programmed)
Ethiopia[1]	Reduced net domestic financing by 100 percent of excess aid	Raised net domestic financing by 50 percent of the shortfall in aid
Ghana[2]	Reduced net domestic financing by 100 percent of excess aid	Raised net domestic financing by some proportion of the shortfall in aid
Mozambique[3]	No adjuster: no effect on net domestic financing	No explicit adjuster: no change in net domestic financing of the budget deficit
Tanzania (2001–04)[4]	No effect on domestic financing of the government budget	Raised net domestic financing by 100 percent of the shortfall in aid; in 2001 adjustment was capped at $60 million
Tanzania (1996–2000)[5,6]	Reduced net domestic financing by 100 percent of excess aid	Raised net domestic financing by 60 percent of the shortfall in aid
Uganda[7]	Reduced net domestic financing by 100 percent of excess aid	Raised net domestic financing by 100 percent of the shortfall in aid

[1]A shortfall (or excess) in foreign program assistance, defined as the cumulative sum of nonproject external funding, excluding assistance under the Heavily Indebted Poor Countries (HIPC) Initiative, from the programmed levels triggers adjustments.

[2]The adjuster allowing for a higher ceiling to account for unexpected aid shortfalls changed from 50 percent of the shortfall to a fixed $50 million cap in June 2001. This cap was raised to $75 million in March 2002.

[3]Domestic primary deficit was the target in Mozambique, which implicitly implied a target for net domestic financing of the government. However, an increase in net domestic assets in response to an unexpected shortfall in program aid implicitly allowed additional domestic financing.

[4]A shortfall in foreign program assistance, which is defined as the cumulative sum of program grants and loans, from the programmed levels, triggers adjustments. For 2001, the trigger was net foreign financing, which was defined as the cumulative sum of program grants and loans minus external debt service paid.

[5]A shortfall (or excess) in net foreign financing, defined as the cumulative sum of program grants and loans minus external debt service paid, from the programmed levels triggers adjustments.

[6]In 1996–97, performance criteria on net credit from the Bank of Tanzania to the government (ceiling) were also in place, adjusted upward by 60 percent (downward by 100 percent) for any shortfall (excess) in net foreign financing.

[7]Net credit to the government (ceiling) adjusted up (down) for any shortfall (excess) in import support (basically, program aid), including debt relief.

selling foreign exchange to sterilize the monetary injection associated with aid-related spending, resulting in a sharp rise in aid absorption and some real exchange rate appreciation. In effect, the authorities moved toward a delayed spend-and-absorb strategy.[41]

In Mozambique, despite more aid absorption than the other countries, the large fiscal expansion was also accompanied by more monetary loosening than in the other countries. Reserve money growth shot up from about 7 percent per annum before the aid surge to 53 percent in 2001. Inflation followed suit, peaking at well over 20 percent in early 2002. From 2002 onward, however, the authorities undertook more sterilization through foreign exchange and treasury bill sales, bringing down reserve money growth. In addition, rapid GDP growth led to an increase in the demand for money. Consequently, inflation was brought under 10 percent by 2003.

[41]Ethiopia in the latter part of its aid-surge period also saw an increase in absorption.

Table 2.7. Policy Response to Aid Surge
(In percent)

	Not Spent[1]	Partly Spent	Mostly Spent	Fully Spent
Not Absorbed[2]	Ghana (0, 7)			Tanzania (0, 91)
Partly Absorbed	Ethiopia (20, 0)		Uganda (27, 74)	
Mostly Absorbed				Mozambique (66, 100)
Fully Absorbed				

[1]"Spent" variable = non-aid fiscal balance deterioration as percent of incremental aid inflow. Truncated at 0 and 100. This variable is the second entry within brackets for each country.

[2]"Absorbed" variable = non-aid current account deterioration as percent of incremental aid inflow. Truncated at 0 and 100. This variable is the first entry within brackets for each country.

Better adherence to the IMF-supported program paths (lower reserves accumulation and greater sales of foreign exchange by the central bank) would have reduced the need for sterilization through treasury bills, helping to avoid crowding out private sector investment in Tanzania and Uganda, and reducing inflation in Mozambique (Figure 2.6). This would have been a more suitable response to the surge in aid inflows because, unlike in Ethiopia and Ghana, the level of import coverage afforded by gross reserves was quite high in all three countries.

Conclusions and Policy Implications

Summary of Findings

Were there significant macroeconomic constraints on aid absorption? Yes, in the sense that in most countries absorption fell significantly short of the increment in aid inflows. Although there is considerable variation from year to year, on a cumulative basis no country entirely absorbed the increased level of aid.[42] Absorption ranged from two-thirds for Mozambique to zero for Ghana and Tanzania. Despite the conjecture that to absorb and spend is generally the best use of aid, no country in the sample systematically pursued this strategy.

Was Dutch disease a problem? There is no evidence in the sample of significant real exchange rate appreciation as a result of a surge in aid. This is consistent with the pattern of aid absorption noted above; if aid is accumulated in reserves, then there is no need for a real exchange rate appreciation to mediate a fall in net exports and thereby absorb the aid. Hence the conclusion that Dutch disease was not a problem ex post for any of the countries studied. Of course, part of the

reason that real appreciation (and consequently, Dutch disease) was not observed is precisely because authorities were concerned with competitiveness and restricted absorption accordingly.

Why did some countries save the increase in aid, neither spending nor absorbing? Two of the countries studied—Ethiopia and Ghana—neither absorbed nor spent a significant part of incremental aid. A number of related but distinct factors seemed to underlie this response. First, both countries went into the aid-surge period with a precariously low level of international reserves and a need to establish macroeconomic stability. Hence, building sufficient import coverage was one motive for accumulating the aid. Second, aid volatility probably played a role in determining absorption behavior in some years. For example, in 2003, when aid surged again in Ghana after collapsing the previous year, part of the motivation for the don't-absorb-don't-spend strategy was to protect against excessive fiscal tightening in the event of a future reduction in aid inflows. Third, nonabsorption may have been governed by a desire to avoid appreciation and preserve international competitiveness and, when coupled with a policy of not increasing government expenditures, to curb inflation (in Ghana's case) or to keep inflation in check (in Ethiopia's case).

Why did some countries fail to use aid to increase net imports at the same time as they increased fiscal spending? That is, why did they spend but not absorb? In Mozambique, Tanzania, and Uganda, and in Ethiopia over 2002–03, government spending out of incremental aid exceeded the amount of aid absorbed. The governments of these countries increased domestic expenditures, but there was a much smaller increase in net imports. This is potentially the most problematic response to aid surges. It can create high inflation, as it did in Mozambique, or require substantial treasury bill sterilization, and hence high interest rates and increases in domestic debt, to keep inflation in check.

---

[42]Heller and Gupta (2002) discuss a number of challenges for aid-recipient countries at both the micro and macro level that could limit aid absorption.

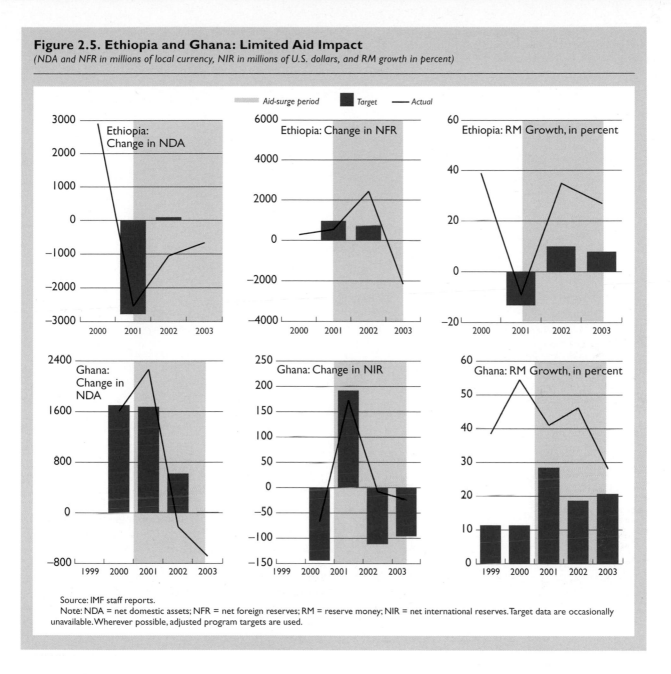

Figure 2.5. Ethiopia and Ghana: Limited Aid Impact
(NDA and NFR in millions of local currency, NIR in millions of U.S. dollars, and RM growth in percent)

Source: IMF staff reports.
Note: NDA = net domestic assets; NFR = net foreign reserves; RM = reserve money; NIR = net international reserves. Target data are occasionally unavailable. Wherever possible, adjusted program targets are used.

What were the main reasons for this policy response? In Ethiopia over 2002–03, absorption was only partial even though the aid increase was largely spent, and the monetary authorities took no obvious actions to reduce absorption, such as sterilizing the associated monetary expansion. However, the monetary authorities' sales of foreign exchange of the aid inflows were dictated by the exchange rate peg to the U.S. dollar. It would have taken further action by the authorities to absorb more of the aid.

In the other countries, the dominant factor behind this response appears to have been a desire to preserve international competitiveness, manifested in an unwillingness to see the nominal or real exchange rate appreciate. Thus, the central banks of each country accumulated international reserves throughout the aid-surge period, despite a relatively comfortable level of import coverage.

This still begs the question of why, in the face of the desire to avoid appreciation, the aid was spent at all? One explanation may be that political pressures make it difficult to resist spending aid money. For example, donors may object to having the aid they provide simply accumulated in government deposits at the central bank. Indeed, loans for projects might require a certain amount of domestic expenditures every year, at the risk of being stopped altogether.

Figure 2.6. Mozambique, Tanzania and Uganda: Spending Exceeds Absorption
(NDA in millions of local currency, NIR in millions of U.S. dollars, and RM growth in percent)

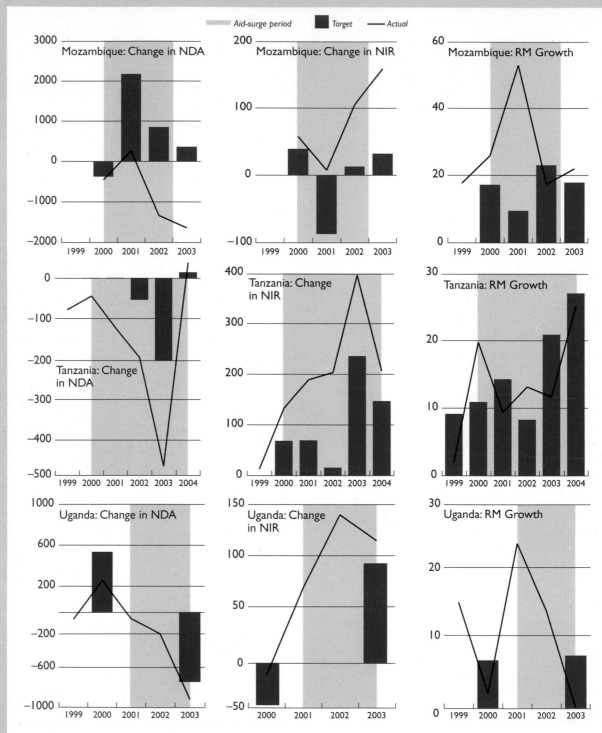

Source: IMF staff reports.
Notes: NDA = net domestic assets; NIR = net foreign reserves; RM = reserve money. Target data are occasionally unavailable. Wherever possible, adjusted program targets are used. In Uganda, the 2000 target for NDA is for the banking system.

These cases illustrate the risk that policies on spending aid inflows may be inconsistent with policies on exchange rate and monetary management of these same inflows. This may be partly because the link between these two sets of issues may not be fully understood by all the relevant policymakers. It may also be because institutional responsibilities for these two sets of issues are separated. Fiscal authorities and donors will find it entirely appropriate that aid inflows to the budget be spent. Central bank officials, on the other hand, may be more concerned about implications for the real exchange rate and the export sector. A spend-but-don't-absorb response may be an unfortunate outcome that neither party fully desires.[43]

Were aid inflows inflationary? Whether the aid surges were inflationary or stabilizing depended on the macroeconomic policy reaction:

- In Mozambique, Tanzania, and Uganda, aid inflows did create inflationary pressures, because the excess of spending over absorption implied an injection of domestic liquidity. In Mozambique, the gap was particularly large, and hence the country experienced high inflation. In Tanzania and Uganda, the inflationary pressures led to various episodes of sterilization through treasury bill sales. Although inflation in these countries was consequently contained below 10 percent, this came at the cost of rising interest rates, and in Uganda's case, a rapidly rising level of domestic debt.
- In Ethiopia and Ghana, the don't-absorb-don't-spend response implied that, over the aid-surge period as a whole, incremental aid did not contribute to inflationary pressures.
- With a different policy response, aid can help reduce inflation. The strategy of absorbing but not spending was executed successfully in some years, notably in Ethiopia and Ghana in 2001. In each case it was part of a successful macroeconomic stabilization program. It was planned but not executed more generally in Ghana during 2001–03, in part perhaps because of concerns about exchange rate appreciation but also as a reaction to the volatility of aid.[44]

---

[43]This issue raises the possibility that there is a potential cost to central bank independence in the context of aid-dependent, low-income countries, as mentioned in Heller (2005). Chapter VIII discusses this issue further.

[44]This is broadly consistent with the conclusions of Buffie and others (2004). However, they assume aid is fully absorbed. Their empirical conclusion that aid is on average 80 percent spent in sub-Saharan Africa also would seem to reflect a wide variety of country experiences, some with full spending and some with none. The inflationary impact evidently depends on the interaction of spending and absorption.

PRGF-Supported Program Design Issues

Strategies for Reacting to Aid Surges

In general, monetary and net international reserve (NIR) targets under the PRGF-supported programs were consistent with a textbook absorb-and-spend response to aid inflows. Where macroeconomic stability had not been established or domestic debt was too high, the programs appropriately envisaged absorbing but not spending.

In practice, these goals typically diverged from the authorities' concerns about international competitiveness and their desire to avoid nominal appreciation. Hence, in those countries where spending exceeded absorption—Mozambique, Tanzania, and Uganda—NIR remained consistently above the programmed path (because of a reluctance to sell foreign exchange to the extent envisaged by the program), while NDA remained below the programmed path (because of attempted treasury bill sterilization to dampen the consequent inflationary pressures). The countries therefore did not benefit from the full extent of aid, inflationary pressures were created, and treasury bill sterilization led to an increasingly high debt service burden on domestic debt.

The consistency of monetary and exchange rate policy with fiscal policy needs greater attention in cases where the authorities spend but do not absorb the aid. Typically, the IMF recommends exchange rate flexibility and foreign exchange sales when a spend-and-don't-absorb outcome emerges. However, where countries are unwilling to follow this advice—perhaps in order to guard competitiveness—more care needs to be taken that an appropriate outcome is achieved.

One option would be to limit spending as well, following the pattern of Ghana and, for part of the time, Ethiopia. This would have the merit of avoiding macroeconomic difficulties while saving the aid for later, and would make sense if Dutch disease concerns outweigh the benefits from the absorption of aid inflows. Even here, the best response would be to work to improve the quality of public expenditures and the quality of aid. However, where aid inflows are volatile, international reserves are too low, or good projects cannot be implemented, reserve accumulation may be the most reasonable short-run response.

Another option is to allow the monetary expansion necessary to accommodate increased expenditures, and accept inflation as the mechanism through which real appreciation occurs. This policy may work well in the short run, especially if a rapid supply response tempers inflation. In the medium term, the incremental domestic expenditures should increase the demand for imports, and the saved foreign exchange should then allow the authorities to accommodate this increased import demand without running low on international reserves. In essence, this is a spend-and-eventually-absorb scenario, of the kind followed by Tanzania after 2003. This requires some tolerance for a period of higher inflation to achieve the required real appreciation and, critically, a willingness on the part of the central bank to defend the nominal exchange rate against depreciation. In other words, the central bank must tolerate the real appreciation and eventually sell foreign exchange as the current account deficit increases.[45]

Most of the countries in the sample—Mozambique, Uganda, and initially, Tanzania—attempted to combat inflationary pressures through treasury bill sterilization. This approach is likely to be suboptimal under many circumstances. Again, aid is not absorbed, while domestic public expenditures in conjunction with higher interest rates potentially crowd out private investment. In addition, where monetary expansion has not yet led to higher inflation and the nominal exchange rate remains stable, programs must exercise care before prescribing treasury bill sterilization that could prevent delayed absorption.

However, sterilization would generally be preferable to inflation as a source of domestic financing (IMF, 2005b). Thus, in a country with a given spend-and-don't-absorb policy, perhaps politically dictated, where inflation is high or rising, there would be a case for sterilization through treasury bills.

Tanzania's experience illustrates how the different policy options work. The aid increases were largely spent. Initially, the monetary authorities attempted to control money growth through sterilization, raising interest rates, and depressing private investment. A subsequent relaxation of monetary policy led to rapid money growth but still no inflation, real exchange rate appreciation, or absorption. Finally, more aggressive sterilization through foreign exchange sales led to an increase in absorption and some real exchange rate appreciation.

Dealing with Aid Volatility

Aid volatility raises a special set of issues. In general, whenever a significant increase in aid was anticipated, program ceilings on the government's primary balance were raised, thereby allowing greater government expenditure. Similarly, reserve targets were also consistent with absorbing expected increases in aid flows.

When there was a deviation from the anticipated aid path, however, programs were more cautious about spending the "excess" aid in most cases. This is because the programs often included adjusters that would fully limit the spending (and absorption) of surprise aid.[46] A symmetric response to aid shortfalls would imply allowing a full increase in domestically-financed spending when aid shortfalls emerged. However, in most cases the PRGF-supported programs limited additional domestic financing of the budget in cases of shortfalls.[47] In practice, however, these adjusters were not a constraint because the budgetary aid outcomes were broadly in line with projections (except in Ghana in 2001).

Further consideration should be given in individual cases to whether such an asymmetric response to aid shocks is appropriate. In general, aid volatility should presumably be smoothed by saving some of the aid in high-aid years (both fiscally and in terms of reserve accumulation that is neither spending nor absorbing) and by dissaving (that is, running down reserves and increasing the deficit after aid) when aid shortfalls emerge. Against this logic must be balanced the temptation to treat positive shocks as permanent and negative ones as temporary, in which case such a policy would lead to a rundown of reserves. Clearly, the level of reserves may itself be an important factor in deciding whether to have symmetric or asymmetric adjusters—countries with lower reserves have less scope to smooth negative aid shocks.

Critically, effective smoothing requires coordinated fiscal and monetary policy responses. Taking the opportunity of a temporary aid surge to build reserves may make sense, but generally only if accompanied by increased budgetary savings as well. Otherwise, the aid surge leads to an increase in the budget deficit that is effectively domestically financed.

Final Considerations

The key long-run strategic choice is whether to use the aid—by absorbing and spending—or not, in which case the aid should be neither absorbed nor spent. The latter choice is equivalent to refusing aid altogether. Other responses should be at most short-run. To absorb and not spend can be very helpful in stabilizing the economy, because it permits a reduction in domestic debt and/or inflation without the fiscal contraction that this would normally require. It cannot be a feasible long-run strategy once stability has been achieved, however, because domestic debt stocks cannot fall indefinitely, and also because donors typically would want their aid spent. To spend and not absorb also is not a desirable long-run strategy because it implies that aid is serving

---

[45]If the authorities fail to defend the nominal exchange rate, inflation will increase without causing real appreciation. This is an inferior response: the aid is not absorbed, while the highly inefficient and regressive inflation tax pays for the spending increase.

[46]In three of five sample countries, spending of excess aid was limited to zero through adjusters on net domestic financing.

[47]For example, in Ethiopia and Ghana, additional domestic financing was restricted to 50 percent of the aid shortfall. Since both countries completely restricted the spending of excess aid, the adjusters in each case were asymmetric.

not to finance additional net imports but to trigger additional domestically-financed spending.

From this perspective, the typical discussion of the monetary management of aid inflows, which centers on the question of how to manage the consequences of aid-related spending, risks missing the point. The common logic proceeds in two steps: (1) the government necessarily spends the aid receipts; and (2) the central bank chooses the appropriate instrument for sterilization—that is, whether to sell foreign exchange causing some real appreciation, sell government bonds inducing an interest rate hike, or employing a combination of both. This line of thought leads to the view that central banks need to balance the risks of excessive exchange rate appreciation against excessive interest rate increases and choose some reasonable middle ground.

This perspective fails to treat the analysis of monetary and fiscal policy jointly. The first consideration should be whether extra public spending at some potential cost to export competitiveness is desirable. If not, the question should immediately arise as to whether the aid should be spent in the first place. After all, additional domestically-financed spending can take place in the absence of aid. Thus, the question becomes whether to spend and absorb or neither spend nor absorb.

In considering this question, it may be helpful to review the nature of macroeconomic absorptive capacity constraints. Frequently, macroeconomic concepts such as inflation and the real exchange rate misalignment are posed as constraints that limit the ability of a country to spend aid on building schools or roads or fighting HIV/AIDS.

However, the real issue is not a trade-off between allowing more inflation and hiring more nurses. The real question is how the productive resources in a country—its workers, natural resources, and physical capital—are to be deployed. Aid raises this question because it allows more domestic resources to be devoted to building physical and human capital at home or to satisfying consumption needs, because fewer domestic resources are needed for producing exports or import substitutes. To the extent that there are domestic projects carrying a high rate of return, or that have an ameliorating impact on poverty, this reallocation of resources is beneficial. The real exchange rate appreciation that may result is not, in itself, a macroeconomic cost of using aid, but rather part of the mechanism whereby aid is useful, because it may be required to draw resources out of the traded goods sector.

When aid comes in the form of grants, the opportunity cost for the recipient of absorbing and spending aid is the foregone use of domestic resources, particularly in the traded goods sector. The traded goods sector—especially nontraditional exports—may play a special role in generating productivity growth. If so, the aid may lower growth by slowing the growth in that sector. It may also have adverse consequences for poverty

by squeezing margins in traditional exports. A related but distinct potential cost has to do with the unpredictability of aid. For example, if aid inflows are high now but fall in the future, then in the presence of transaction costs and imperfect capital markets it may be difficult to resuscitate export firms crowded out by the aid.[48]

The critical strategic question for aid recipients is how to balance these costs and benefits. The question of when the aid-financed investments cease to become sufficiently productive is closely related to the concept of absorptive capacity.[49] The rate of return to investments will likely decline as the rate of investment rises—the best projects should be the first undertaken. Moreover, resources will be drawn out of other uses, and this will likely become progressively costlier—the least-well-used resources should be the first to be drawn away. The implication is that there may be a level of investment beyond which the rate of return will be lower than that achieved in alternative uses. Absorptive capacity has been reached when aid-financed investments do not yield enough to justify the resources used to produce them.

If the judgment is made in a particular situation that the costs of absorbing and spending outweigh the benefits, what is to be done?

One possible solution is to recognize that absorptive capacity cannot be taken as given. It is critical to make expenditures more effective, including by improving project choice and expenditure management, and more broadly the overall policy environment (Bevan, 2005). Attention should be focused on how, and how fast, to scale up aid so as to minimize competitiveness problems, such as by focusing on ways to use aid to increase productivity and critical imports.

For example, a carefully designed and scaled-up investment program may raise the rate of return while minimizing the cost for the traded goods sector. An investment program aimed at improving productivity in the medium term may result in a traded goods sector even larger than it would have been without the aid, as the productivity gains resulting from better roads, education, or health may outweigh the effects of the real exchange rate appreciation (Bourguignon and others, 2005).

Similarly, aid spent directly on noncompetitive imports may create fewer tensions with an export-led growth strategy. For example, using aid to import factors of production used in the export sector (e.g.,

---

[48]The same considerations apply when aid arrives in the form of concessional debt, except that the opportunity cost of aid includes the need to repay the debt. As a result, the risks are higher: if aid is poorly used or Dutch disease effects are strong, the debt burden will be hard to bear.

[49]Adler (1965), Guillaumont (1971), and Berg (1983) are early treatments of this issue.

chemical fertilizer) would not tend to create pressure on the real exchange rate.

However, raising absorptive capacity is easier said than done, and the stakes are high: if the aid-related spending turns out not to be effective, not only is the aid wasted, but scarce domestic resources are misallocated and the traded goods sector is shrunk.

Another possibility is to save the aid until it can be effectively used. This would involve accumulating reserves and avoiding an increase in the budget deficit net of aid. This solution has two major problems. First, it is politically hard to limit government spending of the local currency counterpart to the aid inflows—after all, the aid has been given and the needs are great. This would lead to the spend-and-don't-absorb policy denigrated previously. Second, a country that saves aid inflows in this fashion would alienate donors, who might understandably decide to reallocate the aid to a more eager recipient. Saving a large part of an aid surge is particularly appropriate when there is a concern that the aid boom will prove temporary; however, "treating the aid flow as temporary may well make it so" (Adam, 2001, p. 11).

Donors can help resolve some of these tensions by improving the quality of aid. Aid that is less tied and for which the administration uses up fewer scarce management resources in the recipient country would be more useful. Equally important, aid that is more predictable, and in particular that can be relied on over the medium term, can be spent and absorbed more effectively without the otherwise valid concern that its disappearance will leave the recipient with unsustainable expenditures and an overvalued real exchange rate. Aid that buffers temporary negative shocks may also be more readily used, insofar as stabilization of the exchange rate and aggregate demand in the face of a temporary contraction would not tend to raise competitiveness concerns.

The IMF can provide only supportive guidance regarding the strategic question of how to best absorb and spend aid in the long run. However, the long run famously never arrives. In the meantime, the authorities in aid-recipient countries must balance a complex set of objectives involving fiscal policy and exchange rate and reserve management. But one message is simple: a given aid dollar can be used to build reserves or to increase the fiscal deficit, but not both. The cases reviewed in this paper suggest that trying to do so may make aid less effective.

Appendix 2.1. Methodology for Sample Selection

For each country in the sample, this paper examines the pattern of net aid inflows, which are defined as gross inflows (including debt relief) less amortization, inter-est payments, and arrears clearance.[50] In particular, the paper identifies a year/period in which net aid inflows increased substantially, and a detailed analysis is conducted of the policy responses to increased inflows and macroeconomic outcomes for that year/period and succeeding years. While gross aid flows may be a better aggregate for analyzing donors' leverage in policy dialogue, net aid inflows are a more appropriate measure for assessing the macroeconomic effects of a scaling up of aid. The focus in this paper is on countries characterized by (1) a relatively sound policy record, (2) a large rise in net aid inflows, and (3) net aid inflows that comprise a significant percentage of GDP.

First, the avoidance of the worst performers in terms of institutions and economic policies was driven by a desire to draw lessons of relevance for situations in which, broadly speaking, policymaking is not denominated by macroeconomic disarray, misgovernance, or post-conflict reconstruction. The focus is on how to help those countries that are best positioned, institutionally and in terms of the policy framework, to absorb large quantities of aid. The criteria used were the World Bank's indicators of quality of economic institutions and policies (the CPIA). Only those countries with a CPIA ranking in the third quartile and above were considered.

Second, a country must have experienced a significant rise in net aid inflows as a percentage of GDP. The quantitative screen was for a rise in the net aid/GDP proportion by at least 1 percentage point compared with a period identified by the data as the pre-surge period.

The period at which aid may have begun to rise varies across countries. To divide the 1996–2003 period into two subperiods of pre-surge and ongoing-surge, the "breakpoint" was found that minimizes the sum of squared deviations between annual aid levels and within-period average aid levels. In some cases, aid flows rose linearly, so there was no obvious breakpoint. In these cases, the breakpoint was subjectively and uniformly identified as 2000.

Third, to focus on cases where aid is macroeconomically central, net aid inflows should be large relative to the economy receiving them. The screen applied to capture this feature was that only countries for which net aid was at least 10 percent of GDP over the post/ongoing-surge period were considered.

Excluding small island economies and countries that were emerging from either a major civil conflict or that were not PRGF-eligible, this left seven countries, all of them African (see Table 2.A1; Table 2.A2 presents aid and CPIA data for PRGF-eligible countries). Of these, Mauritania was excluded because of a history

---

[50]Gross inflows include all the resources a low-income country receives in grants (including HIPC debt relief) and loans.

Table 2.A1. Aid Flows: Changes and Levels
(As a percent of GDP)

	Aid-Surge Breakpoint Year[1]	Net Aid: Change Over the Surge Period[2]	Net Aid: Level Following Initial Surge[2]
Ethiopia	2001	11.4	22.1
Ghana	2000	3.0	11.5
Malawi	1998	7.8	24.7
Mauritania	2001	6.6	28.2
Mozambique	2002	6.4	33.0
Tanzania	2002	1.4	13.7
Uganda	2000	2.5	13.5

[1]Where this year came after 2001, 2000 was selected as the breakpoint for the calculations.

[2]Using net aid flow data from the Development Assistance Committee of the Organization for Economic Cooperation and Development.

of significant misreporting. Although Malawi emerged from the quantitative screens, its aid "surge" was in 1998 and reflected a temporary dip in aid flows from the previous year. In contrast to the other countries in the sample, there was no significant and sustained increase in aid, relative to previous periods. As a result, Ethiopia, Ghana, Mozambique, Tanzania, and Uganda were selected.

Appendix 2.2. Dutch Disease: Theory and Evidence

Dutch disease is related to the idea that productivity growth is particularly high when resources are devoted to exports, particularly of nontraditional products, because of learning-by-doing or other dynamic externalities in these relatively competitive and technologically-advanced industries. The decline of the export sector, mediated by an increase in the demand for and price of nontradables, may lower the attainable growth path of the economy. For this argument to hold, dynamic externalities in the export sector would have to outweigh the benefits of capital accumulation associated with aid-financed investment (as well as any related productivity growth). A slightly different argument is premised on imperfect capital markets and hysteresis: if aid is temporarily high and crowds out export firms through real appreciation, it may not be possible to resuscitate these firms once aid falls and the real exchange rate depreciates.

The theoretical case for Dutch disease is ambiguous. For example, when learning-by-doing externalities can also take place in the nontradable sector, the long-run adverse impact will be limited, even if the real exchange rate appreciates in the short term (Torvik, 2001). In the longer run, the investments in physi-

cal and human capital, both in the government and in the private sector, begin to bear fruit and productivity increases not only in the tradable sector but also in the nontradable sector, potentially offsetting the initial loss of competitiveness.[51]

The effects of Dutch disease can be enhanced if the aid-recipient economy has weak financial markets. For example, in thin foreign exchange markets, volatile and lumpy aid disbursements can cause overshooting in the exchange rate or interest rate. Similarly, in the short term, when the real exchange appreciation due to excess demand for nontradables is not yet compensated for by the increase in productivity, firms may be forced out of business if they do not have access to adequate credit to smooth out the shock. Temporary overshooting of the actual real exchange rate after an increase in aid may therefore be more damaging than the longer-term shift in the equilibrium real exchange rate.

Despite a substantial body of theoretical literature on the implications of Dutch disease from aid inflows, empirical work is limited—particularly in low-income countries. Recent cross-country studies find some evidence for the real appreciation effect. For example, Elbadawi (1999) finds that a 10 percent increase in the aid-to-GDP ratio appreciates the real exchange rate by about 1 percent. Individual country studies, however, offer mixed results. Some (e.g., Malawi and Sri Lanka) find that aid inflows cause real appreciation, but others

---

[51]Nkusu (2004a) discusses the theoretical determinants of Dutch disease and emphasizes the mitigating role of excess domestic capacity. Adams and Bevan (2003) describe a nonmonetary theoretical model and calibrate it for Uganda.

Table 2.A2. Net Official Development Assistance (ODA)
(In percent of GDP)

	CPIA Ranking Ranking Quintiles[1]	ODA Average 1996–99	ODA Average 2000–03		CPIA Ranking Ranking Quintiles[1]	ODA Average 1996–99	ODA Average 2000–03
Albania	Third	9.8	6.7	Laos	Fifth	19.6	15.1
Armenia	First	12.5	10.5	Lesotho	Third	7.6	7.3
Azerbaijan	Second	3.5	4.1	Madagascar	Second	13.7	8.7
Bangladesh	Second	2.7	2.3	Malawi	Third	20.9	24.7
Benin	Second	10.2	9.6	Mali	Second	15.8	13.6
Bolivia	Second	8.6	8.8	Mauritania	First	21.3	26.5
Burkina Faso	Second	14.4	13.1	Moldova	Third	4.3	8.1
Burundi	Fifth	9.1	22.8	Mongolia	Third	23.4	20.5
Cambodia	Fourth	10.3	11.6	Mozambique	Third	26.6	33.0
Cameroon	Third	5.1	5.8	Nepal	Second	8.0	7.2
Central African Republic	Fifth	11.9	6.2	Nicaragua	First	32.3	17.7
Chad	Fourth	13.8	10.3	Niger	Fourth	13.5	13.8
Congo, Dem. Rep. of	Fourth	2.6	31.7	Pakistan	Second	1.3	2.4
Congo, Republic of	Fourth	9.5	1.9	Papua New Guinea	Fifth	7.6	7.1
Cote d'Ivoire	Fourth	5.7	4.0	Rwanda	Second	20.8	19.1
Eritrea	Fourth	21.0	36.2	Senegal	First	11.1	8.6
Ethiopia	Third	10.7	18.0	Sierra Leone	Fourth	15.1	39.3
Gambia	Fourth	9.0	14.1	Sri Lanka	First	2.5	2.3
Georgia	Third	7.8	7.4	Sudan	Fifth	2.0	2.2
Ghana	Second	8.5	11.6	Tajikistan	Fourth	10.6	13.5
Grenada	First	2.9	3.0	Tanzania	First	11.6	14.6
Guinea	Fourth	8.7	7.1	Togo	Fifth	8.3	3.9
Guinea-Bissau	Fifth	45.8	39.4	Tonga	Fourth	16.2	14.7
Guyana	Third	20.0	12.3	Uganda	First	11.0	13.6
Haiti	Fifth	9.9	5.5	Vietnam	First	4.2	4.5
Honduras	First	9.1	7.6	Yemen	Second	5.4	3.9
Kenya	Third	4.3	3.9	Zambia	Third	16.2	16.1
Kyrgyz Republic	Third	15.9	12.8	Zimbabwe	Fifth	4.3	2.2

Sources: Organization for Economic Cooperation and Development; International Monetary Fund, *World Economic Outlook;* and World Bank and IMF (2005).
[1]The Country Policy and Institutional Assessment (CPIA) is a measure used by the World Bank. The first quintile is the best ranking.

(e.g., Ghana, Nigeria, and Tanzania) find that aid flows are related to real depreciations.[52]

In a related literature, some papers find evidence of a significant detrimental impact of real appreciation on exports, particularly nontraditional exports (Sekkat and Varoudakis, 2000; Elbadawi, 2002). Empirical evidence also suggests that real appreciation contributed to the widening trade deficits in four African economies (Adenauer and Vagassky, 1998).

A recent approach is to look directly at the impact of aid on exports without attempting to trace through the real exchange rate channel. Rajan and Subramanian (2005a) examine the effects of aid in a sample of 33 countries in the 1980s and 15 countries in the 1990s.

They find that export and labor-intensive manufacturing industries grew significantly slower in those countries that received the most aid, and that a 1 percentage point increase in the ratio of aid to GDP is roughly equivalent to a 4 percentage point overvaluation of the exchange rate. Arellano and others (2005) find that aid significantly depresses the export sector in a sample of developing countries.

The risks of Dutch disease need to be balanced against the potential benefits from the investment that aid can finance. Here, the evidence is also mixed. The benefits of public investment are not clearly established empirically, as a general matter (Leite and Tsangarides, forthcoming). Of course, the rate of return will depend on the particular investment and a variety of country-specific circumstances. A strong case can nonetheless be made for a higher level in poor countries (United Nations Millennium Project Report, 2005). While the systematic evidence for a positive

[52]See White and Wignaraja (1992) for Sri Lanka; Ogun (1995) for Nigeria; Nyoni (1998) for Tanzania; Sackey (2001) for Ghana; Ouattara and Strobl (2003) for the CFA (African Financial Community) countries; and Fanizza (2001) for Malawi.

growth impact of private investment is stronger, it is less clear that aid can be effectively channeled into higher private investment.

More broadly, a huge literature asks directly whether aid affects growth, with somewhat mixed conclusions.[53] However, there is substantial cross-country evidence that exchange rate overvaluations are one of the few policy variables that matter for growth after controlling for institutions. There is also substantial micro-based evidence on the benefits of trade and, to some extent, learning-by-doing associated with exports. Weak exchange rates may also help predict the incidence of episodes of growth acceleration.[54] Case studies that examine the entire chain from aid through export performance to final outcomes include

Nkusu (2004b), who finds little sign of Dutch disease in Uganda.

On balance, the evidence on Dutch disease is mixed. Presumably, the seriousness of the problem and the benefits of aid-financed investments depend on the particular circumstances of each country. A country with strong dynamic externalities in the tradable goods sector may want to carefully consider the level of aid it can absorb without triggering too much real appreciation. It may also wish to seek aid in forms that are less likely to induce real appreciation.[55] It can safely be concluded, however, that the risk of Dutch disease raises the stakes: if aid-financed investments have poor rates of return, not only is the aid wasted, but there is a risk that overall growth may be impaired.

---

[53]See Clemens, Radelet, and Bhavnani (2004) for results showing a positive correlation between aid and growth, as well as Rajan and Subramanian (2005b) and Easterly, Levin, and Roodman (2003) for more skeptical views.

[54]Acemoglu and others (2003) present important evidence on overvaluation and growth, while Easterly, Levin, and Roodman (2003) summarize the literature. Hausmann, Pritchett, and Rodrik (2004) discuss the role of depreciated real exchange rates in sparking growth accelerations. Berg and Krueger (2003) summarize some of the literature on learning-by-doing and exports.

---

[55]This is harder than it seems. It is sometimes argued that aid in kind has no impact on the real exchange rate. This is true, however, only if the transferred good is one for which there was no existing effective demand. If the good transferred was already demanded domestically, then increasing the good's supply would depress the price of tradables relative to nontradables, leading to real appreciation. On the other hand, the transfer of a good for which there is no preexisting demand is clearly of limited utility in general (although not always—for example, one could imagine aid taking the form of expensive drugs or treatments for which there is no effective preexisting demand).

III Ethiopia

Amber Mahone

The Derg regime, a political dictatorship employing socialist central planning, held sway in Ethiopia from 1974 until its overthrow in 1991. After the totalitarian regime fell, the Ethiopian authorities implemented an economic reform program to revive the war-torn economy, and to liberalize many of the central planning policies of the previous government. The authorities made great strides in consolidating the gains of these reforms in subsequent years, with generally favorable results for the economy.

With the new transitional government in place, the country then experienced a surge in aid inflows as it undertook a wide range of structural reforms. These aid flows decreased from 1997 to 2000, when Ethiopia and Eritrea engaged in a violent border conflict. The country's Enhanced Structural Adjustment Facility (ESAF) program with the International Monetary Fund ended in October 1999, with the full amount of programmed funds undrawn. The border conflict was partly resolved in 2000. Shortly thereafter, in March 2001, Ethiopia began a Poverty Reduction and Growth Facility (PRGF) program that accompanied a second period of high aid inflows. It is this second period of increased aid inflows, from 2001 to 2003, that is the subject of this case study.[1]

Since 1992, the country has had nearly consecutive Structural Adjustment Facility (SAF), ESAF, and PRGF programs. Under the most recent PRGF program, Ethiopia achieved a fairly stable macroeconomic position, although growth remains heavily reliant on the success or failure of the annual rains and the agricultural sector.[2] Growth in GDP per capita has averaged 1.4 percent since 2001, even withstanding the country's recession in 2002 and 2003 due to a severe drought.[3] These growth rates, while inadequate, compare favorably to the average GDP per capita growth rate of only 0.04 percent over the previous 10 years.

Ethiopia remains one of the poorest countries in the world, with a per capita income of around $150. The country's 2002 Poverty Reduction Strategy Paper reported a poverty head count of 45.5 percent in 1996, and of 44.2 percent in 2000. The country rates near the bottom of the Human Development Index, at 170th out of 177 countries. As the second most populous country in Africa, with approximately 67 million people, Ethiopia plays a critical role in determining Africa's success in reducing poverty and meeting the Millennium Development Goals (MDGs).

The next section examines the patterns of aid inflows during the study period more closely. To put the subsequent discussions of policy choices in context, this chapter then reviews the behavior of exchange rates and prices, and examines the potential influence of the terms of trade. The core of the chapter is the discussion of the overall pattern of absorption and the fiscal policy response. The final section breaks down the effects of the aid surge on a year-by-year basis in order to understand the authorities' monetary policy responses.

Pattern of Aid Inflows

The year 2001 marked the beginning of the turning point for Ethiopia, with aid flows, (defined as net public inflows) increasing to 8.6 percent of GDP, up from 5 percent of GDP the previous year. The U.S. dollar amount of net public inflows increased by 47 percent from 2000 to 2001. In 2002, aid inflows increased even more dramatically, to 16.1 percent of GDP, an increase of 70 percent over U.S. dollar amounts in 2001. In 2003, aid inflows leveled off, though remaining high, at levels near 15 percent of GDP.

Ethiopia received its largest surge of gross public aid in 1997, with levels of nearly 75 percent of GDP. However, most of this assistance was used for arrears clearance, resulting in net public aid inflows of only 2 percent of GDP that year. Ethiopia received a rescheduling of debt from the Paris Club in 1998 as well as

---

[1]Ethiopia's fiscal year begins on July 7. Throughout the chapter, the fiscal year is referred to by the last year. So for example, fiscal year 2000/01 is simply referred to as 2001.

[2]The IMF's ex-post assessment of its long-term engagement in Ethiopia found that fluctuations in rainfall have a substantial impact on real growth, with a change of 1 percent of rainfall leading to a change in real GDP of 0.3 percent in the next year (IMF, 2004).

[3]The drought during 2002–03 was the most severe the country had seen since 1985, with cereal production declining by 6 percent in 2002 and by a further 26 percent in 2003.

debt relief under the enhanced Heavily Indebted Poor Countries (HIPC) Initiative.[4]

Aid inflows are generally difficult to predict, and Ethiopia is no exception. When actual aid flows through the budget are compared with IMF aid forecasts, it can be seen that the initial surge in aid inflows, in 2001 was far less than predicted (Figure 3.1). In 2002 and 2003, predicted flows were largely on target with actual outcomes.

Net private inflows to Ethiopia are an important factor in the economy as well. They have been relatively stable, however, averaging 7 percent of GDP in the most recent three years, compared to an average of 6 percent between 1996–2000, thus allowing a focus on the macroeconomic impact of public inflows (Table 3.1).

Exchange Rate, Prices, and Terms of Trade

The Ethiopian authorities maintained a close crawling peg to the U.S. dollar over the course of the aid surge. The real effective exchange rate depreciated slightly over the study period, as did the nominal effective exchange rate and the nominal exchange rate against the U.S. dollar (Figure 3.2).

One possible explanation for the stability of the exchange rate despite the aid surge is a decline in food prices of approximately 10 percent in 2001 and 13 percent in 2002. The food surplus experienced in these years was due to a bumper harvest and large amounts of food aid.

A second potential explanatory factor is that Ethiopia's terms of trade fell sharply during the sample period, due to the collapse in coffee prices, the country's primary export (Table 3.2). Nonetheless, an analysis of the relative impact of both the aid inflows and

---

[4]The country reached the HIPC decision point in November 2001, and reached the enhanced HIPC completion point in April 2004.

Figure 3.1. Ethiopia: Programmed vs. Actual Levels of Net Budget Aid
(In percent of GDP)

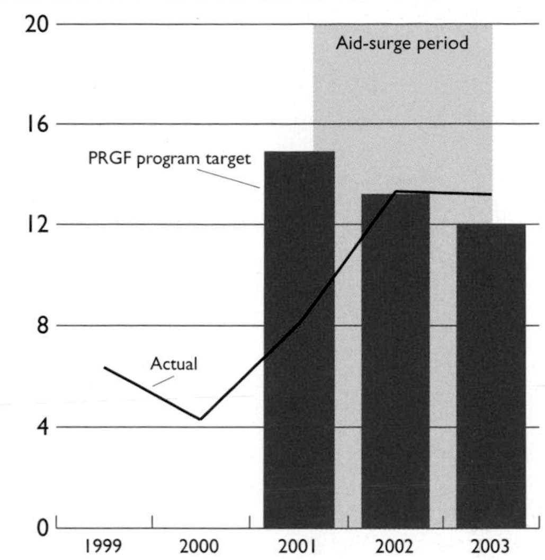

Note: PRGF = Poverty Reduction and Growth Facility.

the declining terms of trade shows that, in the first two years of surging aid inflows, the dollar gain from net aid inflows far outweighed the loss due to declining coffee exports (Table 3.3). The fact that 2001 and 2002 still saw a depreciation in the real exchange rate, despite the overall positive net impact of aid and trade, suggests that the Ethiopian authorities may have pursued policies to avoid an appreciation of the real exchange rate.

On average, across the 2001–03 aid-surge period, Ethiopia absorbed only about one-fifth of the 8 percentage point surge in aid flows (Table 3.4). Most of the

---

Table 3.1. Ethiopia: Aid and Other Inflows
(Percent of GDP)

	1996/97	1997/98	1998/99	1999/00	2000/01	2001/02	2002/03
Net public inflows	1.9	4.9	4.7	6.0	**8.8**	**16.1**	**15.0**
Net private inflows	5.0	5.0	6.6	8.1	**6.8**	**5.7**	**7.7**
Gross public inflows	74.6	13.1	11.7	8.8	**24.3**	**18.1**	**17.5**
Debt relief[1]	68.7	6.8	5.1	1.5	**13.3**	**1.5**	**2.8**
Change in arrears[2]	−59.9	0.8	1.9	0.6	**−12.5**	**0.0**	**0.0**
Memorandum item:							
GDP (real annual percent change)	5.1	−1.4	6.0	5.4	**7.7**	**1.6**	**−3.9**

Note: Figures in bold represent the aid-surge period.
[1]Includes a Paris Club rescheduling agreement in 1997/98 and traditional and Heavily Indebted Poor Countries (HIPC) Initiative debt relief.
[2]Negative values indicate a clearance of arrears.

Figure 3.2. Ethiopia: Exchange Rate and Price Developments

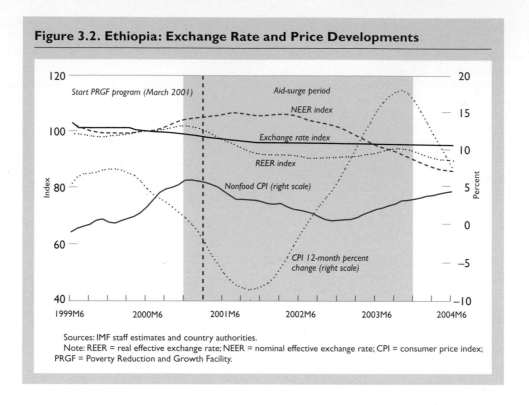

Sources: IMF staff estimates and country authorities.
Note: REER = real effective exchange rate; NEER = nominal effective exchange rate; CPI = consumer price index;
PRGF = Poverty Reduction and Growth Facility.

increment in aid was channeled into increasing official reserves, which rose from 5.2 percent of GDP in 2001 to 14 percent by 2003. The import cover of gross official reserves also improved substantially over the aid-surge period, from 2 to 3.8 months of imports.

Spending Out of Aid

The average fiscal response to the inflows during the three-year period of high aid inflows from 2001 to 2003 was very cautious. Ethiopia saw an increase in aid to the budget of approximately 6 percent of GDP during the aid surge.[5] The average overall fiscal balance (before aid) shows a small improvement, indicating that overall, the government did not spend any increment of the increased aid (Table 3.5). However, these aver-

ages mask significant year-to-year variations, which are taken up in the next section.[6]

The composition of government expenditure showed major improvements over the period in question. Before the aid surge, expenditure was dominated by the war with Eritrea, and defense expenditure reached nearly 13 percent of GDP in 2000. In 2001, the war subsided, and there followed a sharp decline in military defense expenditure. Total social spending (both current and capital), which remained low during the war years, has increased steadily since 2001.

Revenue collection in Ethiopia remained fairly steady, increasing by slightly more than 1 percentage point of GDP. During the aid-surge period, revenue collection fell short of PRGF projections on average by 1.7 percent of GDP. This shortfall is partly explained by the drought years of 2002 and 2003, when tax and nontax revenue collection was lower than expected, largely due to the heavy reliance on the agricultural sector. Overall, the differences between revenue collection before and during the aid-surge period are marginal, and there is no clear evidence that higher volumes of aid inflows reduced the country's revenue collection efforts.

---

[5]Note the distinction between net budgetary aid, as captured by the fiscal data, and net public aid, as captured by the balance of payments data. We use data on net *public* aid when examining the balance of payments, and net *budget* aid for assessing fiscal policy. Differences exist between the two figures because not all aid to a country is necessarily channeled though the government's budget, as a comparison of the aid data in Tables 3.4 and 3.5 shows. The IMF's ex-post assessment of its long-term engagement in Ethiopia notes that aid flows have not been well captured by fiscal data, partly because of the need for better reporting of activities by donors (IMF, 2004).

---

[6]Moreover, the finding that the Ethiopian government did not, on average, increase spending over the period needs to be qualified by noting that defense expenditure fell sharply during the aid-surge period, but total expenditure did not, thus allowing social spending to increase substantially.

Table 3.2. Ethiopia: Trade Indicators

	1998/99	1999/00	2000/01	2001/02	2002/03
Terms of trade index	100.0	70.1	**69.2**	**64.3**	**61.8**
Coffee price (U.S. dollars per thousand metric tons)	2.8	2.3	**1.9**	**1.5**	**1.3**
Annual change in coffee value (millions of U.S. dollars)	−138.8	−19.2	**−80.0**	**−18.8**	**2.0**
Annual change in coffee volume (millions of U.S. dollars)	−18.8	15.4	**−21.0**	**14.7**	**15.8**
Total imports, c.i.f. (millions of U.S. dollars)	1,558.0	1,611.0	**1,557.0**	**1,696.0**	**1,856.0**
As percent of GDP	24.1	24.7	**23.9**	**27.9**	**27.9**
Total exports f.o.b. (millions of U.S. dollars)	484.0	486.0	**463.0**	**452.0**	**483.0**
As percent of GDP	7.5	7.4	**7.1**	**7.4**	**7.3**
Noncoffee exports (millions of U.S. dollars)	203.0	224.0	**281.0**	**289.0**	**318.0**
As percent of GDP	3.1	3.4	**4.3**	**4.8**	**4.8**
As percent of total exports	41.9	46.1	**60.7**	**63.9**	**65.8**
Exports nonfactor services (millions of U.S. dollars)	430.0	498.0	**516.0**	**530.0**	**657.0**
Percent change	−1.1	15.8	**3.6**	**2.7**	**24.0**

Notes: c.i.f. = cost, insurance, and freight; f.o.b. = free on board. Figures in bold represent the aid-surge period. To estimate the dollar size of the terms-of-trade shock, exports and imports are calculated based on what they would have been had prices remained what they were in the previous year.

Monetary Policy Response

Reflecting the overall pattern of absorption and spending, the 2001–03 aid surge presented no major monetary policy challenges on a cumulative basis. By largely saving the aid in the form of higher reserves and reduced fiscal deficits (after aid), the authorities avoided real exchange rate appreciation and the need to manage aid-related increases in liquidity. Thus, on the whole, Ethiopia fits into the don't-absorb-don't-spend category during the period covered. However, this overall picture hides considerable and economically meaningful variation over different subperiods of the aid surge.

Monetary policy was anchored by a close, crawling peg to the U.S. dollar over the period of high aid inflows. The authorities maintained a crawling peg at about 7 percent depreciation annually between 1998 and 2000. With the surge in aid inflows, the authorities moved to a much slower rate of crawl starting in 2001, with an annual rate of depreciation of about 1.6 percent between 2001 and 2003 (Figure 3.3).

The capital account in Ethiopia is largely closed, leaving some scope for monetary policy even given the peg. The Ethiopian banking sector remains underdeveloped, dominated by the National Bank of Ethiopia and the Commercial Bank of Ethiopia. Interest rates remain low and controlled. Moreover, throughout the study period, the banking system contained excess liquidity. All this makes monetary policy somewhat difficult to observe.

Before examining monetary policy during the aid surge, it is useful to investigate the period prior to the aid surge, which was characterized by loose monetary policy, downward pressure on the exchange rate, and a loss of reserves. The 1998–2000 war with Eritrea presented a series of challenges, in particular, escalating defense expenditure. The authorities engaged in a fiscal expansion of 7 percent of GDP, well above the PRGF indicative target for expenditure. In the context of the crawling peg exchange rate, one result was an increase in the current account deficit and a collapse of reserves (Figure 3.4). The fiscal expansion, loose monetary policy, and exchange rate depreciation also began to push up nonfood inflation, which increased from levels near zero in 1999 to 5 percent by December 2000.[7]

During the aid surge, monetary policy was largely driven by how the country addressed the question of spending the aid inflow. Table 3.6 shows the change in the annual averages of the balance of payments and fiscal identity presented previously as period averages. The aid-surge period can be broadly divided into two: 2001: Fiscal contraction in the first year of the aid surge, when aid inflows were saved while none of the aid was absorbed; and 2002–03: The late aid-surge period, when spending of aid inflows exceeded absorption.

---

[7]Even as nonfood inflation rose, headline inflation rates actually fell to negative levels during this period. However, negative headline inflation was due to food surpluses from a bumper harvest and high amounts of food aid.

Table 3.3. Ethiopia: Terms-of-Trade Shocks and Aid Inflows
(In millions of U.S. dollars)

	1998/99	1999/00	2000/01	2001/02	2002/03
Exports					
Actual	484	486	**463**	**452**	**483**
Counterfactual[1]	586	567	**487**	**508**	**497**
Imports					
Actual	1,558	1,611	**1,557**	**1,696**	**1,856**
Counterfactual[1]	1,606	1,207	**1,569**	**1,716**	**1,811**
Trade Balance					
Actual	−1,074	−1,125	**−1,094**	**−1,243**	**−1,374**
Counterfactual[2]	−1,020	−640	**−1,082**	**−1,208**	**−1,314**
Effect of terms-of-trade shock[3]	−54	−484	**−13**	**−36**	**−59**
Aid effect	−15	24	**235**	**417**	**21**
Net effect	−69	−460	**222**	**381**	**−38**

Note: Figures in bold represent the aid-surge period.

[1]Calculated as the value of exports (imports) from the previous year, multiplied by the annual percentage change of the export (import) volume index for the current year.

[2]Calculated as the difference between the counterfactual exports and the counterfactual imports.

[3]Calculated as the difference between the actual trade balance and the counterfactual trade balance.

2001: No Absorption or Spending: Stabilization via Fiscal Contraction

Policy changed substantially in 2001 for two main reasons. First, reduced tensions with Eritrea allowed for reduced military spending and an improvement in the overall fiscal balance. Second, aid inflows surged. The authorities seized this opportunity to undertake a sharp fiscal contraction and increase international reserves. By reducing the fiscal deficit net of aid, even as large amounts of aid began to flow into the economy, the authorities were able to accumulate foreign reserves while eliminating the depreciating pressures on the pegged exchange rate resulting from previous monetization of the fiscal deficit.

In the first year of high aid inflows, Ethiopia cut spending, and so did not spend any of the aid surge through the budget. The government absorbed a negligible portion of total aid inflows, putting most of the aid into international reserves.

The fiscal contraction, of some 4 percent of GDP before aid, allowed a stabilization of the macroeconomic situation. The year 2001 was characterized by a sharp fall in net domestic assets and slowly rising net foreign assets, which reversed their decline of the previous period (Table 3.7). The supply of reserve money decreased as spending was cut. The authorities also were able to retire some domestic debt in 2001 as a part of the stabilization program (Table 3.8).

The increased level of official reserves held by the central bank may also have had a positive effect on expectations, thereby indirectly boosting the authorities' efforts to stabilize the depreciating currency.

Given that Ethiopia was beginning the PRGF-supported program from high levels of spending and such a depleted base of international reserves, holding reserves equivalent to only 2.2 months of imports in 2001, the program encouraged saving, and not absorbing, most of the aid inflows in 2001. In the end, the Ethiopian authorities ended up reducing the fiscal deficit by even more than targeted by the PRGF program, and put most of the increment of aid inflows into reserves, as targeted.

In a country with a liberalized financial market, one would assume that a fiscal contraction and reduced domestic financing would be reflected in falling real interest rates. However, in Ethiopia, as mentioned previously, the financial sector is not liberalized. Interest rates are largely controlled by the government. In addition, the banking system in Ethiopia consistently contained high excess liquidity, reflecting the underdeveloped financial markets in the country. These factors tend to sever the normal relationship between monetary policy and interest rates. Table 3.9 demonstrates that, in 2001, treasury bill rates rose and deposit rates remained fixed, even as Ethiopia cut domestic financing and expenditure.

Perhaps surprisingly, private investment rates showed no increase during this period. One might have expected to see lower interest rates crowding in the private sector. However, the policy objectives in 2001 were to stabilize the post-war economy and increase international reserves. It is questionable whether, in

Table 3.4. Ethiopia: Was Aid Absorbed?
(Annual averages in percent of GDP)

	Pre-Aid-Surge Average, 1999–2000	Aid-Surge Average, 2001–03	Difference	Incremental Aid Absorbed?
Net aid inflows	5.3	13.3	8.0	
Non-aid current account balance	–9.2	–10.8	–1.6	
Non-aid capital account balance	2.0	1.3	–0.7	
Change in reserves (increase –)	1.9	–3.8	–5.7	Partly absorbed

the absence of large-scale banking sector reform, the government could have stimulated private sector investment. Even as real interest rates remained low and the banking sector accumulated more excess liquidity, private sector investment rates remained steady.

2002–2003: Spending Exceeds Absorption

In 2002 and 2003, net aid inflows doubled from the already increased levels of the previous year, hitting 16 percent of GDP in 2002 and 15 percent in 2003. The authorities put about half of the aid increase in reserves, bringing their reserves up to the equivalent of 3.3 months of imports. The rest of the aid increment was absorbed, with the non-aid current account deficit increasing by about 3 percent of GDP. At the same time, the authorities spent most of the second jump in aid, increasing the fiscal deficit cumulatively by about 5 percent of GDP over 2002 and 2003. Domestic debt levels began to rise again, after their brief fall in 2001, as the authorities began increasing spending in 2003, especially on poverty reduction.

The pace of the central bank's sale of foreign exchange was largely dictated by the need to support the crawling peg exchange rate regime. In this context, the degree of absorption of the aid reflects the import component of aid-related spending and possible second-round effects from the fiscal stimulus. It does *not* reflect the effects of an appreciated exchange rate, as there was none: inflation matched the rate of crawl fairly closely. Because spending exceeded absorption, the fiscal expansion implied a potentially inflationary increase in the money supply (for example, by 20 percent in 2002). However, the authorities did not attempt to sterilize through domestic monetary operations in order to achieve money targets and reduce demand.

The increased money supply put some pressure on inflation, but overall, nonfood inflation remained relatively low. Nonfood inflation increased from levels near zero in December 2002 to approximately 5 percent by the start of 2004. It is somewhat surprising that inflation did not increase further still, given that the authorities maintained the currency's nominal peg

to the dollar and also allowed the money supply to increase.

There are several (possibly complementary) explanations for the moderate rise in inflation and lack of a real exchange rate appreciation, despite the fiscal and monetary expansion, which could be expected to increase the price of nontraded domestic goods and thus the real exchange rate. First, a high import content of aid could help avoid appreciation pressures. Second, the income elasticity of import demand could have been very high. Indeed, imports increased by an average of nearly 5 percent of GDP from the pre-aid-surge period (1997–2000) to the aid-surge period (2001–03). Since net aid increased by 9.3 percent of GDP over the same period, the increase in imports represents a sizable fraction of the increase in aid flows. Third, the recession and negative terms-of-trade shocks in 2002 and 2003 may have had a dampening effect on prices and hence the real exchange rate. In 2003, the negative terms-of-trade shock actually outweighed the size of aid inflows. Finally, the banking sector's excess reserves continued to increase as a percentage of deposits, restricting the growth in broad money and thus containing pressures for inflation and a real exchange rate appreciation.

The IMF-supported program did not directly constrain the pace of absorption over 2002–03. The Ethiopian authorities accumulated more reserves than required by the program. During this period, the country authorities exceeded the program floor for net foreign assets (NFA) and net foreign reserves accumulation (Figure 3.5).

Either fiscal policy or monetary policy would have had to have been looser in order to increase absorption further.[8] Some loosening would have been possible under the program. The authorities did not reduce the fiscal deficit (after grants) by as much as expected under the PRGF program in 2002 and 2003. However, the program targeted net domestic assets (NDA) (and

---

[8]This ignores the possibility of tilting the pattern of aid-related expenditures further toward imported goods.

Table 3.5. Ethiopia: Was Aid Spent?
(*Annual averages in percent of GDP*)

	Pre-Aid-Surge Average, 1999–2000	Aid-Surge Average, 2001–03	Difference	Aid Spent or Not?
Net fiscal aid inflows	5.3	11.2	5.9	
Revenue (excluding grants)	18.0	19.4	1.5	
Expenditure (excluding external interest)	31.8	32.5	0.7	
Overall fiscal balance before aid	–13.8	–13.0	0.8	Not spent

net central bank credit to the government), not the deficit itself. The higher-than-expected NFA accumulation kept NDA lower than expected, leaving room under the NDA targets to finance the higher-than-expected deficit.[9]

The program would not have allowed as much absorption as suggested by the NFA floors, however. Program ceilings on NDA would have kept absorption below these levels. Base money demand grew much faster than expected under the program. Had NFA increased only along the lines of the program floors, and had NDA ceilings been respected, money growth would have had to have been slower than was actually observed. Monetary policy would have been tighter and, given fiscal policy, would have encouraged less inflation and hence a more depreciated real exchange rate and less absorption.

Conclusions

Ethiopia experienced a surge in aid inflows beginning in 2001 and continuing through 2003. Overall during this period, only a small portion of the aid was absorbed into the economy, and little of the aid inflows was spent. The cautious fiscal and monetary response to the high levels of aid helped prevent a real exchange rate appreciation, and staved off any symptoms of Dutch disease. Noncoffee export growth remained strong, while the real effective exchange rate showed a slight depreciation.

The lack of Dutch disease symptoms in Ethiopia was due to a combination of factors, including a terms-of-trade shock from falling coffee prices, low inflation due to a food surplus, a fairly high import content to aid, and most importantly, the fact that, overall, very

little of the aid was actually absorbed into the economy. Most of the aid inflows were used for reserve accumulation.

However, this overall picture masks two distinct policy episodes. Coming out of the war period in 2001, the authorities saved and did not absorb the aid, bringing the level of reserves up from very low levels. Because the deficit before grants did not expand (the aid was not spent), the reserve accumulation did not put pressure on domestic monetary policy. Indeed, at the same time, in order to stabilize the exchange rate and stabilize the level of domestic debt, the authorities undertook a fiscal contraction.

Aid increased again sharply in 2002–03 by a further 8 percent of GDP. In response, the authorities spent most of the additional aid, increasing the deficit before grants by a cumulative 4.7 percent of GDP. Absorption was only partial, with the non-aid current account deficit increasing by 3.1 percent of GDP.

This second episode illustrates some of the complexities in the relationship between spending and absorption. The monetary authorities took no obvious actions to reduce absorption, such as sterilizing the associated monetary expansion. The monetary authorities' sales of foreign exchange of the aid inflows were dictated by the exchange rate peg to the U.S. dollar. It would have taken further action by the authorities to absorb more of the aid.

Without the freedom to sell foreign exchange to regulate aid absorption, the authorities were left with two choices, had they wanted to increase absorption. The first would have been to undertake a greater fiscal expansion, because higher fiscal deficits will tend to increase absorption if the associated monetary expansion is not sterilized. Alternatively, the authorities could have allowed looser monetary policy. This might have increased demand through the availability of credit to the private sector, and also increased inflation and hence appreciated the real exchange rate.

Greater absorption of the aid inflows might have been beneficial for Ethiopia. The country had accumulated a comfortable level of reserves by 2002. Ethiopia

---

[9]There was no target on base money, per se. This episode is an example of the fact that interpretation of NDA and domestic financing of the government is not straightforward. In particular, if nonabsorption of aid increases NFA, the resulting fall in NDA and domestic financing may not have the typically expected macroeconomic implications (see Chapter II).

Figure 3.3. Ethiopia: Exchange Rate and Treasury Bill Rates

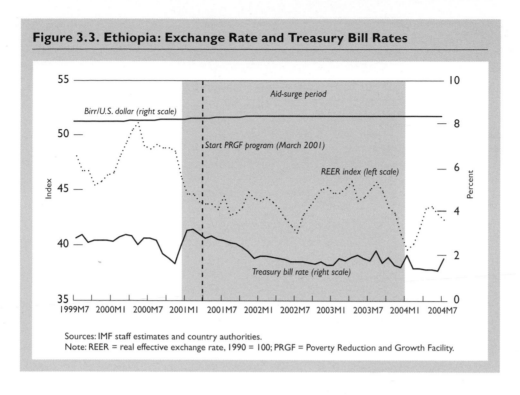

Sources: IMF staff estimates and country authorities.
Note: REER = real effective exchange rate, 1990 = 100; PRGF = Poverty Reduction and Growth Facility.

Figure 3.4. Ethiopia: Gross Official Reserves

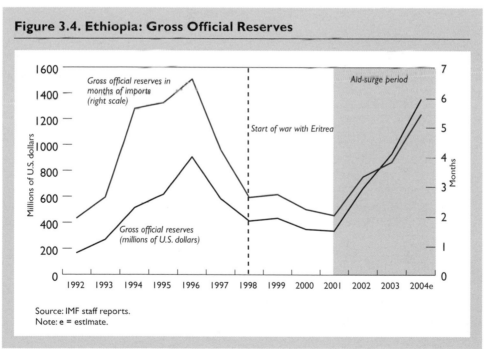

Source: IMF staff reports.
Note: e = estimate.

experienced a retraction in output in 2002 and 2003 due to a severe drought. Consumer demand was stagnating, and poverty levels remained high and persistent. While real annual GDP growth averaged 6.4 percent in 1999 through 2001, the growth rate fell to 1.6 percent in 2002 and to –3.9 percent in 2003. Greater spending or looser monetary policy might have helped to lessen the impact of this recession. It is likely that the resulting possibility of a higher real exchange rate through inflation and a higher national current account deficit could have been accommodated, given the higher aid inflows.

Table 3.6. Ethiopia: Year-on-Year Changes in Absorption and Spending of Aid Inflows
(Change in annual averages in percent of GDP)

Changes	1998/99	1999/00	2000/01	2001/02	2002/03
Balance of payments identity					
Net balance of payment aid inflows	−0.2	1.3	**2.8**	**7.3**	**−1.1**
Non-aid current account balance	−5.7	1.5	**−0.2**	**−3.4**	**0.3**
Non-aid capital account balance	5.7	−5.9	**0.6**	**2.7**	**−0.5**
Change in reserves (increase −)	0.2	3.1	**−3.3**	**−6.6**	**1.3**
Fiscal identity					
Net fiscal aid inflows	2.4	−2.1	**3.8**	**5.2**	**−0.1**
Revenue excluding grants	0.0	−0.1	**0.9**	**1.2**	**−0.5**
Expenditure excluding external interest	6.6	1.3	**−3.0**	**3.7**	**1.7**
Change in overall balance before aid	−6.6	−1.4	**3.9**	**−2.5**	**−2.2**

Note: Figures in bold represent the aid-surge period.

Table 3.7. Ethiopia: Selected Monetary Indicators

	Jul-99	Dec-99	Jul-00	Dec-00	Jul-01	Dec-01	Jul-02	Dec-02	Jul-03	Dec-03
Reserve money										
Percent change (12-month)	...	...	65.4	38.7	**−27.0**	**−9.0**	**20.7**	**34.8**	**27.5**	15.1
Percent change (6-month)	...	−4.4	73.0	−19.8	**−9.0**	**0.0**	**20.7**	**11.7**	**14.2**	0.8
Velocity (GDP/broad money)	2.5	...	2.4	...	**2.2**	...	**1.9**	...	**1.9**	...
Excess reserves (percent deposits)	6.3	...	24.5	...	**5.3**	...	**8.1**	...	**12.8**	...
Broad money										
Percent change (12-month)	13.7	15.9	13.1	14.4	**9.7**	**9.4**	**15.9**	**12.0**	**12.4**	...
Percent change (6-month)	...	8.6	4.1	9.9	**−0.2**	**9.6**	**5.8**	**5.8**	**6.2**	...

Note: Figures in bold represent the aid-surge period.

Table 3.8. Ethiopia: Domestic Debt and Debt Service Indicators
(Percent of GDP)

	1996/97	1997/98	1998/99	1999/00	2000/01	2001/02	2002/03
Domestic debt	31.2	32.1	36.6	39.0	**37.7**	**41.4**	**38.2**
Interest payments on domestic debt	8.4	6.5	7.2	7.6	**5.6**	**5.5**	**5.5**

Note: Figures in bold represent the aid-surge period.

There were also reasons for caution in increasing absorption of the aid inflow. First, the wisdom of increasing aid absorption depends critically on the predictability and durability of the aid inflow. Both higher government spending and an appreciated real exchange rate create risks. If the aid flows recede after a few years, the country would then be in the position of facing difficult adjustment costs. The government would have to make painful spending cuts, and it would be costly for the export sector to recover from the period of appreciated exchange rates.

Second, to suggest that Ethiopia could have absorbed more of the aid through a greater fiscal deficit is to suggest that the country had worthy projects on which to

Table 3.9. Ethiopia: Investment and Interest Rates
(In percent)

	Jun-99	Dec-99	Jun-00	Dec-00	Jun-01	Dec-01	Jun-02	Dec-02	Jun-03
Treasury bill rate	4.1	3.2	3.3	2.2	**3.6**	**2.5**	**1.5**	**1.1**	**1.4**
Deposit rate	6.0	6.0	6.0	6.0	**6.0**	**6.0**	**4.3**	**3.3**	**3.3**
Investment/GDP	16.9	...	15.9	...	**17.8**	...	**20.4**	...	**20.5**
Private investment/GDP	8.9	...	10.7	...	**9.3**	...	**9.0**	...	**10.0**

Note: Figures in bold represent the aid-surge period. Central bank interest rates shown as 6-month backward averages.

Figure 3.5. Ethiopia: Selected Program Targets and Outcomes
(In millions of birr, flow values, unless otherwise specified)

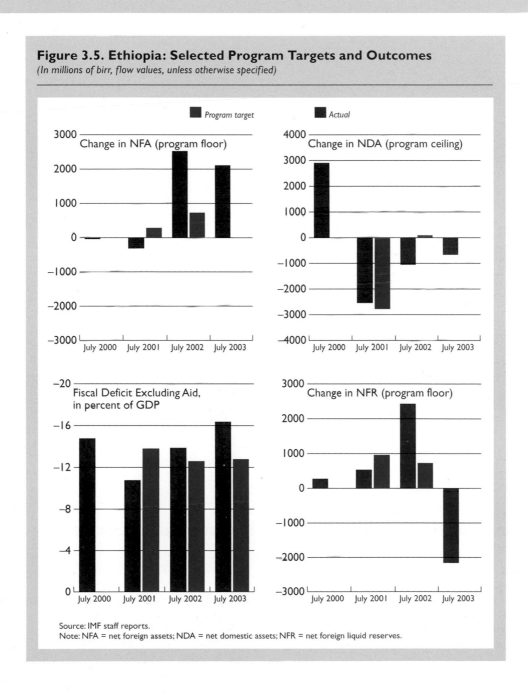

Source: IMF staff reports.
Note: NFA = net foreign assets; NDA = net domestic assets; NFR = net foreign liquid reserves.

spend the aid, as well as the capacity to implement or scale up those projects. It is possible that a more conservative approach to using the aid inflows in Ethiopia might have been appropriate if such projects did not exist or the capacity for project implementation was low.

Finally, the option of increasing absorption through looser monetary policy must also be carefully considered. The monetary authorities could have increased the money supply through purchasing bonds in open market transactions, in an attempt to stimulate demand.

However, increasing the money supply to stimulate demand may be like "pushing on a string," particularly in a country such as Ethiopia, with an undeveloped financial sector. The banking system already contained excess liquidity and there was little private sector demand for credit.

On balance, while there probably was some scope in Ethiopia to increase absorption through looser monetary policy or higher fiscal deficits, the cautious and gradual approach of the authorities was appropriate.

IV Ghana

Shaun Roache

Ghana's economy has performed well in recent years compared with its regional peers. Per capita GDP growth averaged 1.6 percent annually in the 1990s. After a period of economic volatility around the turn of the century, Ghana has pursued economic policies that have delivered a degree of fiscal consolidation, lower inflation, and steadily increasing real GDP growth. Starting in 2000–01, international support jumped by several percentage points of GDP. Net aid averaged 7.3 percent of GDP during 2001–03 compared with 2.8 percent during 1996–2000 (Table 4.1).

This case study looks at Ghana's experience during 1996–2003, a period when the country was almost continuously engaged in economic adjustment programs supported by the International Monetary Fund's Enhanced Structural Adjustment Facility (ESAF) and its successor, the Poverty Reduction and Growth Facility (PRGF).[1]

Pattern of Aid Inflows

The pattern of aid inflows is critical to understanding Ghana's policy response to aid during 2000–03 and the resulting economic outcomes. Net aid jumped in 2001, collapsed in 2002, and jumped again in 2003. This volatility was unexpected, and thus required large and rapid policy adjustments (Table 4.2). Most of these changes were driven by changes in gross aid flows. Debt relief under the Heavily Indebted Poor Countries (HIPC) Initiative was also a major, and much smoother, contributing factor. Ghana reached the HIPC Initiative "decision point" in 2002, and the value of the associated debt service relief was about half that of loans and grants in 2002–03. Private flows, mostly transfers but including unidentified items as well, also rose sharply, amplifying the effects of aid shocks.

Was Aid Absorbed?

During the entire 2001–03 period when aid soared, Ghana's non-aid current account deficit narrowed. In other words, the aid was not used to increase net imports, or more generally to raise investment relative to domestic savings. Rather, inflows were fully accumulated as reserves. The narrower non-aid current account deficit reflected stable or declining import volumes (Table 4.3).

Consistent with Ghana saving the aid as higher reserves, there was little evidence of Dutch disease. The real effective exchange rate changed by less than 1 percent during the period and exhibited little volatility.[2] In view of the absence of real appreciation, it would seem unnecessary to examine the performance of exports for Dutch disease symptoms. Nonetheless, the decline in nontraditional export volumes during the period of higher aid is puzzling (Table 4.3).

This picture for 2001–03 masks three distinct episodes that mirrored the fluctuations in aid:

- About half of the 2001 aid jump (equivalent to 5.1 percent of GDP) remained in reserves, while the rest financed a deterioration in the capital account (indeed, more than the rest, as the non-aid current account deficit shrank).
- The 2002 aid collapse of 5.9 percent of GDP was more than outweighed by a decline of the non-aid current account deficit.[3] This and some capital inflows permitted a further reserve accumulation equivalent to 3.3 percent of GDP.
- Finally, the 2003 aid jump (equal to 6.5 percent of GDP) and a further decline of the non-aid current account deficit (of 1 percent of GDP) fed a further reserve build-up (to 7.3 percent of GDP).[4]

---

[1]An earlier version of this chapter appears in Isard and others (2006).

[2]The real exchange rate versus the U.S. dollar appreciated by roughly 10 percent, mainly when the dollar began to broadly depreciate.

[3]This was driven by a $307 million narrowing in the trade balance, plus an $80 million rise in private transfers, largely made up of remittances.

[4]In one sense, some of the aid could be said to have been absorbed, with the terms-of-trade-related increase in export proceeds going into reserves. However, the terms-of-trade effect simply means that it would have taken a larger real exchange rate appreciation to absorb the aid than otherwise.

Table 4.1. Ghana: Net Aid Inflows and Selected Economic Indicators
(Percent of GDP)

	1997	1998	1999	2000	2001	2002	2003	2004
Gross aid inflows	8.8	8.7	7.5	8.8	14.9	5.9	9.5	7.4
Project aid	7.8	6.9	5.6	5.0	9.3	3.4	4.4	3.3
Program aid	1.0	1.8	1.9	3.8	5.6	2.5	5.1	4.1
Debt service[1]	5.3	5.6	4.7	9.0	4.2	3.4	2.4	−0.6
Net aid inflows	3.5	3.2	2.8	−0.3	10.6	2.5	7.1	8.0
Private inflows[2]	14.0	6.5	12.9	14.8	12.7	13.9	13.7	8.5
Memorandum items:								
GDP (real percent change)	4.2	4.7	4.4	3.7	4.2	4.5	5.2	5.2
Inflation (percent change)	18.4	16.3	13.1	39.3	23.5	14.1	24.0	…
Cedi per U.S. dollar (average)	2,050	2,314	2,669	5,455	7,170	7,932	8,677	9,004
Percent change	−20.1	−11.4	−13.3	−51.1	−23.9	−9.6	−8.6	−3.6
Real exchange rate vs. U.S. dollar (percent change)	−7.6	1.5	−4.1	−34.0	−8.6	1.5	10.8	…
Real effective exchange rate (percent change)	6.0	8.2	0.5	−35.5	0.6	−0.6	1.4	0.0

[1]Net of arrears and debt relief, including Heavily Indebted Poor Countries (HIPC) Initiative.
[2]Includes private transfers (largely remittances) reported in the current account.

GDP growth and the real exchange rate were remarkably steady through the entire period. The nominal exchange rate for the cedi depreciated by nearly 50 percent in 2000, but the use of aid in 2001 helped arrest the decline. Reserve accumulation after 2001 contributed to ongoing nominal depreciation, a policy choice discussed below.

Was Aid Spent?

On a cumulative basis, none of the aid Ghana received was spent in the sense of allowing a widening fiscal deficit (net of aid). This does not mean that aid money itself was not spent, but that if it was, other spending was reduced correspondingly.

Aid going to the budget followed the same pattern as aid measured through the balance of payments (Table 4.4). During 2001–02, fiscal policy was sensitive to aid flows. In 2001, the fiscal deficit widened by half the increase in aid. The next year's large and unexpected aid shortfall triggered a fiscal consolidation that was large but still not enough to close the shortfall. However, fiscal policymakers responded cautiously to the aid surge in 2003; the fiscal balance did not react at all. Although spending rose, it was fully financed by higher nongrant revenues. On a cumulative basis, aid had little fiscal impact during 2001–03.

The volatility of the aid flows seems to have complicated expenditure management and perhaps undermined the efficiency of spending (Figure 4.1). The increase in spending associated with the 2001 aid jump came mainly in the form of higher public capital expenditure, but also recurrent expenditure (Table 4.4). When aid declined by more than 8 percent of GDP in 2002, capital expenditure fell by nearly 7 percentage points of GDP, as current expenditures continued to rise. In 2003, capital expenditures rose with higher domestic revenues, but to levels well below the average of the four pre-aid boom years.

The volatile but increasing trend in net aid did not lead to any apparent reduction in Ghana's revenue efforts. Revenues excluding grants have increased steadily as a share of GDP since 1999.

Why did Ghana not spend the aid on a cumulative basis? Three motivations seem to have been at work:
- A desire to resolve underlying fiscal problems and achieve disinflation;
- IMF conditionality on fiscal policy and its interaction with volatility; and
- An underlying concern for the implications of aid volatility.

Throughout 2001–03, the IMF-supported program targets implied that a large part of the aid increment—between 2 and 4 percentage points of GDP—was not to be spent, in order to reduce the large stock of domestic public debt, high domestic interest rates, and the resulting large share of interest payments in expenditures.

Given the (unpredicted) volatility of aid to Ghana, the interaction between the surprise component of aid flows and the fiscal performance criteria is an important part of the story. The criteria were subject to asymmetric adjustors to account for deviations between expected

Table 4.2. Ghana: Aid Shocks
(In percent of GDP)

	1998	1999	2000	2001	2002	2003
Project grants	−0.1	−0.5	−0.7	1.8	−1.0	−0.2
Program grants	0.3	0.2	−0.6	2.0	−0.1	0.3
HIPC assistance	0.0	0.0	0.0	0.0	0.0	0.2
Project loans	1.9	1.1	−0.7	−0.1	−1.8	0.2
Program loans	0.2	−0.3	−3.9	1.0	−1.2	0.6
Gross aid shock	2.3	0.6	−6.0	4.7	−4.1	1.8
Net aid shock	0.5	0.0	−6.1	4.9	−4.5	1.3

Note: HIPC = Heavily Indebted Poor Countries Initiative. "Aid shocks" are defined as aid received in a given year less aid expected just prior to that year, as reflected in IMF staff projections. A negative number thus implies a shortfall in actual aid compared to the expected level of aid.

and realized aid flows. Positive aid shocks were to be saved and were not to be used to increase spending. Negative aid shocks were to be partially dealt with through a reduction in spending and, hence, a narrower deficit (before grants) (Box 4.1).

As noted earlier, roughly half of each aid jump during 2001–03 was unexpected. In 2001, the increase in domestic credit roughly matched the expected component of the aid inflow. Correspondingly, the actual size of the primary deficit and domestic financing of the budget were close to, though somewhat below, the adjusted program targets. This small degree of outperformance implies that the program was almost binding; there was little scope to boost spending and this led the authorities to save almost all of the aid surprise. Figure 4.2 illustrates this point for domestic financing, which implies the same constraints applied to the fiscal deficit.

In 2002, Ghana's IMF-supported program again called for a large reduction in domestic financing. This was because of the need to begin reducing the large stock of domestic debt—which had reached 20 percent of GDP—and because of high real interest rates. But the substantial fiscal consolidation (equivalent to 6.5 percent of GDP) did not fully compensate for the huge aid shortfall. The adjustors allowed for some rise in domestic financing, but the program's targets were still breached.

In 2003, however, even the expected component of the surge was not spent. In this case, the targets were clearly not a binding constraint on fiscal policy. This is illustrated by the large degree of outperformance against the domestic borrowing criteria in Figure 4.1, indicating that the authorities had room to increase spending under the program. Such increases in government expenditure as were observed were largely financed by terms-of-trade-related increases in tax revenues.

Ghana's choice not to spend the aid surge of 2003 requires further explanation. One obvious inference is

that the largely unexpected aid volatility of the previous few years dictated caution, particularly in view of the impact of aid and, hence, fiscal volatility on capital expenditures.

Ghana's fiscal caution in 2003 is consistent with its policy on reserve accumulation. The authorities saved the entire 2003 aid jump (and more) in reserves. Spending the aid in the face of reserve accumulation would have been equivalent to a domestically-financed fiscal expansion. Thus, the reserve accumulation policy made the fiscal savings more advisable. The reserve accumulation itself may have been driven partly by fiscal policymakers' desire to save the aid jump. In any case, the two policies together served to save the aid inflows.

Finally, the lack of fiscal expansion in 2003 despite the surge in aid afforded the authorities scope to use the aid inflows to stabilize the exchange rate and inflation, which had increased sharply in late 2002 and early 2003. In order to understand this better, we now turn to Ghana's monetary policy response to the aid inflows.

Monetary Policy Response

The pattern of absorption and spending in Ghana—essentially the don't-absorb-and-don't-spend strategy on a cumulative basis—implies that the aid flows in and of themselves had no overall impact on Ghana's monetary policy. In effect, the aid left the country in the form of higher reserves, and the government compensated for any aid-related expenditure increase by cutting spending elsewhere. This contrasts with the strategy outlined in Ghana's PRGF-supported program, which was to mostly absorb and partly spend the expected aid increments in order to reduce the burden of domestic debt on the economy.

Again, this big picture masks some interesting year-by-year variations. Ghana experienced two major

Table 4.3. Ghana: Balance of Payments
(In percent of GDP)

	1997	1998	1999	2000	2001	2002	2003
Levels							
Aid and reserves	6.4	6.2	4.9	4.4	6.9	−2.2	−2.5
Net aid[1]	5.1	6.2	2.4	3.3	8.4	2.4	7.5
Change in gross reserves (decrease −)	1.3	0.0	2.5	1.1	−1.5	−4.6	−10.0
Non-aid balance of payments	−6.4	−6.2	−4.9	−4.4	−6.9	2.2	2.7
Non-aid current account	−15.2	−8.4	−11.7	−9.3	−8.3	−1.1	−1.0
Non-aid capital account[2]	8.8	2.2	6.8	4.9	1.4	3.2	3.6
Changes							
Aid and reserves (changes)	...	−0.2	−1.3	−0.5	2.5	−9.1	−0.3
Change in net aid[1]	...	1.2	−3.8	0.9	5.1	−6.0	5.1
Change in gross reserves (decrease −)	...	−1.3	2.5	−1.4	−2.6	−3.1	−5.4
Non-aid balance of payments (changes)	...	0.2	1.3	0.5	−2.5	9.1	0.5
Change in non-aid current account	...	6.8	−3.4	2.5	1.0	7.3	0.1
Change in non-aid capital account[2]	...	−6.6	4.7	−2.0	−3.5	1.8	0.4
Memorandum items (percent change)							
Real GDP growth	4.2	4.7	4.4	3.7	4.2	4.5	5.2
Gross reserves							
(millions of U.S. dollars)	508.0	508.0	317.0	264.0	344.0	635.0	1,427.0
Cedi per U.S. dollar (average)	−20.1	−11.4	−13.3	−51.1	−23.9	−9.6	−8.6
Real effective exchange rate							
(percent, average)	6.0	8.2	0.5	−35.5	0.6	−0.6	1.4
Trade balance (percent of GDP)	−17.9	−10.8	−16.0	−16.5	−18.2	−10.8	−12.0
Exports f.o.b.	0.0	15.6	−4.1	−3.5	−3.6	10.2	20.1
Export volume	−0.6	16.3	−2.8	2.2	−1.3	−2.1	−6.8
Nontraditional export volumes	2.6	−1.3	−18.2	5.8	6.3	−2.4	−32.9
Imports f.o.b.	32.4	−4.7	12.3	−15.2	2.6	−4.1	20.1
Import volumes	14.4	24.5	10.4	−24.9	10.0	−6.8	6.9
Non-oil import volumes	15.8	23.6	10.3	−30.3	8.6	−7.6	9.0
Terms of trade	−0.7	13.7	−8.7	−16.6	4.8	9.4	14.8
Import cover (months)	2.1	1.9	1.9	1.1	1.5	2.3	4.7

Note: f.o.b. = free on board.

[1]This definition of net aid is taken from the balance of payments and may differ from the net aid inflows reported in the government's accounts and reported in Table 4.1.

[2]Includes unidentified capital flows and errors and omissions.

surges of inflation during the period—in 2000–01 and again in 2002–03. Each followed sharp and unexpected aid declines, and in the first case a major terms-of-trade decline as well. Each was also accompanied by a loosening of domestic monetary and fiscal policy. And each was followed by an aid surge. In the first case, the authorities used aid to help stabilize the economy; in the second, they did not.

The first aid surge came when the Ghanaian economy was still reeling from a terms-of-trade decline of 25 percent during 1999–2000 (Box 4.2).[5] In response

to this shock, and with foreign reserves equal to one month of imports at the end of 2000, the authorities failed to tighten fiscal policy sufficiently; rather, they increased domestic borrowing and ran up domestic arrears to plug the shortfall. Reserve money growth took off and the result was a 50 percent loss in the currency's nominal effective value and a sharp rise in inflation, which rose to an annual average of about 40 percent (Figure 4.3).

The aid surge in 2001 was partly sold into the foreign exchange market, strengthening the cedi and helping reduce money growth. Given the worsening capital account, it is likely that in the absence of the aid surge the nominal exchange rate declines in 2001 would have been much larger than the modest 5 percent experienced.

---

[5]Compounding the effect of the terms-of-trade shock was a decline in net aid inflows of 0.3 percent of GDP, as against IMF staff expectations of a 5.8 percent of GDP increase in aid flows in 2000 (Table 4.1).

Table 4.4. Ghana: Net Aid Flows and the Fiscal Response
(In percent of GDP)

	1997	1998	1999	2000	2001	2002	2003
Change in financing	−0.7	−0.5	0.7	−0.8	4.5	−5.6	1.3
Change in net aid	−1.4	−0.4	−0.3	−3.1	10.9	−8.1	6.1
Of which: unexpected	...	0.5	0.0	−6.1	4.9	−4.4	2.3
Change in domestic financing[1]	0.7	−0.1	1.0	2.3	−6.4	2.5	−4.8
Change in balance (before grants)	1.0	0.9	0.4	−0.2	−4.6	6.5	−0.1
Change in expenditure	−1.3	0.2	−2.4	1.5	5.0	−6.6	2.9
Change in revenue excluding grants	−0.3	1.1	−2.0	1.3	0.4	−0.1	2.8
Memorandum items:							
Revenue and grants	19.2	20.5	18.0	19.8	25.0	21.1	25.5
Revenue	17.3	18.4	16.4	17.7	18.1	18.0	20.8
Grants	1.9	2.2	1.7	2.1	6.9	3.1	4.7
Expenditure	28.4	28.6	26.2	27.7	32.7	26.1	29.0
Recurrent expenditures (excluding interest)[2]	10.3	10.3	10.8	11.1	12.1	13.8	13.8
Wages and salaries	5.3	5.5	5.6	5.2	6.1	8.5	8.4
Capital expenditure	11.6	11.3	9.8	9.2	12.8	6.1	8.9
Poverty expenditure	...	...	...	...	4.5	4.8	6.5
Overall balance	−9.2	−8.1	−8.2	−7.9	−7.7	−5.0	−3.5
Excluding grants	−11.1	−10.2	−9.8	−10.0	−14.6	−8.1	−8.2
Debt service (percent of revenue excluding grants)	37.6	38.0	34.1	42.4	43.1	33.9	29.8
Debt service (percent of exports)[3]	24.7	25.0	21.7	19.4	22.1	19.9	19.8
Interest payments	6.5	7.0	5.6	7.5	7.8	6.1	6.2

[1]Net domestic financing, given by the period's change in the domestic net credit to government.
[2]From 2001 on a cash basis.
[3]Includes subventions in separate line items from 2002 onward.

Figure 4.1. Ghana: Aid Flows and Public Expenditure Patterns
(In percent of GDP)

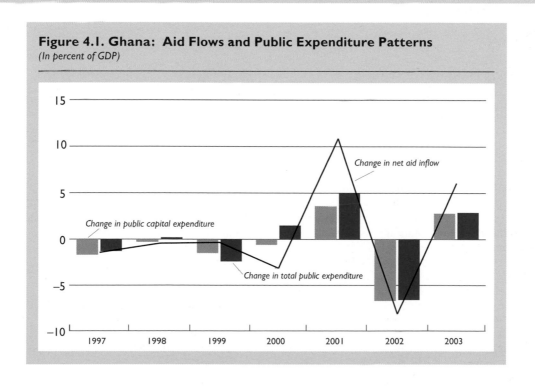

Box 4.1. Ghana: Program Adjustors for Aid Surprises

The criteria set out in the program supported by the Poverty Reduction and Growth Facility for Ghana were subject to asymmetric adjustors to account for deviations between expected and realized aid flows. Positive aid shocks were to be saved in higher net international reserves (NIR) and lower net domestic assets (NDA), while negative aid shocks were to be partially dealt with through a reduction in NIR and some increase in NDA. Some cushion was built in, so that the adjustment was some proportion of the aid shortfall. But if the criteria were binding, shortfalls still implied a tightening of policy.

IMF-Supported Program Aid Flow: Relevant Performance Criteria

	Positive Aid Shock (actual higher than programmed)	Negative Aid Shock (actual lower than programmed)
Performance criteria		
Net domestic financing of government (ceiling)	Lowered by full amount of the aid shock	Raised by some proportion of the aid shock[1]
Net domestic assets of the central bank (ceiling)[2]	Lowered by full amount of the aid shock	Raised by some proportion of the aid shock[1]
Net international reserves (floor)	Raised by full amount of the aid shock	Lowered by some proportion of the aid shock[3]
Indicative targets		
Domestic primary fiscal balance (floor)[4]	No effect	Implicitly raised by some proportion of the aid shock
Reserve money (stock)[2]	No effect	Implicitly lowered by some proportion of the aid shock

[1]The adjustor allowing for a higher ceiling to account for unexpected aid shortfalls changed from 50 percent of the shortfall to a fixed $50 million cap in June 2001. This cap was raised to $75 million in March 2002.

[2]The performance criteria were changed from reserve money to net domestic assets in June 2001. Reserve money became an indicative target.

[3]The adjustor allowing for a lower floor to account for unexpected aid shortfalls changed from 50 percent of the shortfall to a fixed $50 million in June 2001. This limit was raised to $75 million in March 2002. Aid shortfalls could therefore only be partly financed by drawing down reserves.

[4]Excludes grants and foreign-financed capital expenditure.

In 2001, IMF staff supported the Ghanaian monetary authorities' strategy, advising that aid flows be used to support the currency as a way to curb inflation. The IMF-supported program specified a floor for the accumulation of net international reserves (NIR) and a ceiling for central bank net domestic assets (NDA). Both targets were generally met in 2001, except that NDA targets were waived as money demand increased more than what was forecast, while inflation eased.

As the aid shortfall hit in 2002, monetary policy was eased. The fiscal contraction was less than the aid decline, and the government borrowed directly from the central bank to partly cover the resulting financing gap. There was little sterilization of these liquidity injections during this period, either domestically or in terms of foreign exchange, as reserves continued to be accumulated. In part, reserve accumulation was programmed, because import cover at the start of 2002 remained fairly low (at just 2.3 months). The nominal exchange rate depreciation accelerated and inflation began to pick up by the end of 2002.[6]

The monetary and fiscal targets under the IMF-supported program were overshot by the end of 2002. These slippages prevented the IMF's Executive Board from completing the final review of the 2002 PRGF-supported program.[7] Reserve floors under the program were exceeded, however. Thus, the program left substantial room to sell reserves; indeed, reserves ended the year $80 million above the adjusted program floor. Selling some reserves would have reduced monetary expansion without requiring further contraction of domestic credit by the central bank.[8]

---

[6]In early 2003, inflation pressures were exacerbated by one-off petroleum price hikes linked to the removal of subsidies.

[7]It would seem unlikely that this event contributed much to the shortfall in aid, which had already mostly emerged by then.

[8]The monetary performance criterion was changed from reserve money to net domestic assets in June 2001. Reserve money became an indicative target.

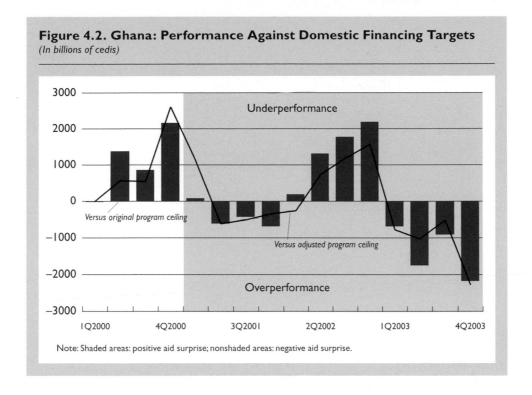

Figure 4.2. Ghana: Performance Against Domestic Financing Targets
(In billions of cedis)

Note: Shaded areas: positive aid surprise; nonshaded areas: negative aid surprise.

In 2003, the authorities faced a need to stabilize. One approach might have been to sell some reserves to reduce money growth and stabilize the exchange rate. The authorities in fact steadily reduced the rate of nominal exchange rate depreciation, contributing to the inflation stabilization. However, the authorities could have made more aggressive use of foreign exchange sales. Instead, as discussed above, the authorities continued to accumulate more reserves. One motivation, emphasized earlier, was the need to create a buffer for volatile aid flows. A desire to keep the real exchange rate from appreciating may have also played a role, however, as the authorities actually bought reserves in the foreign exchange market and accumulated more than would be implied by the aid jump.

To reduce inflation, the authorities conducted policy through domestic monetary operations, selling treasury bills for local currency and increasing reserve requirements for domestic banks to reduce money supply growth and raise interest rates. In the event, inflation fell to less than 5 percent on a six-month annualized basis by the end of 2003.

IMF staff urged the authorities to avoid further reserve accumulation and once again use the aid to allow the currency to adjust, in order to slow the pace of monetary expansion, restrain inflation expectations, and avoid the crowding-out effects of domestic sterilization. Reserve accumulation exceeded the program floor by $310 million, approximately $200 million more than the positive aid surprise. Despite this, high-powered money was just 7 percent above its indicative target as a result of the aggressive domestic monetary tightening.

The potential costs of domestic sterilization were twofold: the possible effect on private investment and the quasi-fiscal costs of the higher domestic debt level. Excluding the early part of the year, when petrol prices affected inflation, real interest rates in Ghana tended to rise from already high levels in 2003 (Figure 4.4). Private investment remained stable, at about 14 percent of GDP. Meanwhile, domestic debt remained high, at 20 percent of GDP, and with interest rates high, domestic debt service continued to absorb 5 percent of GDP, or 17 percent of total public expenditure.

One aim of policy over this period was to reduce the domestic debt burden in order to lower real rates, stimulate private investment, and reduce the burden of domestic interest payments on the budget. A number of factors supported higher private investment after 2001, including improving terms of trade, recovering GDP growth, and fiscal consolidation.[9] It is possible that the domestic sterilization policy may have kept real interest rates higher, the domestic debt burden higher, and private investment lower than otherwise would have

---

[9] Private investment is only an estimate, constructed by IMF staff, and therefore any inference about its level or change needs to be treated with appropriate caution. Ghana's Statistics Service does not produce expenditure components of GDP.

Box 4.2. Ghana: Terms-of-Trade Shocks and Aid Inflows

The table below illustrates the relative importance of net aid flows, private flows, and the trade balance for overall foreign exchange flows to Ghana between 1998 and 2003. Three commodities dominate the terms of trade: gold and cocoa exports, and oil imports. Price volatility in these commodities can greatly influence the flow of foreign exchange into the economy.

In 1996, two commodities, gold and cocoa, accounted for roughly equal shares of 74 percent of exports; by 2003, this had declined modestly to roughly equal shares of 64 percent (i.e., one-third each). Price independence provides some diversification (the correlation of annual price changes of the two commodities since 1996 is not significantly different from zero), but overall exposure to prices remains high. Between 10 and 20 percent of imports are accounted for by oil.

In 2000, Ghana suffered a large negative terms-of-trade shock that amplified the impact of the aid decline. During 2001–03, terms-of-trade effects were not as large as aid movements but were still important. In 2002, they offset some of the decline, and in 2003 they moved in the same direction as the large jump in aid, driven largely by export price increases.

Net Aid and Terms-of-Trade Effects
(In millions of U.S. dollars)

	1998	1999	2000	2001	2002	2003
Exports (higher export values +)	282	−86	−70	−69	190	414
Of which: price effects	−11	−28	−112	−44	234	594
Imports (lower import values +)	144	−355	493	−72	117	−545
Of which: price effects	714	−49	−422	185	−81	−335
Trade balance (narrower deficit +)	426	−441	423	−141	307	−131
Of which: terms-of-trade effect	703	−77	−534	141	153	259
Net aid (higher net aid flows +)	−7	−15	−233	576	−406	409
Private capital (higher inflows +)	−350	405	−305	132	10	285
Total	69	−51	−115	567	−89	563
Memorandum items:						
Change in gross reserves (millions of U.S. dollars)	−62	−62	−182	80	291	792
Terms of trade (annual percent change)	14	−9	−17	5	9	15

---

been the case (Table 4.5). While some of this may have been appropriate in view of the need to reduce inflation, a more aggressive use of aid—via sales of foreign exchange—may have mitigated some of these problems.

Conclusions

Ghana avoided real exchange rate appreciation and Dutch disease during a three-year period when aid flows were 4.4 percentage points of GDP higher than during the previous five years. This cannot be attributed to offsetting exogenous forces, as Ghana's terms of trade improved and private inflows rose significantly during the same period. Rather, the fact that Ghana effectively saved all of the aid and prevented it from having a cumulative impact on the economy explains the lack of a real exchange rate effect.

The aid inflows and Ghana's policy response differed in each of the three years:

- In 2001, aid inflows jumped unexpectedly. Fiscal policy was restrained, in keeping with the IMF-supported program, which did not allow spending of aid surprises. Much of the extra aid was absorbed in that it was sold in the foreign exchange market, putting this episode in the category of aid mostly absorbed but not spent. The sale of foreign exchange and associated policies allowed the exchange rate to stabilize and inflation to fall.
- In 2002, aid inflows fell just as unexpectedly. Fiscal policy contracted, but not proportionally, leaving a net increase in domestic financing of the deficit. Reserves were further accumulated, in excess of the actual aid flows. The combined impact of the less-than-full fiscal adjustment and the accumulation of reserves was a loose monetary policy that contributed to an increase in inflation by the end of 2002.

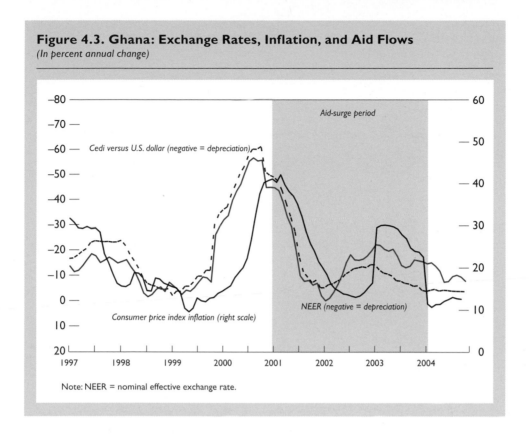

Figure 4.3. Ghana: Exchange Rates, Inflation, and Aid Flows
(In percent annual change)

Note: NEER = nominal effective exchange rate.

- In 2003, aid again surged unexpectedly. This time, the authorities more than accumulated the jump in reserves and avoided any increase in the fiscal deficit before grants. Aid was neither absorbed nor spent. Inflation was stabilized, in part through the sale of government paper that contracted the money supply, which contributed to high interest rates and a large stock of domestic public debt. The authorities did not take the opportunity to stabilize through more aggressive foreign exchange sales, a more appreciated real exchange rate, and a reduction in the level of domestic public debt.

A number of conclusions emerge. First, why did policymakers limit the impact of aid on the economy? The answer does not seem to lie in the strictures of the IMF-supported program. Most notably, the lack of fiscal and exchange rate reaction to the 2003 aid inflow expansion cannot be ascribed to program fiscal and reserve accumulation targets.

Part of the reason for the reserve accumulation was presumably Ghana's desire to rebuild reserves from low levels. And part of the reason for the lack of proportionate increase in the fiscal deficit was a desire to "crowd in," that is, to reduce the large stock of domestic public debt that had led to high real interest rates and incurred large interest costs for the budget.

However, these explanations are perhaps not the full story. The clearest indication of this is that IMF floors

for reserve accumulation and ceilings on domestic financing of the deficit were substantially exceeded in 2003. In addition to the above motivations, the policy may have reflected a desire to avoid real exchange rate appreciation. However, there is little direct evidence on this point.

Aid volatility—particularly unexpected and large swings—has contributed to Ghana's policy difficulties and, most likely, to the authorities' caution in spending the 2003 aid surge. The volatility of aid carried other costs as well. It is surely more difficult to revert to a given level of expenditure after an increase than to simply maintain the current level of spending. In this sense, the volatility in 2001–02 contributed to the fiscal, and then monetary, policy relaxation, and to high inflation in 2002. Moreover, recurrent expenditures appear to have been harder to restrain than capital spending during the 2002 downturn. This implies that spending the aid as it arrives could help reduce the share of capital expenditures over time. Recent improvements in donor coordination in Ghana should help limit the volatility of aid flows in the future.[10]

---

[10]The government takes the overall lead in coordinating external assistance and has introduced a "mini-Consultative Group" process, in which it meets with external partners on a quarterly basis. The World Bank has stepped back from its traditional role to leave scope for the government to lead external partner coordination.

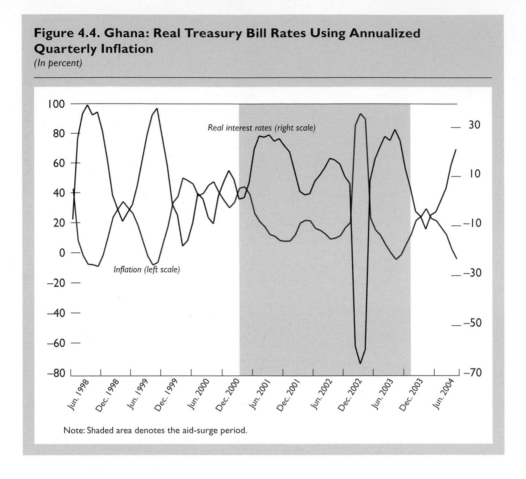

Figure 4.4. Ghana: Real Treasury Bill Rates Using Annualized Quarterly Inflation
(In percent)

Note: Shaded area denotes the aid-surge period.

Table 4.5. Ghana: Monetary Conditions
(In millions of cedis, except where indicated)

	1997	1998	1999	2000	2001	2002	2003
Change in reserve money	301	315	584	1,145	1,333	2,116	1,882
Change in net foreign assets	111	294	−550	−930	1,405	1,752	6,115
Change in net domestic assets	189	21	1,133	2,076	−72	364	−4,233
Memorandum items:							
Net aid flows (millions of U.S. dollars)	243	236	221	−13	563	157	566
Change in gross reserves (millions of U.S. dollars)	−91	0	−62	−182	80	291	792
Percent change in nominal effective exchange rate (average)	−16	−5	−21	−49	−5	−18	−16
Percent change in real effective exchange rate (average)	6	8	1	−36	1	−1	1
Inflation, percent change (average)	18	16	13	39	23	14	24
Treasury bills (average nominal rate)	43	27	30	41	33	26	22
Treasury bills (average real rate)	25	11	17	2	10	12	2
Reserve money (percent change)	33	26	38	55	41	46	28
Broad money (percent change)	44	17	25	54	32	49	34
Velocity	5	4	4	4	4	4	3
Private investment (percent of GDP)	12	12	13	15	14	14	14
Private investment (percent of investment)	49	52	58	62	52	69	60

IMF-supported program targets, with their asymmetric adjustors, may significantly affect how aid surprises are absorbed. The system of adjustors in Ghana was, in part, designed to reduce the risks of excessive public domestic borrowing and facilitate crowding in. With these objectives in mind, although the asymmetric adjustors may have appeared excessively tight ex ante, in the event, they turned out to be useful. Had the aid jump of 2001 been fully spent, the collapse of 2002 would have been even harder to manage.[11] Had the effect of the aid collapse on policy been fully smoothed by domestic borrowing, the public debt stock would have risen from already high levels, while the emerging inflation problem of 2003 would have been worse.

---

[11]The assumption is that the aid collapse of 2002 was not a result of donor or recipient dissatisfaction with the partial failure to spend the aid in 2001.

V   Mozambique

Shekhar Aiyar

Mozambique received high levels of aid throughout the late 1990s, with a substantial increase beginning in 2000, a year when the country was hit by torrential rains and flooding. The aid inflows were accompanied by increased government expenditures, especially in priority social sectors. GDP and export growth rates were high, and social indicators improved.

However, during the aid surge period (2000–03), aid absorption lagged far behind spending out of aid. While about 65 percent of the increment in aid was absorbed by higher net imports, government expenditure increased by well over 100 percent of the increment in aid. Consequently there was a large injection of domestic liquidity. Despite some attempts at sterilization through treasury bill sales, the result was high inflation, nominal depreciation, and substantial currency substitution, especially in 2001.

A policy of selling foreign exchange to curb domestic liquidity could have helped contain inflation. The feasibility of such a strategy is indicated by the large depreciation that occurred in both nominal and real exchange rates, giving room for foreign exchange sterilization without a large risk of crowding out exports, and by the comfortable reserve position throughout the period.

Pattern of Aid Inflows

Gross inflows of aid were high throughout 1998–2003, but spiked in 2000, following the floods that affected the country that year. Although aid inflows decreased as a percentage of GDP after 2000, they remained at a higher level than the pre-2000 average (Table 5.1). The same pattern held for net public inflows, which rose sharply in 2000 and then remained at an elevated level. Debt relief under the Heavily Indebted Poor Countries (HIPC) Initiative accounted for a large part of the inflows, averaging more than $400 million annually from 2000 to 2002.

Private inflows also were substantial. Foreign direct investment and private sector net borrowing accounted for less than 6 percent of GDP until 1998, but then rose sharply to almost 16 percent in 1999, mainly to finance imports for an aluminum smelting plant. After 1999, private inflows exhibited considerable volatility, but always remained higher than the pre-1999 period.

Aid Absorption

The higher aid inflows in the post-2000 period were partly absorbed by a higher average non-aid current account deficit (Table 5.2). But a substantial part of the increase in aid was also channeled into increasing international reserves, which rose from 16.4 percent of GDP at end-1999 to 21.9 percent at end-2003.[1] Finally, there was also a cumulative deterioration of the non-aid capital account. This may have been partly due to the currency substitution during the period, with depositors switching from local currency deposits to dollar deposits.

Spending Out of Aid

Despite the less than full absorption of aid noted above, government expenditures increased by more than twice the increment in aid. Allowing for the fact that government revenues also increased over the surge period, there was still an increase in the fiscal deficit before aid of almost twice the increment in aid (Table 5.3). Thus, almost 200 percent of the additional aid was spent, despite only about 65 percent of incremental aid being absorbed. This implied an injection of liquidity into the domestic economy and determined the challenge for monetary policy.

Starting from a low base, revenues maintained a steady upward path under the Poverty Reduction and Growth Facility (PRGF) program, rising from about 11 percent in 1998 to 14 percent in 2003. Revenues increased even in 2000, when flood damage shrunk the tax base. Although some quarterly revenue targets under the program were missed, these episodes did not

---

[1]International reserves in months of imports (excluding imports for large projects, notably the aluminum smelting plant) rose from 6 months at end-1999 to 6.7 months at end-2003.

Table 5.1. Mozambique: Aid and Other Inflows
(Percent of GDP, unless specified otherwise)

	1998	1999	2000	2001	2002	2003
Gross public inflows	13.4	13.4	**20.0**	**16.7**	**18.5**	17.4
Net public inflows	11.6	11.4	**20.4**	**15.4**	**16.4**	15.0
Net private inflows	5.9	15.8	**10.7**	**6.3**	**15.1**	7.7
Net total inflows	17.6	27.2	**31.1**	**21.8**	**31.5**	22.7
Memorandum item:						
GDP growth rate	11.9	7.5	**1.5**	**13.0**	**7.4**	7.1

Note: Figures in bold represent the aid-surge period.

Table 5.2. Mozambique: Was Aid Absorbed?
(In percent of GDP)

	Pre-Aid-Surge Average, 1998–99	Aid-Surge Average, 2000–03	Difference
Net aid inflows	11.5	16.8	5.3
Non-aid current account balance	−19.7	−23.1	−3.4
Non-aid capital account balance	8.7	7.7	−0.9
Change in reserves (increase −)	−0.5	−1.4	−0.9

Note: Errors and omissions included in capital account.

appear to be the result of moral hazard arising from increased aid inflows.[2]

Government expenditures increased at a much faster rate than revenues (Table 5.4). It appears that the increased government expenditures were generally well directed. Growth was strong throughout the period, except for the flood year of 2000. Under the National Action Plan for Reduction of Absolute Poverty (PARPA), expenditures were targeted at priority social sectors, which included education, health, infrastructure development, governance, and the judicial system. PARPA priority sector expenditure rose from 13.3 percent of GDP in 1999 to 18 percent in 2002, and from 55.2 to 65.3 percent of total expenditure.[3] Gross enrollment rates in primary school increased from 69 percent in 1996 to 91 percent in 2000, and from 18 to 24 percent for secondary education. The poverty rate declined from 69.4 percent in 1996 to 54.1 percent in 2002.

With the aid surge in the form of grants and debt relief, there is little indication of an unsustainable debt accumulation over the period. The net present value (NPV) of debt-to-exports declined sharply, mainly due to HIPC debt relief, from 212 percent in 1998 to 88 percent in 2002. The debt-service-to-exports ratio also declined considerably, from 20 to 4 percent.

Real Exchange Rate and Terms of Trade

The terms of trade remained fairly stable, apart from a sharp fall in 1999 due to a decline in world agricultural prices.[4] Over 2000–03, when aid inflows increased considerably, the terms of trade actually strengthened mildly. Both exports and imports grew rapidly, with exports rising especially sharply in 2000 and 2001 due to the completion of an aluminum smelting plant (Table 5.5).

---

[2]In particular, in 2002 the revenue target was breached in every quarter. However, these breaches occurred against the backdrop of an ambitious revenue target (in fact, actual revenues increased by almost 1 percentage point of GDP over the year), and were caused mainly by a drop in excise and import taxes arising from an increase in world oil prices.

[3]Excluding bank restructuring costs and interest payments.

[4]Excluding cotton, sugar, and copra.

Table 5.3. Mozambique: Was Aid Spent?
(In percent of GDP)

	Pre-Aid-Surge Average, 1998–99	Aid-Surge Average, 2000–03	Difference
Net budgetary aid	13.1	16.5	3.4
Revenue (excluding grants)	11.7	13.8	2.1
Expenditure (excluding external interest)	22.4	31.1	8.7
Overall fiscal balance before aid	−10.8	−17.3	−6.6

Table 5.4. Mozambique: Central Government Budgetary Operations
(In percent of GDP)

	1998	1999	2000	2001	2002	2003
Revenue and grants	19.4	23.7	**21.2**	**28.1**	**26.0**	24.9
Revenue	11.3	12.0	**13.2**	**13.3**	**14.2**	14.3
Grants	8.1	11.7	**8.0**	**14.8**	**11.8**	10.6
Expenditure and net lending	21.6	24.7	**27.3**	**34.6**	**34.1**	29.4
Overall balance	−2.4	−1.5	**−6.0**	**−6.6**	**−7.9**	−4.9

Note: Figures in bold represent the aid-surge period.

Despite elevated aid inflows, a rapid growth of exports and a stable terms of trade, the real effective exchange rate declined sharply, especially in 2001. This is consistent with the pattern of aid absorption lagging behind aid expenditure, and the consequent large injection of domestic liquidity. The real depreciation remained much less than the nominal depreciation due to the high level of inflation (Figure 5.1). Because of the failure of the real exchange rate to appreciate, there was no ex-post evidence of Dutch disease. However, to the extent that the lack of aid absorption may have been driven by the authorities' reluctance to sell foreign exchange and allow nominal appreciation, a fear of Dutch disease effects may have led to the policy responses observed.

Monetary Policy Response

This section chronologically examines the monetary policy response, beginning in 2000, the first year when there was a substantial increase in net inflows of aid. Although total inflows jumped during 1999, this was due to an increase in private inflows, as shown in Table 5.1. In particular, the climb in private inflows was due to foreign direct investment in an aluminum smelting plant. Because the inflow was used to finance capital imports for the project, it presented no new challenges for macroeconomic policy.

Table 5.6 shows the evolution of basic monetary aggregates and macroeconomic indicators. The loosening of monetary policy is apparent from the rapid growth in reserve money from 2000 onward, accompanied by high inflation, currency depreciation, and a substantial shift within domestic portfolios toward dollar deposits (Figure 5.1).

2000: Year of Floods

From early February to March 2000, Mozambique was buffeted by torrential rains and a cyclone, causing floods and heavy damage to housing, crops, and infrastructure. GDP growth fell to 1.5 percent, from an average of more than 10 percent during the three preceding years. Inflation doubled from the previous year due mainly to supply shortages, and the currency depreciated. The natural disaster also elicited a sharp increase in aid inflows, much of it as humanitarian assistance but also to finance reconstruction activities.

Because of lags in government spending on reconstruction, the aid inflows were effectively sterilized

Table 5.5. Mozambique: Exchange Rates, Net Exports, and the Terms of Trade
(In millions of U.S. dollars, unless otherwise specified)

	1998	1999	2000	2001	2002	2003
Exports f.o.b.	244.6	283.7	**364.0**	**703.0**	**682.0**	1,044.0
As percent of GDP	6.2	6.9	**10.0**	**20.4**	**18.9**	24.2
Imports c.i.f.	817.0	1,199.8	**1,162.3**	**1,063.0**	**1,263.0**	1,767.0
As percent of GDP	20.6	29.4	**32.0**	**30.9**	**35.0**	40.9
Export price index	117.0	100.0	**99.4**	**100.1**	**101.6**	—
Import price index	100.3	100.0	**102.3**	**97.5**	**98.3**	—
Terms of trade (percent change)	–3.4	–14.2	**–2.8**	**5.7**	**0.6**	—
Nominal effective exchange rate (percent change; depreciation –)	6.1	–2.9	**–9.6**	**–19.5**	**–13.1**	–10.9
Real effective exchange rate (percent change; depreciation –)	3.5	–3.5	**–1.5**	**–15.2**	**–2.6**	–2.8

Notes: c.i.f. = cost, insurance, and freight; f.o.b. = free on board. Figures in bold represent the aid-surge period.

during the first half of the year through an accumulation of reserves in the government's account at the central bank. With the increase in net foreign assets (NFA) offset by a large fall in net domestic assets (NDA), reserve money grew by only 3 percent from January through June (Table 5.7). As reconstruction gathered pace in the second half of the year, NDA stopped declining, leading to a spurt in reserve money, which grew by almost 23 percent over the last six months of 2000. Despite the rise in aid inflows, the currency depreciated sharply. This may have been caused partly by the central bank's reluctance to supply dollars to the foreign exchange market, perhaps due to a desire to keep reserves high. Evidence from the parallel market supports this view: a dollar premium on the parallel market, which had first emerged in November 1999, widened to about 10 percent by March before slowly narrowing over the rest of the year.

The nominal depreciation exacerbated the effect of supply shortages on the price level, causing inflation to jump to over 11 percent during the first half of the year.[5] Subsequently, however, inflation was kept in check, as supply shortages eased and the demand for money picked up along with reconstruction activities.

The currency depreciation and inflation caused an erosion in the returns on deposits in domestic currency, leading to a strong currency substitution effect. Foreign currency deposits as a percentage of total deposits in the banking system rose from 33 percent at the end of 1999 to almost 50 percent by the end of 2000.

The spurt in reserve money over the year could have been avoided to some extent by making more dollars available to the foreign exchange market. Net international reserves remained comfortably above the program floor throughout the year, so selling more foreign exchange would have been compatible with the PRGF program.

2001: Loose Monetary Policy

In 2001, aid inflows remained high, although they came down from the elevated level of 2000. Reconstruction continued and the real economy rebounded strongly, with GDP growth of 13 percent. There was a large increase in government expenditure, which rose to almost 35 percent of GDP from about 27 percent in the previous year. These expenditures were accommodated by continuing with the monetary loosening that started in the second half of 2000, leading to large increases in reserve money (breaching the program target in every quarter), high inflation, and nominal depreciation.

During the first half of the year, reserve money increased by almost 20 percent and the consumer price index (CPI) increased by over 5 percent. This was accompanied by a nominal depreciation of more than 25 percent. Thus, the erosion of returns on local

---

[5]With imported food accounting for a considerable share of the consumer price index, the nominal depreciation contributed significantly to the jump in inflation. Due to the high level of inflation, the real effective exchange rate depreciated only mildly, by 1.5 percent over the year, despite the sharp nominal depreciation. Also, the depreciation of the nominal effective exchange rate was less sharp than the nominal depreciation against the dollar, because of the weakness of the rand and the euro. (South Africa and the European Union are Mozambique's major trading partners.)

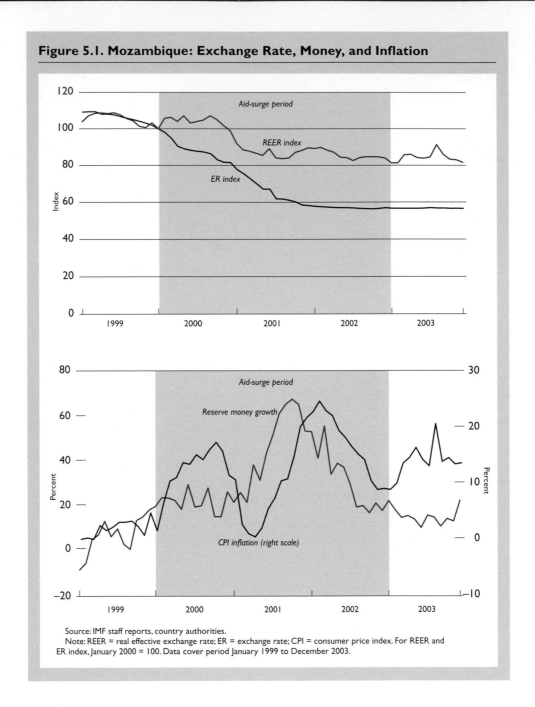

Figure 5.1. Mozambique: Exchange Rate, Money, and Inflation

Source: IMF staff reports, country authorities.
Note: REER = real effective exchange rate; ER = exchange rate; CPI = consumer price index. For REER and ER index, January 2000 = 100. Data cover period January 1999 to December 2003.

currency deposits continued from the previous year, with the proportion of foreign currency deposits in total deposits rising to 55 percent.

During the second half of the year, the authorities, with the IMF's encouragement, tried to reign in the growth of domestic liquidity to some extent. Treasury bill sales increased, reserve requirements were increased, and enforcement of reserve requirements was tightened. Despite these measures, however, reserve money grew by a further 29 percent during this period, the CPI increased by 16 percent, and the

currency depreciated by 9 percent (Table 5.8).[6] A better outcome over the whole year could have been achieved by increasing net central bank sales of foreign exchange. Throughout the year, the central bank's net

_____

[6]It is almost certainly the case that part of the high inflation was attributable to supply shortages in the wake of the natural disaster, rather than to loose monetary policy. But the floods occurred at the beginning of 2000, and supply shortages were most acute in that year. Yet inflation in 2001 exceeded inflation in 2000, suggesting that the looser monetary policy of the latter year played a role.

Table 5.6. Mozambique: Selected Macroeconomic Variables

	June 1999	Dec. 1999	June 1999	Dec. 2000	June 2001	Dec. 2001	June 2002	Dec. 2002	June 2003	Dec. 2003
Central bank assets					*(Billions of meticais)*					
Net foreign assets	−1,274	−1,384	−798	−99	1,451	1,764	1,727	3,935	3,108	7,104
Net domestic assets	3,774	4,501	4,009	4,039	3,246	4,293	4,640	3,197	3,862	1,578
Change in net foreign assets	699	−110	586	699	1,550	313	−37	2,208	−827	3,996
Change in net domestic assets	−891	727	−492	30	−793	1,047	347	−1,443	665	−2,284
Reserve money	2,500	3,117	3,211	3,940	4,697	6,057	6,367	7,132	6,970	8,682
Percent change (12-month)		15.8	28.4	26.4	46.3	53.7	35.6	17.7	9.5	21.7
Percent change (6-month)	−7.1	24.7	3	22.7	19.2	29	5.1	12	−2.3	24.6
Commercial bank interest rates					*(6-month backward averages)*					
Deposit rate	7.9	7.9	9.2	10.2	13.5	16.7	19.4	18.1	14.5	10.5
Lending rate	22.7	22.6	22.4	22.4	25.2	32.2	36.6	37	32.5	29.3
Inflation					*(End-of-period)*					
Consumer price index										
12-month percent change	4	6	13.5	11.3	5.1	22	18.5	9.7	14.3	13.7
6-month percent change	4	1.9	11.3	0	5.1	16.1	2.1	7.5	6.3	6.9
Dollar/meticais exchange rate					*(End-of-period; depreciation −)*					
Nominal exchange rate										
(6-month percent change)	−1.9	−5.6	−15.4	−11.1	−25.4	−8.7	−2.1	-0.8	0.2	0.2

international reserves remained comfortably above the program floor, suggesting that the opportunity for foreign exchange sales always existed. Foreign exchange sales would have reduced the growth in reserve money by reducing NFA, thereby abating the steep depreciation, attenuating the high rate of inflation, and possibly having a salutary effect on inflationary expectations.[7]

The argument against foreign exchange sales as a sterilization instrument usually rests on the crowding of net exports. But in the case of Mozambique, especially in 2001, the facts suggest that such a strategy would have been justified to curb surging domestic liquidity. Over the year, not only was there an extremely large nominal depreciation, but the real effective exchange rate (REER) depreciated by more than 15 percent. Moreover, this occurred against a backdrop of surging exports and high aid inflows during a period of rebounding economic activity. This suggests that in the absence of a policy geared toward building up international reserves, the currency could have been more

stable, and that the central bank had ample scope for selling foreign exchange.[8]

2002: Fighting Inflation

In 2002, aid inflows remained high, increasing by 1 percent of GDP compared with the previous year. Agriculture continued its recovery from the floods, and the construction sector continued to boom, leading to high GDP growth of more than 7 percent. Government expenditure remained at a high level of 34 percent of GDP. However, the effort to tighten monetary conditions that began in the middle of the previous year continued, leading to a fall in the growth of reserve money to about 18 percent, compared with 54 percent the previous year. NDA and reserve money were contained below program targets throughout, and both foreign exchange sales and treasury bill sales were also used to keep reserve money in check, especially during the first half of the year (Table 5.9).

Tighter monetary conditions yielded lower inflation, with the rise in the CPI kept under 10 percent, compared with 16 percent in 2001.[9] The currency depreciation was also largely halted, with both nominal and real

---

[7]In this context, it is noteworthy that the program's performance criterion—the NDA ceiling—proved to be of limited usefulness in containing inflation, given the authorities' response to the aid inflows. Thus, reserve money—which was only a benchmark, not a performance criterion—increased rapidly with the rise in international reserves, and inflation took off. Accordingly, the current PRGF program has adopted reserve money as the performance criterion.

[8]Gross international reserves increased from 7.2 to 7.8 months of imports from 2000 to 2001, excluding imports for large projects (which were mainly foreign-financed).

[9]Inflation would have been lower in the absence of a drought that caused some increase in agricultural prices late in the year.

Table 5.7. Mozambique: Poverty Reduction and Growth Facility Benchmarks and Performance Criteria, 2000
(In billions of meticais, unless otherwise specified)

	March 2000		June 2000		December 2000	
	Programmed	Actual	Programmed	Actual	Programmed	Actual
Central government domestic primary deficit (ceiling)	703	369	1,191	1,026	4,014	3,923
Central government revenue (floor)	1,614	1,620	3,270	3,321	7,471	7,463
Net domestic assets of Bank of Mozambique (ceiling)	5,008	4,749	5,127	3,934	4,126	4,039
Reserve money (ceiling)	3,256	3,076	3,204	3,211	...	...
Net international reserves of Bank of Mozambique (floor) (millions of U.S. dollars)	434	451	424	480	508	526
Memorandum items:						
Money and quasi money (M2)	11,418	12,539	11,646	13,624	15,791	16,779
Of which: Foreign currency deposits	4,049	4,736	4,119	5,535	5,891	7,107
Foreign currency deposits/total deposits (percent)	42.5	44.7	42.2	47.5	45.0	49.5

Table 5.8. Mozambique: Poverty Reduction and Growth Facility Benchmarks and Performance Criteria, 2001
(In billions of meticais, unless otherwise specified)

	March 2001		June 2001		September 2001		December 2001	
	Programmed	Actual	Programmed	Actual	Programmed	Actual	Programmed	Actual
Central government domestic primary deficit (ceiling)	1,417	1,227	2,613	1,711	3,771	3,589	4,340	4,207
Central government revenue (floor)	1,893	2,043	3,902	4,140	6,039	6,186	8,670	9,616
Net domestic assets of Bank of Mozambique (ceiling)	5,365	3,987	4,980	3,246	5,162	4,715	6,215	4,293
Reserve money (ceiling)	3,642	3,729	4,133	4,697	4,826	5,518	5,122	6,056
Net international reserves of Bank of Mozambique (floor) (millions of U.S. dollars)	425	518	385	525	451	496	439	533
Memorandum items:								
Money and quasi money (M2)	15,917	17,637	16,238	19,547	19,128	21,104	19,967	21,763
Of which: Foreign currency deposits	5,834	7,876	5,767	9,361	9,650	9,799	9,614	9,897
Foreign currency deposits/total deposits (percent)	44.0	51.8	42.4	55.3	58.1	53.9	55.6	52.7

effective exchange rate depreciation kept under 3 percent. Currency substitution was consequently curtailed, with foreign currency deposits stabilizing at about 50 percent of total deposits.

2003: A Tale of Two Halves

In 2003, the effort to control inflation through tighter monetary policy continued through the first half of the year. Sterilization through foreign exchange sales continued, with NFA falling considerably. Consequently, the nominal exchange rate appreciated slightly, and reserve money fell over the first half of the year. Although the PRGF program had expired, the IMF continued to monitor the authorities' performance against their own macroeconomic targets. All the monetary targets for June 2003 were met (Table 5.10).

In the second half of 2003, the previous pattern of money growth driven by a reluctance to sell foreign

Table 5.9. Mozambique: Poverty Reduction and Growth Facility Benchmarks and Performance Criteria, 2002

(In billions of meticais, unless otherwise specified)

	June 2002		September 2002		December 2002	
	Programmed	Actual	Programmed	Actual	Programmed	Actual
Central government domestic primary deficit (ceiling)	1,971	2,031	3,579	3,273	3,224	3,068
Central government revenue (floor)	5,383	5,321	8,409	8,200	12,406	12,057
Net domestic assets of Bank of Mozambique (ceiling)	4,896	4,640	5,600	4,962	5,145	2,953
Reserve money (ceiling)	6,412	6,366	6,931	6,683	7,450	7,134
Net international reserves of Bank of Mozambique (floor) (millions of U.S. dollars)	516	533	506	530	546	638
Memorandum items:						
Money and quasi money (M2)	23,861	24,575	24,901	26,093	25,942	26,145
Of which: Foreign currency deposits	10,567	10,714	11,107	11,034	11,554	11,544
Foreign currency deposits/total deposits (percent)	50.6	49.6	51.4	48.1	51.8	50.9

Table 5.10. Mozambique: Poverty Reduction and Growth Facility Benchmarks and Performance Criteria, 2003

(In billions of meticais, unless otherwise specified)

	June 2003		December 2003	
	Programmed	Actual	Programmed	Actual
Central government domestic primary deficit (ceiling)	2,509	2,179	3,821	4,108
Central government revenue (floor)	6,375	6,374	14,703	14,717
Net domestic assets of Bank of Mozambique (ceiling)	4,568	3,672	3,316	1,309
Reserve money (ceiling)	7,399	6,970	8,238	8,682
Net international reserves of Bank of Mozambique (floor) (millions U.S. dollars)	581	611	670	797
Memorandum items:				
Money and quasi money (M2)	28,563	26,975	29,674	32,257
Of which: Foreign currency deposits	12,924	11,418	12,751	12,716
Foreign currency deposits/total deposits (percent)	51.3	48.8	49.7	45.4

exchange reappeared. International reserves increased by $186 million, a level well above the indicative target. Reserve money increased by almost 25 percent over the period, breaching the indicative ceiling, and inflation remained well above single digits for the year.

The rand and the euro strengthened significantly against the U.S. dollar in 2003. Hence, despite the mild nominal appreciation over the year, there was a significant depreciation of the nominal effective exchange rate. Coupled with high inflation, this led to a mild depreciation of the REER.

Conclusions

In Mozambique, there was a significant increase in aid inflows starting around 2000, the year that floods hit the country. Over a four-year period, aid absorption, though considerable, lagged well behind spending out of aid. In fact, government expenditures increased by well over 100 percent of the increment in aid. Hence, there was a large injection of domestic liquidity into the economy.

Sterilization through treasury bill sales proved insufficient to check inflationary pressures. Inflation remained in the 10 to 15 percent range for most of the period. The authorities proved reluctant to use foreign exchange sales as a means of sterilizing the liquidity injection, except in 2002, when the strategy did yield some lowering of inflation. In terms of program targets, this policy response implied that net international reserves remained well above program targets, while reserve money growth exceeded target growth for most of the aid-surge period. Implicitly, the PRGF program implied greater aid absorption via more sales of foreign exchange by the central bank. This would have reduced the money supply and helped check nominal depreciation and curb inflationary pressures.

VI Tanzania

Mumtaz Hussain

Tanzania's good record of sound macroeconomic policies and structural reforms has earned it the support of the donor community and debt relief under the Heavily Indebted Poor Countries (HIPC) Initiative. While structural adjustment started in the early 1990s, the government has increased its reform efforts since the late 1990s. Strong support from the donor community and from programs supported by the International Monetary Fund has helped the authorities implement prudent macroeconomic policies and economic reform. Aid inflows have been high throughout the period and have continued to increase in recent years. In 2004, budgetary aid inflows financed about 40 percent of public spending and stood at about 10 percent of GDP.

Large and increasing levels of aid inflows provide new opportunities for Tanzania, but also pose a number of macroeconomic policy challenges for the government. This case study covers the most recent seven-year period—from the 1997/98 through the 2003/04 fiscal years—during which Tanzania continuously implemented programs supported by the Poverty Reduction and Growth Facility (PRGF).[1]

Pattern of Aid Inflows

Net aid inflows have increased substantially more than gross inflows, reflecting partly lower debt service payments following the debt relief received under the HIPC Initiative (Table 6.1).[2] Moreover, donors are increasingly channeling their assistance through the government budget; the net resource transfer to the budget has quadrupled (from 2.2 percent of GDP in 1996/97 to 9.4 percent in 2003/04). This shift in

favor of budget aid reflects a number of factors such as improvement in public expenditure management and increased donor confidence in the poverty reduction budget support (PRBS) mechanism and sector-wide assistance programs (SWAPs) in Tanzania.[3] In fact, Tanzania is considered a success story in terms of the usefulness of both the PRBS and SWAPs as tools for increasing program support.

Aid Absorption

This section focuses on absorption of aid inflows and real exchange rate trends. Table 6.2 reports changes in net aid inflows and corresponding changes in the balance of payments. In Tanzania, net aid during the aid-surge period increased substantially. However, the current account deficit excluding aid narrowed over most of the aid-surge period, and a significant portion of incremental aid was saved as international reserves. The reserves rose from two months coverage of imports in 1997/98 to about seven months in 2002/03 (from $500 million to almost $1.7 billion). The authorities generally accumulated more reserves than was targeted under the PRGF-supported programs. More recently, however, aid absorption has increased, as evidenced by the expansion of the non-aid current account deficit by about 3.4 percent of GDP—more than the size of the aid surge.

Real Exchange Rate and Dutch Disease

Consistent with partial absorption of aid, the real effective exchange rate did not appreciate much over the aid-surge period (Table 6.3). The real exchange rate trends do not provide any evidence of Dutch disease.

This overall story for the aid-surge period, however, hides significant year-to-year fluctuations in the real exchange rate (Figure 6.1). Before the aid surge, the

---

[1]Following the presidential election in late 1995, the new government implemented a short staff-monitored program from January-June 1996. An Enhanced Structural Adjustment Facility (ESAF) arrangement was implemented between July 1996 and August 1999. This was followed by another PRGF arrangement between April 2000 and July 2003. Almost all of the disbursements under both arrangements were made on time. Currently, a third PRGF arrangement is in place.

[2]Tanzania reached the HIPC decision point in April 2000 and the completion point in November 2001.

[3]For example, Tanzania met 11 of the 16 benchmarks used to assess public expenditure management systems (IMF, 2005b).

Table 6.1. Tanzania: Aid Flows
(In percent of GDP, unless otherwise indicated)

	1996/97	1997/98	1998/99	1999/2000	2000/01	2001/02	2002/03	2003/04
Official aid flows in the balance of payments[1]								
Gross inflows	15.2	13.3	12.7	**12.8**	**12.7**	**10.5**	**10.5**	**12.1**
Debt service paid	−6.5	−4.8	−2.3	**−2.7**	**−2.4**	**−2.0**	**−1.6**	**−1.3**
Net inflows	3.9	4.6	6.6	**7.5**	**8.0**	**6.6**	**7.6**	**9.4**
Official assistance for budget[2]								
Gross inflows	4.4	5.1	5.6	**7.3**	**5.9**	**6.6**	**9.2**	**10.6**
Of which: Grants	3.6	3.0	4.0	**4.5**	**3.7**	**4.5**	**6.2**	**6.7**
Debt service paid	2.2	2.4	2.1	**1.9**	**1.7**	**1.5**	**1.4**	**1.2**
Net inflows	2.2	2.7	3.5	**5.4**	**4.2**	**5.2**	**7.7**	**9.4**
Net inflows (millions of U.S. dollars)	157	220	306	**461**	**395**	**482**	**780**	**983**

Note: Figures in bold represent the aid-surge period.
[1]IMF staff reports. Fiscal year data except for 1999/2000, which is the average of 1999 and 2000 data.
[2]IMF staff reports. Fiscal year data.

Table 6.2. Tanzania: Aid Absorption
(Annual averages in percent of GDP)

	Pre-Aid-Surge Average	Aid-Surge Average	Difference	Incremental Aid Absorbed?
	1998–99	2000–04		
Net aid inflows	5.6	7.8	2.2	
Non-aid current account balance[1]	−9.2	−6.8	2.3	
Non-aid capital account balance[2]	4.1	1.7	−2.4	
Change in reserves (increase −)	−0.6	−2.7	−2.2	Not absorbed
	1998–99	2000–01		
Net aid inflows	5.6	7.8	2.2	
Non-aid current account balance	−9.2	−6.9	2.3	
Non-aid capital account balance	4.1	1.4	−2.7	
Change in reserves (increase −)	−0.6	−2.3	−1.8	Not absorbed
	2002–03	2004		
Net aid inflows	7.1	9.4	2.3	
Non-aid current account balance	−5.7	−9.1	−3.4	
Non-aid capital account balance	2.1	1.6	−0.4	
Change in reserves (increase −)	−3.5	−2.0	1.5	Absorbed

Source: IMF staff reports.
[1]Current account balance before official transfers.
[2]Errors and omissions are included in the capital account.

Tanzanian schilling appreciated significantly in real terms at a time when the authorities implemented an exchange-rate based stabilization program. This trend of real appreciation continued through 2000 despite a brief period of depreciation in 1999; the currency appreciated by about 15 percent in 2000. Concerned with Dutch disease, the authorities took a policy stance—lack of aid absorption—that subsequently encouraged depreciation of the real exchange rate. The currency depreciated in real terms over 2001–04

Table 6.3. Tanzania: Real Effective Exchange Rate and Its Components
(Percent change)

	June 1995–June 1998	June 1998–June 2001	June 2001–June 2004
Change in REER (depreciation –)	64.3	–0.2	–35.4
Change in NEER (depreciation –)	8.6	–12.7	–36.6
Change in relative prices	51.3	14.4	1.8
Change in NER (depreciation –)	–9.0	–25.5	–20.2
Change in RER (depreciation –)	38.3	–17.1	–19.1

Notes: REER = real effective exchange rate; NEER = nominal effective exchange rate; NER = nominal exchange rate of local currency with respect to U.S. dollar; RER = real exchange rate of Tanzanian shilling against the U.S. dollar.

despite a significant increase in aid inflows over the same period.

Despite the real depreciation of the currency during most of the aid-surge period and significant structural reform over the past decade, the performance of the export sector was mixed. Following a good performance of both traditional and manufactured exports in the first half of the 1990s, exports declined over 1997–99, partly because of a sharp real appreciation of the currency (Figure 6.2). Since 2000, growing gold exports have helped aggregate exports to recover. How-

ever, traditional exports such as coffee, cotton, and tea have not recovered, despite favorable developments in the real exchange rate.

Spending Out of Aid

Net aid resources for the budget have increased dramatically over the past seven years, from 2.7 percent of GDP in 1997/98 to 9.4 percent in 2003/04. All of the budget aid was spent. As a result of increased aid, public

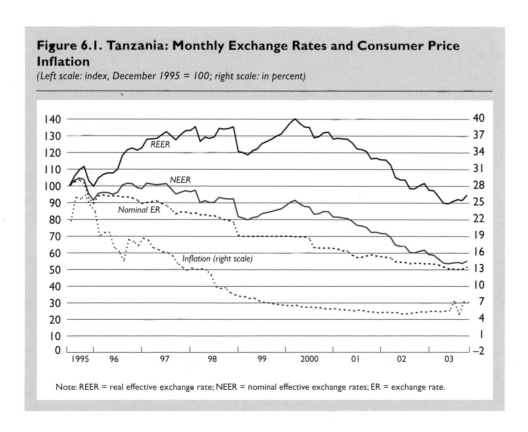

Figure 6.1. Tanzania: Monthly Exchange Rates and Consumer Price Inflation
(Left scale: index, December 1995 = 100; right scale: in percent)

Note: REER = real effective exchange rate; NEER = nominal effective exchange rates; ER = exchange rate.

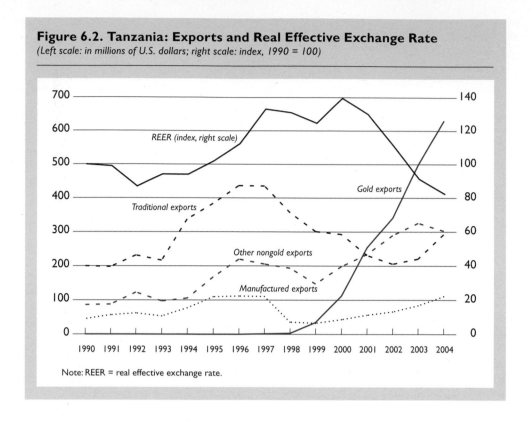

Figure 6.2. Tanzania: Exports and Real Effective Exchange Rate
(Left scale: in millions of U.S. dollars; right scale: index, 1990 = 100)

Note: REER = real effective exchange rate.

expenditures increased significantly and the fiscal deficit before aid increased (Table 6.4). On average, net aid to the budget rose by 3.3 percent of GDP over 2000–04 and the fiscal deficit before aid grew by about 3.1 percent.

The changes in net aid inflows and expenditures were highly correlated (Table 6.5). In particular, changes in capital expenditures were highly correlated with changes in net aid inflows to the budget—the correlation coefficient was about 0.97. Although foreign assistance was not absorbed in the early years of the aid surge, it played a role in encouraging the government to improve the pro-poor orientation of public expenditures. Between 1998/99 and 2003/04, the central government's spending on priority sectors such as health, education, and other poverty reduction programs increased by 5 percentage points of GDP (from 4.8 percent of GDP to 9.9 percent).

Revenue collection remained fairly steady, but fell short of the indicative targets under the PRGF programs. While domestic revenues remained stagnant at around 12 percent of GDP over the sample period, revenue collection has improved substantially in the last two years, partly as a result of tax administration reforms.[4] Given current expenditures (including social

spending) well above domestic revenues, budgetary spending is highly vulnerable to aid shocks.

In Tanzania, PRGF-supported programs allowed substantial fiscal space to spend the aid inflows. These programs anticipated the aid increments reasonably accurately and accordingly allowed for a larger fiscal deficit before aid. Moreover, IMF program targets generally allowed for the spending of the aid in excess of program levels and did not require a reduction in domestic financing of the budget (Table 6.6). In the event of a negative aid surprise, the PRGF-supported programs (especially recent ones) allowed for an increase in net domestic financing of the government and lowered international reserve targets. The generally predictable aid increments combined with the flexibility of the PRGF program targets allowed Tanzania to spend almost all of the aid increments.

Monetary Policy Response

Incremental aid in Tanzania was spent by the government, but for most of the aid-surge period (2000–04) the additional aid was not absorbed and the current account deficit before aid narrowed. This pattern of the spending of aid exceeding absorption has macroeconomic consequences similar to that of domestically-financed public spending.

---

[4]Revenues as a percentage of GDP declined slightly over 1998–2000 owing mainly to trade liberalization that lowered revenue from trade taxes. For a more detailed discussion of revenue performance, see IMF (2006).

Table 6.4. Tanzania: Allocation of Incremental Net Budgetary Aid Spent or Saved
(In percent of GDP)

	Pre-Aid-Surge Average[1]	Aid-Surge Average[1]	Difference	Incremental Aid Spent or Not?
Net fiscal aid inflows	3.1	6.4	3.3	
Revenue (excluding grants)	11.8	12.1	0.3	
Expenditure (excluding external interest)	15.3	18.5	3.3	
Overall fiscal balance before aid	−3.6	−6.7	−3.1	Spent

[1]For Tanzania, 1998–99 is before the aid-surge period and 2000–04 is the aid-surge period.

The monetary policy stance varied significantly during 1997–2004. From 1997–99, the government's main objective was to bring down inflation from relatively high levels and to build sufficient international reserves to support the exchange rate and ensure against exogenous shocks. To maintain price stability in the wake of the first aid surge in 1999/2000, the Bank of Tanzania resisted the monetization of aid-related fiscal spending by selling domestic securities

and raising interest rates and public debt. Once inflation dropped to single digits, policymakers became increasingly concerned about the adverse impact of high interest rates and the costs of sterilizations. Consequently, the authorities let the money expand as the government spent aid. This also led to a large buildup of international reserves and excess money growth, particularly in 2002–03. By late 2003, however, concerns about overheating the economy became

Table 6.5. Tanzania: Changes in Net Aid Inflows to Budget and Fiscal Spending
(In percent of GDP, unless otherwise specified)

	1997/98	1998/99	1999/00	2000/01	2001/02	2002/03	2003/04
Levels							
Net aid inflows (in budget)	2.7	3.5	5.4	4.2	5.1	7.7	9.4
Of which: Grants (program and project)	3.0	4.0	4.5	3.7	4.3	6.2	6.7
Program aid	2.0	1.8	2.3	2.7	3.8	5.1	6.1
Net aid inflows (millions of U.S. dollars)	219.8	305.6	461.4	394.7	481.5	779.9	983.2
Revenues	12.0	11.5	11.3	12.0	12.1	12.1	12.9
Expenditure and net lending (excluding interest)	14.5	16.1	17.9	16.4	17.0	19.5	22.1
Current expenditures	10.6	11.9	12.6	12.7	13.6	14.5	16.3
Development expenditures	3.8	4.1	5.3	3.7	3.4	5.0	5.7
Of which: Foreign financed	3.4	3.8	5.0	3.3	2.8	4.0	4.5
Overall balance before net aid	−2.4	−4.7	−7.1	−4.7	−4.9	−7.4	−9.2
Domestic financing (net)	−0.4	−0.2	0.1	−0.0	−0.3	−0.4	−0.2
Of which: Bank financing	−0.9	−0.0	−0.4	−0.2	−0.7	−0.1	−0.3
Changes[1]							
Net aid inflows (in budget)	...	1.0	1.8	−0.7	0.9	3.0	1.9
Revenues	...	0.5	−0.4	1.6	−0.0	0.9	1.2
Expenditure and net lending (excluding interest)	...	2.8	1.6	−0.1	0.5	3.8	3.3
Overall balance before grants and interest	...	−2.4	−2.4	1.9	−0.2	−2.9	−2.1
Domestic financing (net) (decrease −)	...	0.2	0.3	−0.2	−0.2	−0.1	0.2

Source: IMF staff reports.
[1]Changes are calculated in nominal values and reported as a percent of current-year GDP.

Table 6.6. Tanzania: Aid Fluctuations and Domestic Financing of the Budget

	Excess Aid	Shortfall in Aid
2002–04[1]	No effect on domestic financing	Raised domestic financing of the budget by 100 percent of the shortfall
2001[2]	No effect on domestic financing	Raised domestic financing of the budget by 100 percent of the shortfall, up to a maximum of $60 million
1996–2000[2,3]	Reduced domestic financing by 100 percent of the excess	Raised domestic financing of the budget by 60 percent of the shortfall

[1]A shortfall from the programmed levels in foreign program assistance, defined as the cumulative sum of program grants and loans, triggers adjustments.

[2]A shortfall (or excess) from the programmed levels in net foreign financing, defined as the cumulative sum of program grants and loans minus actual payments of external debt service, triggers adjustments.

[3]In 1996–97, performance criteria on net credit to the government from the Bank of Tanzania (ceiling) that was also in place was adjusted upward by 60 percent (downward by 100 percent) for any shortfall (excess) in net foreign financing, defined as the cumulative sum of program grants and loans.

important, and policymakers took steps to increase aid absorption and actively managed excess liquidity through large foreign exchange sales—a policy consistently encouraged by the IMF-supported programs in the aid-surge period. The rest of this section discusses these varying policy responses.

Pre-Aid-Surge Period: Achieving Macroeconomic Stability

Formulated against the backdrop of significant macroeconomic instability, monetary policy during this period was aimed at reducing the inflation rate and building international reserves. Policymakers took steps to achieve programmed levels of money growth, largely through the sale of government securities. Both reserve money growth and broad money growth was reduced from above 20 percent to single-digit levels (Figure 6.3). Real interest rates became positive, and interest rate volatility increased significantly (Figure 6.4). Consequently, inflation was brought down to single digits from about 25 percent. Fiscal policy was also geared toward achieving macroeconomic stability. Domestic financing of the budget deficit was curtailed substantially, which opened up room for an increase in credit to the nongovernmental sector (Table 6.7). In order to build up reserves, the Bank of Tanzania was a net purchaser of foreign exchange from the market.

1999–2003: Aid Spent but Not Absorbed

In 1999–2000, the authorities aggressively sold domestic securities to mop up the liquidity resulting from aid-related expenditures. The results were stable inflation, higher interest rates, a decline in private investment, and an increase in reserves. Aid to

the budget rose by about 2 percent of GDP and the government spent this incremental aid on social and other development projects. However, the central bank accumulated almost all of the additional aid in official reserves. To limit upward pressure on the currency, the central bank had also purchased over $100 million worth of foreign exchange from the market (Table 6.7). The currency appeared to be pegged against the dollar from mid-1999 to end-2000 (Figure 6.1). The excess liquidity associated with spending but not absorbing this incremental aid created potential inflationary pressures.

To offset the excess liquidity, the Bank of Tanzania undertook open market operations and sold liquidity papers of about 1 percent of GDP. The treasury bill rate increased from 6 percent in May 1999 to 15 percent in October, where it remained until April 2000. In addition to monetary tightening, "corrective" actions also were taken on the fiscal front in early 2000. Nevertheless, broad money growth was above the authorities' target in this period. The private sector was crowded out, as credit to the nongovernmental sector grew by only 9 percent, compared with a 29 percent expansion in the previous period (Table 6.7). Private investment declined, although that decline was more than offset by the increase in public sector investment.

Overall, monetary policy was successful in limiting inflation to single digits. While broad money expansion was well in excess of the program targets (Figure 6.3), inflation remained low, especially nonfood inflation, which declined to 2.5 percent a year. A structurally higher demand for money following the achievement of price stability in the preceding years may have helped in achieving low inflation. In sum, the domestic sterilization restricted the benefits from the higher aid resources in this period.

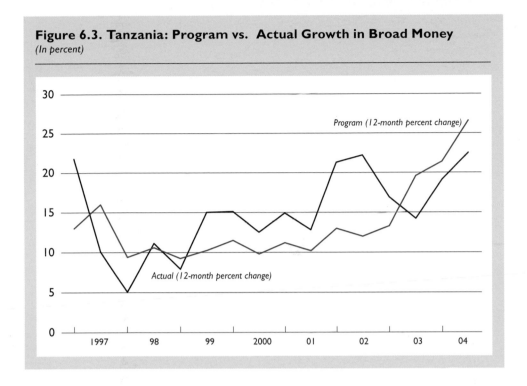

Figure 6.3. Tanzania: Program vs. Actual Growth in Broad Money
(In percent)

While net aid inflows declined slightly in 2000/01, they recovered in 2001/02 and surged by 2.7 percent of GDP in 2002/03.[5] The authorities were concerned that high interest rates could hinder development of the private sector. At the same time, a resurgence of real appreciation of the currency in 2000 increased policymakers' concerns about external competitiveness. Sterilization through the sale of treasury bills was curtailed and the Bank of Tanzania accumulated more than $1 billion in gross foreign exchange reserves in order to limit further real appreciation of the currency. Thus, this period could be characterized as an increased "fear of floating" policy regime, though such fear was present in the previous period as well.

In order to reconcile the objectives of limiting interest rate increases and avoiding appreciation of the currency, authorities had to let the money supply increase even more rapidly. Policymakers were convinced that there was a structural increase in money demand in response to stabilization and economic reforms. For example, they noted that currency in circulation grew by only 5 percent in 2001, but bank deposits increased by 22 percent. This conviction justified very limited open market operations to control liquidity generated from spending of the budgetary aid.

In its efforts to avoid appreciation, the central bank intervened heavily in the foreign exchange market and

this, along with the aid inflows, accelerated the pace of reserves accumulation (Table 6.7). By August 2003, gross international reserves reached almost $2 billion (or seven months of imports). This policy stance contributed to the depreciation of the currency, which fell against the U.S. dollar by more than 30 percent from January 2001 to August 2003. Combined with low inflation, the real exchange rate also depreciated to levels of early 1996.

The combination of reserve accumulation and low domestic interest rates resulted in money growth well above the program targets (Figure 6.3). Nonfood inflation rose from nearly zero in late 2001 to almost 10 percent in early 2003. The impact on overall inflation was not large, however, because food accounts for about three-quarters of the consumer basket and food prices remained stable. Overall inflation remained relatively low and stable (Figure 6.5). Banks had substantial excess reserves—for example, at one point in 2002, excess bank reserves reached as high as 12 percent of these banks' deposits. Treasury bill yields fell even below the rate of inflation (Table 6.7). In 2003, the IMF Financial Sector Assessment Program team evaluated banking system performance in Tanzania and identified management of excess liquidity and large excess reserves of banks as important policy concerns for maintaining macroeconomic stability (IMF, 2003b).

Tanzania overperformed under the PRGF-supported programs. The central bank accumulated more reserves than PRGF targets and, consequently, net domestic

---

[5]In 2000/01, net aid to the budget declined by 1.2 percent of GDP and recovered only partially (about 0.8 percent) in 2001/02.

Figure 6.4. Tanzania: Bank Reserves and Treasury Bills/Liquidity Paper Holdings
(In percent)

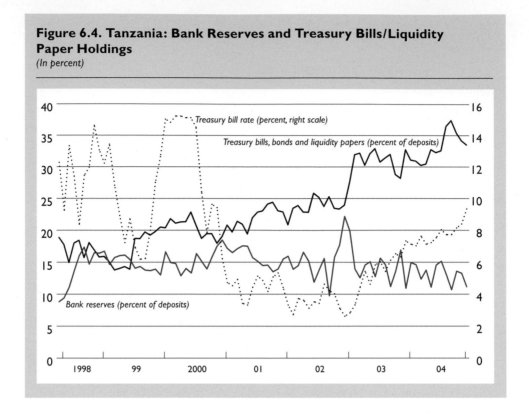

assets levels also overshot (that is, were below) program targets. The PRGF programs were designed to allow greater absorption of aid inflows. For example, during 2001–03, program targets on international reserves were not adjusted upward for any unanticipated additional aid, and these targets were revised downward in case of a shortfall in aid. Despite this flexibility in the program, most of the aid increments were not absorbed in this period.

In sum, policy during this period was in effect to finance aid-related expenditures largely through a domestic monetary expansion. Compared with the previous policy of aggressive domestic sterilization, the benefit was that interest rates came down. The feared rapid inflation did not materialize, despite very rapid money growth. However, there were limits to the scope for monetary financing, and authorities had to pursue a relatively tight fiscal policy in 2000/01, which helped control inflationary pressures by cutting capital spending well beyond the drop in aid inflows (Table 6.4). The cost of this strategy, in addition to the risk of inflation, is that the country did not fully benefit from the higher aggregate demand and net imports that the aid inflows might have allowed. Achieving real depreciation through a 30 percent decline in nominal value of the currency within two and a half years while accumulating about $1.1 billion in official reserves did not result in aid absorption.

Since Mid-2003: Aid Spent and Absorbed

The policy dilemmas of effectively managing higher aid became increasingly obvious over this period. Aid inflows continued to increase, with net aid inflows to the budget up by a further 1.7 percent of GDP in 2003/04. In mid-2003, the government delayed some capital spending financed by foreign assistance because of concerns about excess money growth and inflation. The large aid inflows, the failure of the Bank of Tanzania to sterilize the liquidity emanating from spending of these inflows, and the lack of adequate lending avenues for the commercial banks had created large structural excess liquidity in the banking system.

Although this excess liquidity did not produce higher inflation, the authorities and IMF staff were concerned about the inflationary pressures. First, net aid inflows in 2003/04 were much higher than in previous years. Second, with foreign exchange reserves equal to seven months of imports, authorities ran out of room for a further rapid build-up of reserves. Third, the costs of sterilization were becoming significant: the quasi-fiscal cost was rising, as outstanding liquidity papers were about 23 percent of the broad money supply in September 2003, and treasury bills rates started to pick up (Figure 6.4).

In this period, the authorities moved to more use of foreign exchange sales to reduce aid-related liquidity injections. After consultation with IMF staff, the

Table 6.7. Tanzania: Policy Response to Aid Surges

	Before aid surge[1]	Aid Spent But Not Absorbed		Aid spent and absorbed[4]
		Domestic sterilization[2]	Monetary expansion[3]	
Average annual overall inflation (percent)	8.1	6.0	4.5	6.3
Nonfood inflation (percent)	7.5	2.5	1.5	0.9
Gross international reserves (millions of U.S. dollars)	604.9	814.6	1,908.9	2,003.1
In months of imports coverage	3.3	4.2	6.9	7.0
Change in gross reserves (millions of U.S. dollars)	364.8	209.8	1,094.2	94.3
Bank of Tanzania's intervention in foreign exchange market (–, net sales) (millions of U.S. dollars)	209.3	101.8	1.5	–323.1
Reserve money growth rate (percent)	8.2	22.3	17.5	10.9
Average treasury bill rate (percent)	10.7	12.8	4.3	7.7
Average deposits rate (percent)	10.9	8.1	3.7	4.0
Bank reserves (percent of deposits)	15.7	14.4	16.9	11.2
Treasury bills and liquidity papers (percent of deposits)	16.0	20.7	25.8	33.1
Government deposits at the Bank of Tanzania (12-month growth rate)	–1.8	49.0	47.5	–13.1
Credit to nongovernmental sector from banking sector (12-month growth rate)	29.3	9.3	41.5	31.7

[1]Pre-aid-surge period is July 1996 to May 1999.
[2]Period of aid surge and active liquidity management (June 1999 to May 2000).
[3]Period of aid surge and large accumulation of reserves (January 2001 to August 2003)
[4]Second aid-surge period (September 2003 to September 2004).

Bank of Tanzania started to make adjustments in its monetary operations to meet the challenge of aid absorption. The bank was no longer reluctant to carry out sterilization operations through sales of foreign exchange, which it had not done previously owing to considerations about appreciation of the currency. In fact, the Bank of Tanzania sold more than $300 million of foreign exchange (3 percent of GDP) in this period (Table 6.7). Sales of liquidity papers were also sizable. The domestic and foreign exchange sterilization operations reduced excess liquidity in the banking system to 11.2 percent of total deposits in September 2004—barely above the 10 percent required reserve ratio. The tightening of liquidity increased short-term interest rates, although the real deposit rate remained negative and the nominal exchange rate did not appreciate much (Figure 6.1).

With this policy switch, the incremental aid was absorbed. The non-aid current account deficit expanded more than the incremental aid inflows, financed partly by drawing down international reserves (Table 6.2). On the fiscal front, the budget deficit before aid increased, as spending went up by about 2.6 percent of GDP, partly

reflecting higher development expenditures. Combined with good performance in revenues and a small amount of bank financing, the higher aid financed these expenditures (Table 6.5). Moreover, the government deposits at the Bank of Tanzania declined, which suggests that the fiscal policy was focused on full utilization of aid resources instead of delaying the spending of aid to limit inflationary pressures (Table 6.7).

Increasingly passing on incremental aid inflows to the foreign exchange market, the Bank of Tanzania was able to bring money growth in line with the program targets. Food prices drove a small increase in inflation, as nonfood inflation was reduced below 1 percent (Figure 6.5). Despite the tightening of liquidity and some bank financing for the budget, credit to the private sector continued to grow rapidly (by about 32 percent over a 12-month period). There also was a significant pick-up in economic growth. In sum, the recent increase in aid inflows is being absorbed and its effects on the exchange rate, interest rate, and prices have been well managed, although the currency has started to appreciate in real terms in recent months.

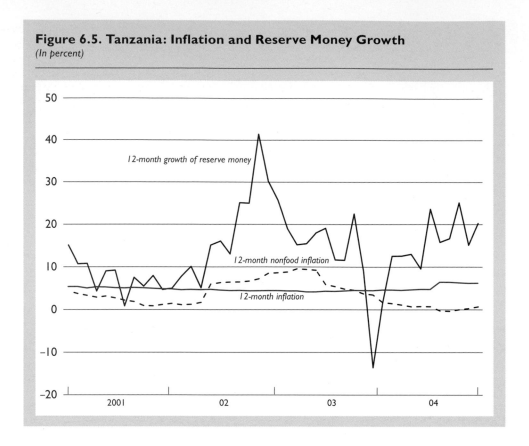

Figure 6.5. Tanzania: Inflation and Reserve Money Growth
(In percent)

Findings and Conclusions

The major findings of this chapter are as follows:

- The increased aid to the government budget was spent. Total public expenditures and the fiscal deficit before aid expanded in line with the increased budgetary aid. Spending of the aid was focused on priority and development expenditures. Public investment appears to have encouraged real GDP growth, which rose from 3.2 percent on average during the pre-surge period to 5.9 percent in the most recent three years.

- For most of the period, the incremental aid was not absorbed. A significant portion of aid resources was saved through a large build-up of reserves, which rose from two months of import cover in 1997/98 to about seven months in 2002/03. Moreover, the current account excluding aid narrowed for most of the period, despite increased financing via higher aid inflows.

- Recently, absorption of aid inflows has been improving. In 2003/04, the current account deficit before aid widened by 3.7 percent of GDP, well above the aid increment.

- Tanzania avoided appreciation of the real exchange rate. In fact, the real exchange rate depreciated by about 30 percent over the aid-surge period. The Bank of Tanzania intervened heavily in the foreign exchange market to purchase dollars, depreciating the exchange rate and accumulating international reserves well above the level envisaged under the IMF-supported programs. However, this policy stance has also discouraged absorption of the incremental aid.

- IMF-supported programs allowed Tanzania sufficient fiscal space to spend the expected increase as well as most of the unexpected increase in budgetary aid. The targets for the fiscal deficit before aid were expanded considerably with the additional projected budget aid.

- The reserve targets envisaged under these programs were modest, reflecting a desire to increase aid absorption. However, the Bank of Tanzania accumulated reserves well in excess of these targets.

- The authorities struggled with tensions resulting from the competing objectives of external competitiveness and absorbing the increased aid. The authorities opted to spend but not absorb the incremental aid in the early years of the aid-surge period. The Bank of Tanzania had to undertake aggressive open market operations to sterilize excess liquidity emanating from increasing public spending locally and saving aid dollars as reserves. As a result, interest rates remained high and the credit growth for the private sector was rather limited in some years.

- Over the last year, policymakers have been adopting a policy of spending and absorbing additional aid. They are sterilizing liquidity emanating from the fiscal spending of aid inflows through large foreign exchange sales and some open market operations. This policy has resulted in some appreciation of the exchange rate, but aid absorption has also improved. Moreover, the recent increased emphasis on infrastructure spending is likely to help in absorbing aid by increasing the import content of aid expenditures.

VII   Uganda

Shekhar Aiyar

In the early years of the new millennium, Uganda represented the paradigm of a poor but well-governed country receiving high levels of aid inflows. After attaining political stability in the late 1980s, the government committed itself to a strong program of economic reform and prudent macroeconomic management, with commensurately strong involvement by the donor community. Aid inflows were high throughout the 1990s, but there was a sharp increase in aid in 2000/01. This makes the country an interesting case study both in terms of the general macroeconomic management of high levels of aid inflows, and in terms of policies to deal with a sudden spurt in aid.

This chapter examines the period from 1997/98 through 2002/03.[1] Uganda's macroeconomic policies were supported by Enhanced Structural Adjustment Facility (ESAF) and Poverty Reduction and Growth Facility (PRGF) programs through much of this period. Social expenditures increased significantly, with a corresponding improvement in education, health, and poverty indicators.[2] The inflows did not lead to appreciation in the real effective exchange rate (REER), which depreciated steadily, at least partly because of collapsing world coffee prices. A rapid rate of growth of both GDP and noncoffee exports was maintained.

External debt burden indictors improved over the period. The main policy concern was that spending out of aid exceeded aid absorption, resulting in a substantial injection of domestic liquidity over the period as a whole. Inflationary pressures were countered with sterilization through treasury bill sales, leading to rising interest rates and potential crowding out of private sector investment, as well as to a rapid accumulation of domestic debt.

Pattern of Aid Inflows

Gross aid inflows were already high from 1997 to mid-2000 at about 9 to 11 percent of GDP. This was followed by a sharp increase, with inflows reaching almost 14 percent of GDP during the following two years.[3] This pattern was not generated by project aid (which remained quite stable), but by program assistance, which rose sharply from 3 to 4 percent of GDP in 1998–2000 to 6 to 9 percent in 2001–03 (Table 7.1).

Net aid inflows were lower than gross aid inflows in most years but still very high, and they followed the same pattern, rising from 8 to 10 percent of GDP in 1998–2000 to 12 to 15 percent over 2001–03.

Private sector inflows remained relatively stable at about 3 percent of GDP throughout the period. This stability, and the small size of private relative to public sector inflows, enables a focus on the latter when considering macroeconomic management.

Real Exchange Rate and Terms of Trade

Despite the surge in aid inflows from 2000/01 onward, the real and nominal effective exchange rates depreciated considerably over the period (Table 7.2). In general, a real depreciation in the face of surging aid inflows may be indicative of three factors: (1) real features of the economy, such as a rapid supply response to aid expenditures or high import propensities, although this would tend to mitigate the appreciation rather than cause a depreciation; (2) a policy stance that leans against real appreciation through some combination of fiscal and monetary policy; or (3) other exogenous events, most notably a terms-of-trade shock that adversely impacts the country's primary export commodity. The first two factors will be examined in the subsequent sections.

In 1997/98, coffee comprised 59 percent of Uganda's exports. After a period of rising prices in the mid-1990s, world coffee prices began to fall precipitously

---

[1]The Ugandan fiscal year begins in July.

[2]There is some evidence, however, that in recent years the decline in poverty may have been arrested or even reversed (Kappel, Lay, and Steiner, 2005).

[3]From 2000/01 onward, official data include off-budget donor inflows of about $80 million annually. This tends to bias upward the amount of the aid increase. However, even if these inflows are excluded, there is still a substantial aid surge, and the analysis remains fundamentally unchanged.

Table 7.1. Uganda: Aid and Other Inflows
(In percent of GDP)

	1997/98	1998/99	1999/00	2000/01	2001/02	2002/03
Gross aid inflows	10.7	9.8	10.3	**13.9**	**13.8**	**12.9**
Project aid	7.3	6.8	6.8	**7.0**	**5.5**	**4.7**
Program aid	3.5	3.0	3.5	**6.8**	**8.3**	**8.2**
Net aid inflows	9.0	8.4	9.4	**14.2**	**13.7**	**12.9**
Private sector inflows	2.8	3.0	3.2	**2.8**	**3.2**	**3.3**

Note: Figures in bold represent the aid-surge period. The pre-aid-surge period is from 1999–2000 and the aid-surge period is from 2001–03. Errors and omissions included in the capital account.

Table 7.2. Uganda: Exchange Rate Movements and the Terms of Trade
(In millions of U.S. dollars, unless specified otherwise)

	1997/98	1998/99	1999/00	2000/01	2001/02	2002/03
Coffee price (U.S. cents/kilogram)	156.6	136.3	102.5	**63.7**	**53.2**	**60.9**
Terms of trade (index, 1995/96 = 100)	99.4	88.8	73.4	**65.6**	**63.6**	**65.5**
Percent change in nominal effective exchange rate (depreciation −)	0.0	−14.0	−3.2	**−6.9**	**2.3**	**−12.7**
Percent change in real effective exchange rate (depreciation −)	2.2	−13.0	−0.2	**−6.5**	**−1.7**	**−10.6**
Exports f.o.b.	459	549	453	**446**	**475**	**508**
Coffee	270	307	187	**110**	**85**	**105**
Noncoffee	189	242	266	**336**	**390**	**403**

Notes: f.o.b. = free on board. Figures in bold represent the aid-surge period.

during the period studied here.[4] This fall was mirrored by the terms of trade, which declined by 34 percent between 1997/98 and 2002/03. Box 7.1 attempts to disentangle the effects of this decline in coffee prices from the surge in aid.

The falling REER probably helped cushion the effect of the decline in world coffee prices. Apart from tempering the decline in local currency earnings in the coffee sector, it may have helped nontraditional exports, which more than doubled over the period, and accounted for a much larger share of exports than coffee by 2002/03. Since the REER fell substantially over

the aid-surge period, there is no ex-post evidence of Dutch disease.

Aid Absorption

Despite substantially higher aid inflows in the surge period, the non-aid current account deteriorated by only 1.3 percent of GDP (Table 7.3). Much of the incremental aid appears to have escaped through the capital account. In addition, the authorities' concern over the exchange rate translated into a reluctance to sell foreign exchange, resulting in gross international reserves rising substantially over the period.[5]

[4]This was the second prolonged shock to world coffee prices since the Museveni government came to power. The first began around 1986 and reached its trough in 1992, after which prices climbed for a few years. Prior to the first shock, Ugandan coffee exports were even more important to the country's economy, comprising 95 percent of all exports in 1986.

[5]However, in terms of months of imports, reserves fell slightly, from an average of 6.2 months from 1998/99 to 1999/2000 to 5.9 months from 2000/01 to 2002/03.

Box 7.1. Uganda: Terms-of-Trade Shocks and Aid Inflows

Because high levels of aid inflows in Uganda coincided with a terms-of-trade shock, including during the period of sharply elevated aid levels, it is useful to compare the effect of these separate factors on the net inflow of dollars into the economy. The table below measures the change in dollar inflows into the economy compared to the previous year, both as a result of changes in aid and as a result of terms-of-trade movements. The net changes in dollar inflows are then compared with movements in the real and nominal exchange rate.

Until 1999/2000, the terms-of-trade shock combined with a fall in annual aid inflows, causing both the nomi-

nal and real exchange rates to depreciate. In 2000/01, however, a steep increase in aid inflows dominated the adverse effect of price movements, leading to a net increase in dollar inflows to the economy. The continuing sharp depreciation of the nominal and real exchange rates partly indicates a policy stance that leaned against nominal appreciation and curbed inflation through sterilization. The same trend is apparent in an average of the post-aid surge period (2000–03)—despite the fact that incremental aid dominated the loss in dollar inflows from the terms-of-trade shock, the real and nominal effective rates depreciated substantially.

Uganda: Terms-of-Trade Shocks and Aid Inflows: Net Effect on Dollar Inflows From Trade and Aid

	1997/98	1998/99	1999/00	2000/01	2001/02	2002/03
	(Millions of U.S. dollars)					
Exports f.o.b.	459	549	453	**446**	**475**	508
Imports c.i.f.	966	1,039	978	**973**	**1,085**	1,131
Counterfactual exports[1]	459	633	532	**501**	**513**	446
Counterfactual imports[1]	966	1,070	951	**976**	**1,134**	1,129
Net effect on dollar inflows	—	–89	–52	**194**	**9**	70
Of which: From trade[2]	—	–53	–106	**–52**	**11**	60
From aid[3]	—	–36	54	**246**	**–2**	10
	(Annual percentage change)					
Nominal effective exchange rate	0.0	–14.0	–3.2	**–6.9**	**2.3**	–12.7
Real effective exchange rate	2.2	–13.0	–0.2	**–6.5**	**–1.7**	–10.6

Note: f.o.b. = free on board; c.i.f. = cost, insurance, and freight. Figures in bold represent the aid-surge period.

[1]Current year export and import volumes multiplied by export and import price indices of the previous year.

[2]Counterfactual net exports minus actual net exports.

[3]Net aid inflows in the current year minus net aid inflows in the previous year.

Spending Out of Aid

As shown in Table 7.4, most of the incremental aid was spent, in the sense that the aid-surge period was characterized by a deterioration in the fiscal balance before aid. Almost 80 percent of the additional aid was spent, even though only about a quarter of incremental aid was absorbed. Thus, over the period as a whole, Uganda's aid expenditure greatly exceeded its aid absorption. This implied an injection of liquidity into the domestic economy and determined the challenge for monetary policy, as discussed in the next section.

Most of the aid-surge dollars were sold by the central bank, but went into capital outflows rather than a current account deficit. There are subtle questions about how to interpret policy in this context (see Box 2.3 in

Chapter II), but it remains the case that a given aid dollar can be used either to accommodate a capital outflow or to finance government spending, but not both. Thus, the spending in excess of absorption still shapes the monetary policy challenge.

How well was the aid spent? On the face of it, the aid was a success. In general, governance in Uganda was relatively good, with the authorities firmly committed to economic reforms. Real GDP grew at between 5.5 and 7.5 percent annually over the period under consideration. Given Uganda's low (albeit rising) revenue mobilization, official inflows were important in enabling the government to spend on areas such as health, education, and other poverty-reduction programs. The Poverty Action Fund (PAF), an accounting mechanism within the government budget, linked donor assistance

Table 7.3. Uganda: Was Aid Absorbed?
(In percent of GDP)

	Pre-Aid-Surge Average 1999–2000	Aid-Surge Average 2001–03	Difference
Net aid inflows	8.9	13.6	4.7
Non-aid current account balance	−10.1	−11.4	−1.3
Non-aid capital account balance	1.6	−1.1	−2.7
Change in reserves (increase −)	−0.4	−1.1	−0.7

Note: The pre-aid-surge period is from 1999–2000 and the aid-surge period is from 2001–03. Errors and omissions included in the capital account.

Table 7.4. Uganda: Was Aid Spent?
(In percent of GDP)

	Pre-Aid-Surge Average	Aid-Surge Average	Difference
Net budgetary aid	9.3	12.5	3.2
Revenue (excluding grants)	12.6	12.8	0.1
Expenditure (excluding external interest)	22.2	24.7	2.5
Overall fiscal balance before aid	−9.6	−12.0	−2.4

Note: The pre-aid-surge period is from 1999–2000 and the aid-surge period is from 2001–03.

to poverty-reduction spending and allowed for better monitoring. Between 1997/98 and 2001/02, budgetary expenditures on education and health increased by 1.5 percentage points and 0.8 percentage points of GDP, respectively, along with substantially increased spending on roads, water supply, and agricultural support services. The share of expenditures on poverty-related programs increased from 39 percent in 1997/98 to 46 percent in 2001/02.

Increased social spending appears to have laid the foundation for sustained growth in Uganda, particularly by enhancing human capital.[6] Educational outcomes have improved, and the adult prevalence rate of HIV/AIDS declined from 30 percent in 1992 to 6.5 percent in 2001. However, Kappel, Lay, and Steiner (2005) argue that in recent years growth ceased to be pro-poor. Household surveys show that

while the poverty headcount fell from 55.7 percent in 1992/03 to 33.8 percent in 1999/2000, it increased to 37.7 percent by 2002/03. Moreover, income inequality increased throughout, with the Gini coefficient rising from 0.36 over 1992–2003 to 0.39 in 1999–2000, and to 0.43 in 2003/04. The steep fall in world coffee prices could be partly responsible for the recent increase in poverty.

Table 7.5 shows that despite the substantial aid inflows, and despite the rising share of grants as a percentage of GDP, it seems that the government did not succumb to potential adverse incentives on the revenue generation front. Revenue as a percentage of GDP rose from 11.6 percent in 1997/98 to 13.2 percent in 2002/03, albeit with some volatility in the interim.

There is little indication that the debt situation worsened significantly. The debt-to-GDP ratio fell from the high level of 43.1 percent in 1999 to 34 percent in 2001. Debt service decreased substantially, with the debt service-to-exports ratio declining from 27 percent in 1997/98 to under 10 percent by 2000/01. This reflected both a brisk growth rate of GDP and debt relief granted

---

[6]For example, Deninger and Okidi (2001) calculate that over the last decade, a rise in the education level of the head of the household by one year was associated with a statistically significant increase of about 0.6 percentage points in the growth rate of household income in Uganda.

Table 7.5. Uganda: Central Government Budgetary Operations
(In percent of GDP, unless specified otherwise)

	1997/98	1998/99	1999/00	2000/01	2001/02	2002/03
Revenue and grants	17.4	18.3	18.7	**20.0**	**21.0**	**20.8**
Revenue	11.6	12.8	12.4	11.8	13.3	13.2
Grants	5.8	5.5	6.3	8.3	7.7	7.6
Expenditure and lending	18.6	21.3	24.6	**23.3**	**27.2**	**25.5**
Overall balance	−1.2	−3.0	−5.9	**−3.2**	**−6.2**	**−4.7**
Excluding grants	−7.0	−8.5	−12.2	**−11.5**	**−13.9**	**−12.3**

Note: Figures in bold represent the aid-surge period. The pre-aid-surge period is from 1999–2000 and the aid-surge period is from 2001–03.

to Uganda under the Heavily Indebted Poor Countries (HIPC) and enhanced HIPC frameworks.[7]

Monetary Policy Response

Throughout the period, and especially from 2000 onward with the sharp increase in aid, policymakers were concerned with keeping the exchange rate from appreciating. This concern was driven by collapsing world coffee prices and the consequent shrinking of the important coffee sector. The other main objective of policy was to keep inflation low and stable.

Put together, these policy objectives implied that the target was a stable REER. Although this target was indeed reached, it is debatable whether it represented an optimal policy response (Figure 7.1). In particular, the REER depreciation may have been too high during the period of sharply increased inflows, when the net effects of terms-of-trade shocks and aid inflows are taken into account.

The main instruments at the disposal of policymakers were transactions in treasury bills, transactions in the foreign exchange market, and the rate of spending of aid inflows. It is instructive to look more closely at the way these instruments were deployed to meet the twin policy objectives when aid inflows surged in mid-2000.

June 2000 to December 2000

Net foreign assets (NFA) increased sharply in response to greater aid inflows starting around the middle of 2000 (Table 7.6). The central bank, concerned with the exchange rate, set net interventions in the foreign exchange market to prevent nominal appreciation. At the same time, to temper the injection of domestic liquidity that this exchange rate policy entailed, the authorities sterilized by means of selling treasury bills. Table 7.6 shows the combined effect of these policies on reserve money, inflation, and interest rates. Although there was a spurt in the growth of reserve money, underlying inflation (excluding food prices) remained relatively low at 4.7 percent in December 2000. The rate of interest on treasury bills jumped to 15 percent, and the lending rate of commercial banks followed suit, climbing to over 24 percent.

There were apparently two main reasons for the pattern of foreign exchange intervention, which aimed at preventing nominal appreciation, rather than at sterilizing government spending out of aid. First, an appreciating nominal exchange rate may have had adverse effects on poverty by compounding the effect of falling world coffee prices. A lower local currency price for coffee may have lowered farmgate prices correspondingly, thus squeezing rural incomes. Second, the central bank maintains that attempts to sterilize government spending through sales of foreign exchange would have been quickly limited by the commercial banks' limited appetite for foreign exchange assets. The argument is that commercial banks could not buy much foreign exchange without facing a currency mismatch between assets and liabilities.[8] For these reasons, treasury bill sales were the only instrument used to attempt to sterilize government expenditures.

It is interesting to compare this policy response to the IMF stance implicit in program targets and in the short-term macroeconomic framework. Table 7.7 shows

---

[7]Uganda reached its completion point under the HIPC Initiative in April 1998. The resulting debt relief was followed by a further debt stock operation in May 2000, when the country reached its completion point under the enhanced HIPC Initiative.

[8]This argument is perhaps unlikely to hold for countries with relatively open capital accounts like Uganda, where the ultimate counterparty to the central bank's foreign exchange sales would be the nonbank public and foreign investors.

Figure 7.1. Uganda: Exchange Rates and Monetary Indicators

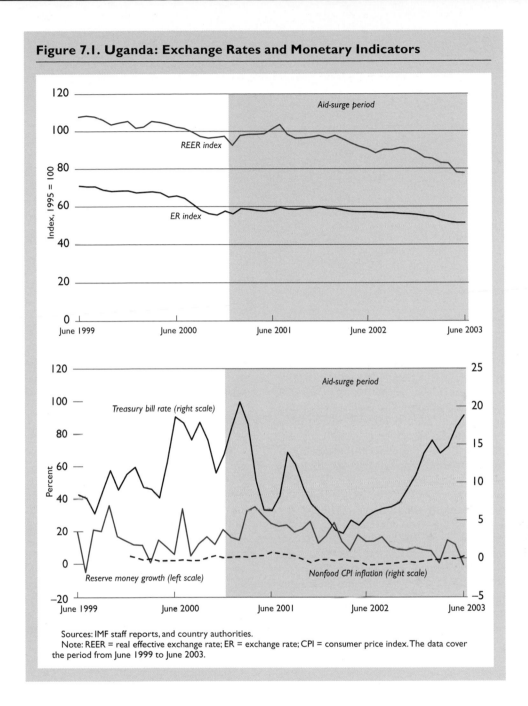

Sources: IMF staff reports, and country authorities.
Note: REER = real effective exchange rate; ER = exchange rate; CPI = consumer price index. The data cover the period from June 1999 to June 2003.

quantitative targets and programmed growth in reserve money for June, September, and December 2000, and compares them to the outcome. All quantitative targets were met over this period. In particular, net domestic assets (NDA) remained well under the program ceiling. On the other hand, reserve money grew much faster than programmed. This implies that the increase in reserve money was due to the rapid increase in NFA, which in turn was partly due to the pattern of central bank net interventions in the foreign exchange market to prevent nominal appreciation. Given the level of net

foreign exchange intervention, the sterilization through treasury bill sales was actually insufficient to keep reserve money under the programmed level.

The IMF's program implied much greater net sales of foreign exchange by the central bank, which would have allowed the nominal exchange rate to appreciate (or moderated the nominal depreciation). From June through December, the increase in the central bank's net international reserves remained well above the program floor. The authorities' aggressive stance was fueled by concerns over export earnings in the

Table 7.6. Uganda: Policy Instruments and Outcomes
(In billions of Ugandan shillings)

	June 1999	Dec. 1999	June 2000	Dec. 2000	June 2001	Dec. 2001	June 2001	June 2003
Net foreign assets	585	604	614	886	792	1,237	1,091	1,500
Net domestic assets	−153	−137	−172	−339	−242	−619	−461	−869
Change in net foreign assets	146	19	10	272	−94	445	−146	409
Change in net domestic assets	−137	16	−35	−167	97	−377	158	−408
Reserve money	432	467	442	547	550	618	630	631
Reserve money growth (12-month percent change)	15.8	10.4	2.3	17.1	24.4	13.0	14.5	0.2
Underlying consumer price index inflation (12-month percent change)	4.5	6.2	2.9	4.7	7.9	3.3	0.1	1.6
Treasury bill rates (percent, 6-month average)	6.1	8.8	11.4	15.0	12.8	9.2	4.2	15.4
Lending rate (percent, 6-month average)	22.0	21.1	21.8	24.1	24.3	21.0	19.4	18.1

face of the shock to coffee prices. Who was correct? On balance, it seems fair to conclude that the central bank had ample room for more net sales of foreign exchange. There were two opposite influences on the REER during this period: reduced export earnings due to the coffee price shock, and increased aid inflows. But the net effect of the two appears to have been an increase in dollar inflows (Box 7.1). So the fact that there was a sharp depreciation in the REER and in the nominal effective exchange rate (NEER) over the period indicates that net foreign exchange sales by the central bank were too low—so low as to reverse the expected direction of the REER.

Although reserve money growth was far more rapid than programmed, consumer price index (CPI) inflation remained broadly in line with the program forecast. This implies that the IMF's program framework was perhaps unnecessarily restrictive. In fact, given the level of foreign exchange interventions, keeping reserve money at the programmed level would have required even more sterilization through treasury bill sales than actually transpired and would have almost certainly been counterproductive, raising interest rates to unacceptably high levels.

Taken together, these points imply that a more appropriate response would have been to increase net sales of foreign exchange, allowing some nominal appreciation to occur (or moderating the rate of depreciation). This would have helped to keep interest rates lower through two channels. First, it would have reduced the need for sterilization through treasury bills, especially because faster reserve money growth was clearly compatible with maintaining low and stable inflation. Second, the expected erosion of the Ugandan shilling compared with the dollar meant that higher nominal interest rates

needed to be offered on domestic borrowing and lending. This effect would have been moderated by more sales of foreign exchange.

December 2000 to June 2001

With the successful containment of inflation in the previous period, and the sharp rise in interest rates, sterilization through the sale of treasury bills was curtailed. NFA over the period declined slightly, probably due to a combination of lower aid inflows and larger net sales of foreign exchange. This policy led to a fall in treasury bill rates, and the rapid growth of reserve money in the preceding period was curtailed. Although underlying inflation increased to almost 8 percent, this largely reflected a rise in electricity tariffs by the state-owned utility.

The PRGF arrangement expired in March 2001, and it was not until September 2002 that a new arrangement was put in place. Hence it is not possible to compare the authorities' macroeconomic performance over this period against program benchmarks or performance criteria. However, it seems clear that IMF staff shared the authorities' concerns about the rise of reserve money and inflation; the general goal was to keep inflation at or under about 5 percent. Again, it seems that better results may have been achieved through higher net sales of foreign exchange. More nominal appreciation could have been allowed to counter the sharp depreciation of the previous period. This would have moderated the inflationary impact via the exchange rate as well as further reduced the need for treasury bill sterilization. Such a policy may have led to moderating the decline in the REER compared with the actual outcome, in line with net dollar inflows over 2000–01.

Table 7.7. Uganda: Macroeconomic Performance Against Poverty Reduction and Growth Facility Targets

	March 2000		June 2000		September 2000		December 2000		June 2001[1]	
	Programmed	Actual	Programmed	Actual	Programmed	Actual	Programmed	Actual	Programmed	Actual
	(Billions of Ugandan shillings)									
Benchmarks and performance criteria										
Ceiling on increase in net domestic assets	306.2	130.5	587.8	307.0	75.8	−4.8	−7.4	−102.1	—	—
Ceiling on increase in net claims on government	319.4	204.2	638.3	542.5	73.6	9.0	−40.2	−97.8	—	—
	(Millions of U.S. dollars)									
Minimum increase in net international reserves of Bank of Uganda	8.4	106.6	−42.0	−12.9	−30.0	−15.2	−35.6	57.3	—	—
	(12-month percentage change)									
Memorandum items:										
Reserve money	7.7	3.8	7.1	2.3	3.9	12.8	1.7	20.0	15.2	24.2
Consumer price index	—	—	5.0	5.8	—	—	—	—	5.6	4.5
Underlying consumer price index	—	—	0.0	5.0	—	—	—	—	5.0	5.0

[1]Not a program target. The Poverty Reduction and Growth Facility program expired in March 2001.

June 2001 to June 2002

Aid inflows remained high in 2001–02, and government expenditures increased.[9] A greater willingness to engage in net sales of foreign exchange led to a mild appreciation of the NEER. Treasury bill sales continued to be used as a sterilization instrument, as indicated by the fall in NDA over the period. Overall reserve money growth fell from 24 percent the previous year to about 14 percent, and inflation fell sharply.

Why did treasury bill sales not lead to a spike in interest rates as they did in the preceding year? Greater net sales of foreign exchange allowed the nominal exchange rate to appreciate mildly. This in turn probably helped lower inflation. Both the fall in inflation and the reduced need for treasury bill sterilization may explain the lack of an interest rate response.

June 2002 to June 2003

The mild NEER appreciation over the previous year appears to have sparked renewed concern about international competitiveness over 2002/03. It is evident from Table 7.6 that NFA climbed sharply, as aid inflows went into reserve accumulation, with low net sales of foreign

exchange. In June 2003, the PRGF floor on net international reserves was exceeded by over $20 million.[10]

Again in 2002/03, there was much sterilization through treasury bill sales to keep inflation low. This kept the central bank's NDA well below the program ceiling, and resulted in zero growth in reserve money over the year.[11] Consequently, underlying inflation remained very low, but at the cost of another spike in the treasury bill rate, which jumped up to over 18 percent by June 2003.

Conclusions

Despite some policy variations from year to year, government expenditure out of incremental aid generally exceeded absorption over the aid-surge period. The central motive for this appears to have been a desire on the authorities' part to preserve international competitiveness. Foreign exchange sales by the central bank were limited to a level consistent with a stable or depreciating nominal exchange rate.[12] This response avoided exacerbating the effects of the terms-of-trade shock on the coffee sector,

---

[9]As noted in Table 7.5, government expenditures increased substantially from about 23 percent of GDP to about 27 percent, and the share of poverty-related expenditure rose from 39 percent in 1997/98 to 46 percent in 2001/02.

[10]A new PRGF arrangement commenced in 2002/03.

[11]The new PRGF program explicitly targeted reserve money rather than NDA. The NDA target referred to here was therefore only an indicative component of the macroeconomic framework.

[12]Some of this depreciation may also be attributable to the capital outflow over the period.

and allowed nontraditional exports to continue their healthy rate of growth. However, the policy also entailed a rapid increase in domestic liquidity. This led to episodes of heavy sterilization through treasury bill sales.

The spend-but-don't-absorb strategy followed by Uganda, coupled with treasury bill sterilization, had at least two negative consequences. First, interest rates rose significantly as a result of treasury bill sales. This potentially crowded out private sector investment.[13] Second, the treasury bill sales led to a rapid accumula-

---

[13]It is difficult to ascertain how much crowding out actually occurred due to the absence of a counterfactual. This is especially true in low-income countries where the private sector is often small and dependant on government patronage. The private investment-to-GDP ratio improved from an average of 11.2 percent in the pre-surge period to 13.9 percent during the aid surge, but given that interest rates rose substantially during the sterilization episodes, it is possible that more improvement may have occurred in the absence of treasury bill sterilization.

tion of domestic debt, which rose as a percentage of GDP from an average of 2.9 percent in 1999–2000 to 6.9 percent during the aid-surge period, and a corresponding rise in debt service.

It seems likely that greater net sales of foreign exchange, and therefore a greater degree of exchange rate adjustment, might have alleviated some of the macroeconomic imbalances that arose, while not unduly compressing exports. Real and nominal exchange rate stability, as opposed to the depreciation that occurred, would have curtailed domestic liquidity to some extent and reduced the need for treasury bill sterilization. In turn, this would have further spurred private sector activity and reduced the build-up of domestic debt. Hence the optimal response would have been to absorb and spend, with sales of foreign exchange by the central bank enabling absorption through increased imports. Implicitly, this is the outcome that was targeted by the PRGF program.

VIII Modeling Aid Inflows in a Small and Open Economy

Tokhir Mirzoev

This chapter examines the dynamics of adjustment to changes in aid inflows in a stochastic general equilibrium model of a small and open economy. In particular, it explores the dynamic response to changes in aid under various combinations of spending and absorption policies.

The experiments exploit a theoretical model of a small and open economy that features monopolistic competition (Blanchard and Kiyotaki, 1987), sluggish price adjustment (Calvo, 1983), and the presence of traded and nontraded goods. When applied to open economies, this class of models is also known as the new open economy macroeconomics (NOEM) literature (Obstfeld and Rogoff, 1995).

The model reflects key features of low-income countries, in contrast to the usual application to emerging or developed economies. Low-income countries typically have less access to foreign borrowing and lower levels of foreign direct investment. To capture this feature, a closed capital account is assumed. As a result, the exchange rate is mostly determined by external trade and central bank actions, rather than by international capital flows, and the only source of financing for the trade deficit is the sale of aid dollars by the central bank. The authorities are assumed to target a constant nominal money supply, except insofar as spending differs from absorption. The exchange rate regime is thus a float. Prior to the aid shock, inflation and the exchange rate are stable.

The model is designed to be as simple as possible while still capturing the basic intuition of Chapter II in a micro-founded general equilibrium dynamic framework. As a result, much of potential interest is not modeled. First, there are no bonds, so that the option of sterilizing cannot be discussed. More broadly, the set of policy choices open to the authorities is limited. Second, given the short-term focus of the model, the stock of physical capital is fixed. Third, productivity is also fixed. In particular, a higher level of exports does not raise aggregate productivity through positive spillovers of "know-how" or through a dynamic "learning by doing" process. Fourth, the social value of government spending is ignored. In reality, foreign aid is often provided with the hope that government expenditures will lead to higher private sector productivity. To the extent that these gains are realized with lags, they should not affect our short-term analysis. Fifth, foreign currency is only used as a medium of exchange (to purchase imports) and not as a means of saving.[1] Finally, the model is not calibrated to any particular country but with broadly sensible parameter values.

This model is a first effort toward a more complete characterization of the monetary policy challenge facing aid-dependent low-income countries. The list of omissions thus also represents an agenda for future work. The model is nonetheless sufficiently rich to confirm and illustrate many of the basic points from the previous chapters, as well as assess some questions that the intuition provided there cannot readily address:

- Spending without absorption must be financed domestically, here by seigniorage. It raises government spending and lowers private consumption. Aid that is associated with this response results in macroeconomic instability, specifically higher inflation. The real exchange rate tends to appreciate in the long run but is more likely to depreciate in the short run (but neither of these exchange rate results are robust to plausible alternative parameter values).
- An absorb-and-don't-spend response appreciates the real exchange rate and raises private consumption. The model is too simple to capture the channel by which lower public debt (or lower inflation) encourages private investment and thus growth.
- An absorb-and-spend response increases net imports. The real exchange rate is likely to appreciate, in the short and long run, by more than the spend-and-don't-absorb response.

The next section describes the model and policy choices, while the rest of the chapter presents the implications of aid shocks and how these depend on different policy choices with respect to absorption and spending.

---

[1]Buffie and others (2004) and O'Connell and others (2006) examine the effects of aid inflows in a model with currency substitution with a focus on various monetary and exchange rate policies. The model presented in this chapter is more explicit in accounting for the consumption-labor choice and for the effects of profitability of domestic firms on household income and focuses more closely on the interactions of monetary and fiscal policy.

The Model

The economy has two sectors, producing nontradable and exportable goods.[2] Nontradable goods producers are monopolistic competitors. Prices in this sector exhibit sluggish adjustment as in Calvo (1983).[3] Exportable goods producers, on the other hand, take the foreign currency value of their price as given by the world market. Hence, in the absence of changes in world prices, the domestic currency value of traded goods prices is entirely determined by the nominal exchange rate. Foreign demand for domestic exports is infinitely elastic, i.e., exporters can sell any amount at the given international price. However, their output is restricted by the diminishing marginal product of labor.

Domestic households (consumers) and the government purchase nontraded goods, domestically-produced exportables, and imported goods, although their preferences over various types of goods may differ. Household consumption is financed by their labor income, dividends from firm ownership, and returns on financial assets.[4] Consumers hold two financial assets: domestic currency and nominal nonstate-contingent bonds that are traded only among consumers. Because all households are identical, the equilibrium bond holding is always zero. The (negative) return on money holdings is equal to price inflation.

The capital account is closed, i.e., the country's residents and the government neither lend nor borrow from abroad. Therefore, in the absence of foreign exchange interventions by the central bank, the country's trade balance must always be zero for the foreign exchange market to clear.[5] Alternatively, in any period imports can only exceed exports by the amount of foreign exchange sold by the central bank.

Government spending is financed by labor income taxes and by foreign aid in the form of grants.[6] Upon the receipt of aid, the government places aid dollars in the central bank and receives a domestic currency equivalent on its account. Next, it decides on the fraction of the aid money to be spent, while the central bank determines whether to add the aid dollars to foreign exchange reserves or whether to sell them on the market. The government's budget constraint can be expressed as follows:

$$P_{gt} G_t = \tau W_t L_t + \gamma S_t A_t^*, \qquad (1)$$

where P_{gt} is the price of a unit of the government's consumption basket, G_t is the number of baskets purchased by the government, or the real value of government spending, τ is the tax rate, W_t is nominal hourly wage, L_t stands for aggregate labor hours, or aggregate employment, A_t^* is the dollar value of aid received in period t, S_t is the nominal exchange rate, and γ is one of our key policy variables, measuring the fraction of aid spent by the government. The nominal money supply evolves as follows:

$$M_t - M_{t-1} = (\gamma - \theta) S_t A_t^*, \qquad (2)$$

where M_t is the nominal money supply in period t, and θ is the fraction of aid dollars sold on the market by the central bank. Equation (2) states that the net effect of aid on the money supply is jointly determined by the government's decision on spending (through γ) and the central bank's decision on absorption/sterilization (θ). In the absence of absorption ($\theta = 0$), higher government spending is entirely financed by money creation and, ultimately, inflation. On the other hand, full foreign exchange sterilization ($\theta = 1$) could generate a real appreciation that would accommodate higher domestic aggregate demand through an increase in net imports.[7] The experiments presented in the next section study the effects of random changes in A_t^* under various combinations of spending (γ) and absorption (θ).

The exact parameter values used in the experiments are presented in Appendix 8.1.[8] The assumed values imply that in the steady-state government spending is roughly 20 percent of GDP; nontraded goods firms' prices are set with a 20 percent markup over marginal costs (an elasticity of substitution between goods of 6); consumers treat tradables and nontradables as equally important, whereas the government in its spending basket places a 90 percent weight on nontradables and a 10 percent weight on domestically-produced tradables and does not purchase imports; and aid finances about 8 percent of government spending. In dynamic simulations, each nontraded goods firm is assumed to face a 50 percent probability of adjusting its price each period. Finally, the experiments examine the effects of a 30 percent increase in aid (0.5 percent of the steady-state GDP). The possible effects of different

---

[2]A detailed description of the model and the solution method is presented in Appendices 8.1 and 8.2.

[3]Monopolistic competition is a standard device to allow a role for aggregate demand in output determination and for price-setting behavior, which in turn generates nominal rigidities. The empirical relevance of this assumption will presumably depend on the country in question, and parameters can be chosen to yield any desired degree of monopolistic competition.

[4]All domestic firms are assumed to be owned by domestic consumers. Consumers receive dividends from firms, but take them as given, i.e., they do not actively participate in firms' decision-making.

[5]This assumption is less appealing for countries with market access and substantial levels of foreign direct investment. However, we view it as a useful first-step approximation in keeping the analysis simple and tractable.

[6]We do not examine optimal tax policies and therefore keep the tax rate fixed.

[7]This is likely to be true even when the government only spends aid proceeds on nontradables. A real appreciation would shift private demand toward imports, allowing the government to consume more nontraded goods.

[8]Instead of a linearization-based solution, we used the collocation method to solve this model (Appendix 8.2).

parameter values are discussed in the context of each experiment.

Anatomy of Macroeconomic Adjustment to Aid Inflows

Spend and Don't Absorb

A well-known property of New Keynesian models is that the real effects of permanent increases in the nominal money supply are short-lived because they are driven by nominal rigidities that disappear in the long run. In contrast, a permanent shock to aid inflows, when aid is spent but not absorbed, is in essence an amalgam of a pure monetary expansion because higher government spending is financed by liquidity injection, and a shock to the structure of aggregate demand when the government's spending habits differ from those of the private sector.[9] When, as here, the government strongly favors nontraded goods over tradables, such an increase in spending would have two opposing effects on the real exchange rate. A monetary expansion tends to generate nominal and, in the periods of incomplete price adjustment, real depreciation. On the other hand, a higher relative demand for nontraded goods would tend to raise their prices relative to prices of traded goods and result in real appreciation. If the aid shock is permanent, then these two effects compete in the short run, but only the second effect persists. A slow pace of domestic price adjustment may thus result in a short-run depreciation followed by a permanent real appreciation. Such overshooting is likely to lead to overshooting of other variables and implies that aid inflows may generate larger short-run volatility than is implied by the new long-run equilibrium. Therefore, distinguishing between the short-term and long-term effects of shocks to aid is important in this scenario.[10]

Figures 8.1 and 8.2 present the effects of, respectively, permanent and temporary increases in the level of aid in the model. The first panel displays the different short- and long-run effects on the real exchange rate discussed above. In the short run, while nontraded goods prices have not completely adjusted to higher demand, the real exchange rate depreciates. As prices adjust, the effects of higher government spending push the real exchange rate toward appreciation. An interesting implication illustrated by Figure 8.2 is that if price rigidities are strong enough and the aid increase is tem-

porary and not very persistent, then real appreciation may be very small or may never materialize, since it would happen late in the adjustment process. This may in part explain the real depreciation observed in some of the case studies.[11]

The real value of government spending in Figure 8.1 also overshoots its long-run equilibrium value due to sluggish price adjustment. Inflation rises rapidly due to the instant adjustment of the nominal exchange rate and the prices of traded goods and gradually returns to a new higher level. The effects on private consumption can be explained by the behavior of the three components of household income. First, a permanent increase in the inflation tax, which finances government spending, permanently lowers household income. Second, wage income rises as consumers try to compensate for a higher inflation tax and increased labor supply. Wage income rises more in the short run when real wages are higher due to price rigidity. Third, firms' profits (households' dividend income) fall in the short run, driven by lower profits of firms with unadjusted prices, but rise in the long run due to higher aggregate demand. The offsetting effects of higher wage and dividend income imply that consumption[12] falls gradually due to the overshooting of real wages, and that in the long run it falls by less than the amount of inflation tax. This results in a positive net long-term effect on domestic aggregate demand.[13]

The short-run shift of demand toward nontraded goods combined with real depreciation depresses aggregate demand for traded goods. On the other hand, as the real exchange rate appreciates over time, households increasingly substitute tradable goods for nontraded goods produced domestically and imported. Despite lower aggregate private consumption, the effect on the net demand for tradable goods is ambiguous, and depends on the relative strength of the substitution and income effects in consumer demand. Our particular parameter values lead to an unchanged net demand (and supply) for tradables as shown in Figure 8.1. Note that if the elasticity of substitution between the tradables and nontraded goods and labor supply elasticity were very low, then output in the traded goods sector would most likely decline in the long run.

---

[9]Note that an increase in government spending in the absence of aid would be a similar amalgam of a pure monetary shock and a change in the structure of aggregate demand.

[10]For simplicity, we focus on the extreme cases when θ and γ are either 0 or 1. Intermediate cases can be interpreted as more moderate versions of the scenarios presented here. For example, when $\gamma > \theta$, the interpretation would be similar to the case of spending without absorption.

[11]Other parameter values, such as those creating differences in sectoral productivity, high elasticity of substitution between traded and nontraded goods, and a higher share of traded goods in the government's consumption basket may also result in real depreciation both in the short and long run.

[12]"Consumption" is used interchangeably with "private consumption."

[13]Output increases in the long run mainly because (1) the increase in government consumption is greater than the decline in private consumption, and (2) the government consumes domestic goods disproportionately, requiring higher domestic output. Even if private consumption demand fully offset government consumption demand in (1), the effect of (2) would still increase long-run output.

Figure 8.1. Spend and Don't Absorb, Permanent Shock

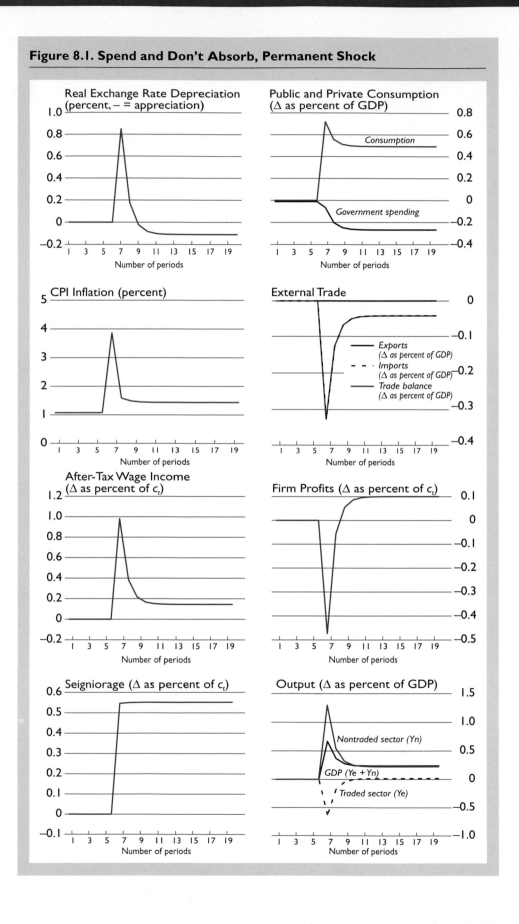

Figure 8.2. Spend and Don't Absorb, Temporary Shock

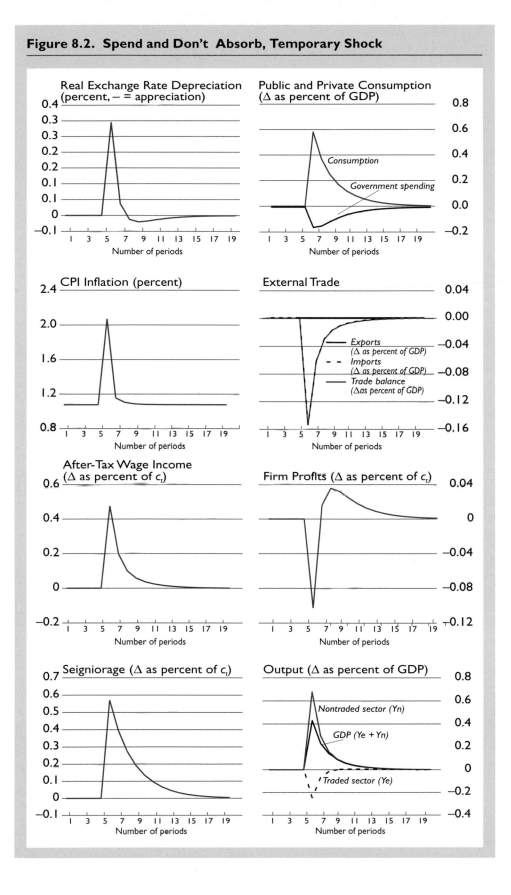

Finally, note that in the absence of aid absorption the trade balance is unchanged, i.e., aid does not lead to any resource transfer from abroad. The fiscal expansion examined here could in principle be undertaken even without aid by borrowing directly from the central bank. The only difference is that central bank reserves are higher in the scenario with aid.

Absorb and Don't Spend

A sale of aid dollars ($\theta = 1$) without an associated increase in government spending ($\gamma = 0$) generates a real resource transfer through higher net imports, but produces a monetary and real tightening. The pattern of adjustment to a permanent shock to aid is displayed in Figure 8.3.[14] A monetary contraction reduces inflation, increasing consumers' real income. A real appreciation in this case is unambiguous, although it is larger in the short run when some of the nontraded goods prices are fixed. Higher income provides an incentive for consumers to increase consumption and to supply less labor.[15] Aggregate output and government revenues therefore decline, and more so in the short run. Note that this result differs from the analysis in Chapter I, which argues that an absorb-and-don't-spend policy can be used to crowd in private sector investment (for example, by using aid to retire domestic government debt) and thereby stimulate growth. The model presented here, for considerations of tractability, does not model government debt or private investment behavior, both of which are important considerations for an absorb-and-don't-spend strategy.

Real exchange rate overshooting generates quite different responses of sectoral output. In the short run, when the appreciation is large and government spending is low, nontraded output declines while traded goods output expands. On the other hand, as the real exchange rate returns to the long-run level, output in both sectors declines. Nevertheless, household consumption of all types of goods rises at the expense of lower government spending and lower exports.

Absorb and Spend

When aid is spent and absorbed, the nominal money supply remains constant (see equation 2). Hence, the main effect on the real exchange rate comes from higher government spending, which explains the absence of exchange rate overshooting in the first panel of

Figure 8.4; instead, the real exchange rate gradually appreciates as nontraded goods prices adjust to the new demand structure. The long-run real appreciation is higher than in the spend-and-don't-absorb case.

In the absence of an inflation tax, household income is affected by wage income and profits. Profits are mostly driven by nontraded goods producers, whose profits rise significantly due to higher government demand and firms' monopoly power. Wages rise in the short run, due to a large output response in the nontraded sector, but fall in the long run. Lower employment in the long run results from the assumption of identically diminishing marginal products of labor in both sectors, combined with monopolistic competition in the nontraded goods sector. These assumptions imply that in the steady state, output is lower and marginal productivity of labor is higher in the nontraded sector. Therefore, a given expansion in the nontraded sector would require less labor resources than the same contraction in the traded sector. Alternatively, a given amount of labor resources freed as a result of a contraction of traded goods output would generate higher output in the nontraded goods sector. In the new long-run equilibrium, a mixture of these two effects is observed: lower aggregate employment and higher aggregate output. This outcome is not robust to various plausible alternative parameter assumptions. A lower assumed monopoly power in the nontraded sector, absence of perfect competition in the traded sector, and different sectoral technologies can nullify the implication that a demand-induced reallocation of resources toward nontraded goods improves aggregate efficiency.[16] In any case, the increase in output in Figure 8.4 (about 0.02 percent of GDP) is negligible compared with the size of the aid shock (0.5 percent of GDP).

Discussion of the Appropriate Policy Response

Even in this simple framework, countries may face difficult choices in responding to aid inflows, because each policy scenario has potentially negative effects on at least some variables. The model can be used to show how the expected utility of consumers depends on the nature of the policy response to aid shocks. However, it lacks too many features, notably investment and any explicit benefit to government spending, to provide much direct insight on this basis.[17] But in anticipation of a more fully worked-out model, the results presented so far, applied somewhat loosely, can shed light on the

---

[14]The effects of a temporary aid shock are qualitatively similar and are omitted.

[15]This is related to the concept of the backward-bending labor supply curve. An early reference for this possibility in the developing country context is Berg (1961), who discusses conditions under which labor supply elasticity turns negative beyond some target level of income.

[16]For example, a high elasticity of substitution between traded and nontraded goods and/or higher labor productivity in the traded sector, among other factors, could reverse the output outcome.

[17]For similar reasons, the long-run effects on output do not allow a useful ranking of the merits of the different policy responses.

Figure 8.3. Absorb and Don't Spend, Permanent Shock

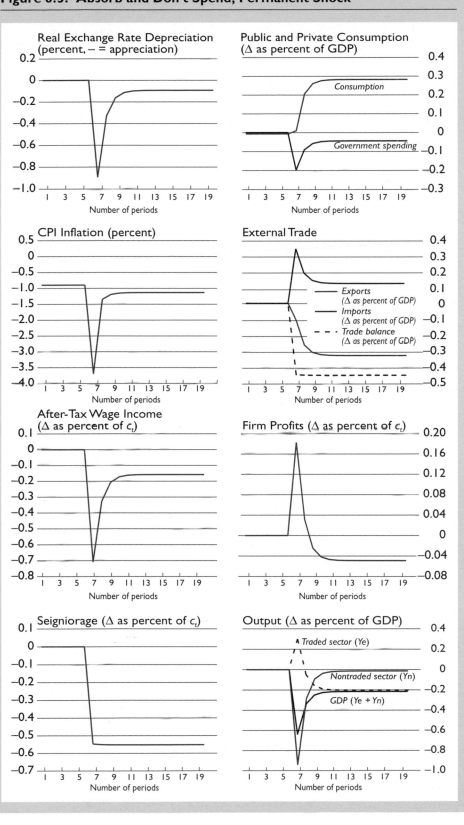

Figure 8.4. Absorb and Spend, Permanent Shock

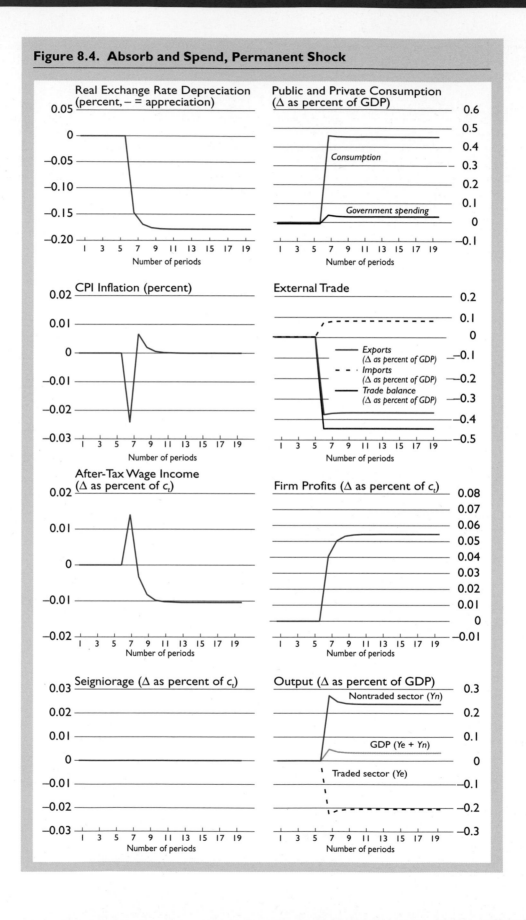

relative merits of the different choices with respect to absorbing and spending.

It is useful to compare two responses: that which would be optimal given overall policy preferences of the authorities and that which would be the outcome of separate decisions by the government (for fiscal policy) and an independent central bank (for monetary policy). A useful starting point is to note that a spend-and-don't absorb response would not likely be the optimal choice of a single authority. This reflects the idea that any benefits of domestically-financed fiscal expansions have already been exploited or do not arrive with aid shocks, not that they do not exist in general.[18] To absorb and not spend is likely to be suboptimal when the initial rate of inflation is appropriate, but may be desirable in a highly inflationary environment. Thus, in the absence of high initial inflation, the two optimal long-run responses are likely to be spend and absorb or neither spend nor absorb. The long-run trade-off is between the potentially negative effects on the export sector and the stimulus to long-run growth provided by government investments.[19]

It is possible that separate, uncoordinated decisions by the central bank and the government would result in a suboptimal outcome. The objectives of central banks typically involve maintaining macroeconomic stability through low and stable inflation. Another common objective is to maintain competitiveness by avoiding real exchange rate appreciation. The fiscal authorities share similar objectives, but it is reasonable to suppose that they place more weight on the benefits associated with government spending, less on macroeconomic stability, and less on the costs of exchange rate appreciation.

Consider first the decision of the ministry of finance. In general, its choice may depend on whether it expects the central bank to absorb or not. However, it is plausible that the ministry will choose to spend whatever the decision of the central bank with respect to absorption, as long as it considers that the benefits of spending outweigh either the costs of appreciation in the case of absorption or the costs of higher inflation in the case of nonabsorption.

The central bank thus may have to decide how to respond to the decision to spend. The central bank faces a trade-off. Absorption (i.e., the sale of aid dollars) avoids a rise in inflation and results in much smaller short-term volatility of other variables; however, it also results in a more appreciated real exchange rate (Figures 8.1 and

8.4). When it is not too concerned about real appreciation, the central bank will choose to absorb. If the central bank sufficiently dislikes real exchange rate appreciations, however, then it will choose not to absorb.

In sum, a central bank mostly concerned about real appreciation and a ministry of finance mostly concerned about spending might separately choose policies that result in a spend-and-don't-absorb response, despite the fact that together they would not choose such an outcome. The case studies suggest that this situation may be common.

This analysis of policy responses is only suggestive. A next step would be to write down well-defined preferences for the two institutions and derive the noncooperative and coordinated equilibria. More generally, the model presented here abstracts from several important considerations. A more complete version of the model, calibrated to a specific country case, is the subject of ongoing work.

Appendix 8.1. Model Description

This appendix presents the details of the model used in the experiments.

Consumers

Each consumer maximizes life-time utility that depends on consumption, real money balances, and labor:[20]

$$\max E_0 \sum_{j=0}^{\infty} \beta^j u\left(C_t, \frac{M_t}{P_{ct}}, L_t\right), \tag{A.1}$$

where C_t is private consumption expressed in units of domestic consumption baskets (to be defined below), $\frac{M_t}{P_{ct}}$ is the consumers' holding of real money balances, and L_t is their labor effort. The consumers' budget constraint is given by

$$\underbrace{C_t P_{ct}}_{\text{cons. spend.}} \leq \underbrace{-B_t^c + (1+i_{t-1})B_{t-1}^c - M_t + M_{t-1}}_{\text{change in asset (bonds and money) holding}} + \underbrace{(1-\tau_t)W_t L_t + \Pi_t^n,}_{\text{after-tax labor income}}$$

where B_t^c is the consumers' holding of domestic nominal nonstate-contingent bonds, τ is the income tax rate, W_t is the nominal wage, and Π_t^n denotes the nominal profits of domestic firms, which are taken as given by consumers. Dividing both sides of the budget constraint by the price of the domestic consumption basket P_{ct} and

---

[18]It is possible that optimal domestically-financed spending would be greater with higher reserves, because the higher reserves might lower the country risk premium. However, this is likely to be a small effect. Moreover, borrowing domestically while building reserves would imply losses on the spread between the cost of borrowing and the yield on reserves. These considerations are outside the scope of the model presented here.

[19]As noted earlier, this trade-off cannot be formally addressed with the model presented here. See Prati and Tressel (2005).

[20]The benchmark model employs the following period utility function:

$$u\left(C_t, \frac{M_t}{P_{ct}}, L_t\right) = \ln C_t + \frac{x}{1-\varepsilon}\left(\frac{M_t}{P_{ct}}\right)^{1-\varepsilon} - \frac{\kappa}{\psi}L_t^{\psi}.$$

employing smaller case letters to denote real values of nominal variables, we can rewrite the budget constraint in real terms[21] as follows:

$$C_t \le -b_t^c + (1+i_{t-1})\frac{b_{t-1}^c}{1+\pi_{ct}} - m_t + \frac{m_{t-1}}{1+\pi_{ct}} + (1-\tau_t)w_t L_t + \Pi_t^r. \quad (A.2)$$

Maximizing (A.1) subject to (A.2) yields the following first order conditions:

$$u_{ct} = \beta E_t \left\{ \frac{u_{ct+1}(1+i_t)}{1+\pi_{ct+1}} \right\} \quad (A.3)$$

$$u_{mt} = u_{ct} \frac{i_t}{1+i_t} \quad (A.4)$$

$$-u_{Lt} = (1-\tau_t)w_t u_{ct}, \quad (A.5)$$

where u_c, u_m, u_L denote partial derivatives of the utility function with respect to consumption, real money balances, and labor, respectively.

Consumption Baskets and Demands and Price Indices

The three types of goods traded in the economy are indexed by superscript (N) for nontradables, (e) for exportables, and (F) for foreign imported goods. Consumption sub-baskets of each type of goods aggregate consumption of individual products using a constant elasticity of substitution (CES) function:

$$C_t^N = \left(\int_0^1 C_{it}^{N\frac{\lambda-1}{\lambda}} di \right)^{\frac{\lambda}{\lambda-1}} ; \; C_t^e = \left(\int_0^1 C_{it}^{e\frac{\lambda-1}{\lambda}} di \right)^{\frac{\lambda}{\lambda-1}} ; \; C_t^F = \left(\int_0^1 C_{it}^{F\frac{\lambda-1}{\lambda}} di \right)^{\frac{\lambda}{\lambda-1}}$$

The total consumption basket of the consumers combines the three sub-baskets:

$$C_t = \left(n_1^{\frac{1}{\omega}} (C_t^N)^{\frac{\omega-1}{\omega}} + n_2^{\frac{1}{\omega}} (C_t^e)^{\frac{\omega-1}{\omega}} + n_3^{\frac{1}{\omega}} (C_t^F)^{\frac{\omega-1}{\omega}} \right)^{\frac{\omega}{\omega-1}} \quad (A.6)$$

where $n_1 + n_2 + n_3 = 1$. Here, λ and ω represent elasticity of substitution between various types of goods.[22] The government also spends money on goods, but has a different consumption basket:

$$G_t = \left(v_1^{\frac{1}{\omega}} (G_t^N)^{\frac{\omega-1}{\omega}} + v_2^{\frac{1}{\omega}} (G_t^e)^{\frac{\omega-1}{\omega}} + v_3^{\frac{1}{\omega}} (G_t^F)^{\frac{\omega-1}{\omega}} \right)^{\frac{\omega}{\omega-1}} \quad (A.7)$$

where $v_1 + v_2 + v_3 = 1$. Varying v_i's stresses differences in government's preferences over different varieties of goods.

Price indices associated with each basket of goods follow similar notation and are defined as the minimum nominal cost of buying one unit of each (sub-) basket. They are given by

$$P_t^N = \left(\int_0^1 P_{it}^{N1-\lambda} di \right)^{\frac{1}{1-\lambda}} ; \; P_t^e = \left(\int_0^1 P_{it}^{e1-\lambda} di \right)^{\frac{1}{1-\lambda}} ; \; P_t^F = \left(\int_0^1 P_{it}^{F1-\lambda} di \right)^{\frac{1}{1-\lambda}}. \quad (A.8)$$

The law of one price (LOP) holds in the tradables sector. Furthermore, the foreign price is normalized to unity ($P_t^{*F} = 1$), so that the domestic nominal price of exportables and imports are both equal to the nominal exchange rate: $P_t^F = S_t P_t^{*F} = P_t^e = S_t$, where S_t is the nominal exchange rate and P_t^{*F} is the foreign currency value of the import price.[23]

Price indices associated with the baskets of consumers and the government, respectively, are

$$P_{ct} = \left(n_1 (P_t^N)^{1-\omega} + n_2 (P_t^e)^{1-\omega} + n_3 (S_t P_t^{*F})^{1-\omega} \right)^{\frac{1}{1-\omega}}$$

$$P_{gt} = \left(v_1 (P_t^N)^{1-\omega} + v_2 (P_t^e)^{1-\omega} + v_3 (S_t P_t^{*F})^{1-\omega} \right)^{\frac{1}{1-\omega}}.$$

Dividing both sides of these equations by P_{ct} provides an expression for "real" prices, or prices in terms of the private consumption basket. Using the LOP assumption $P_t^{*F} = P_t^e = S_t$ implies the following expressions:

$$1 = \left(n_1 (p_t^N)^{1-\omega} + (1-n_1)(p_t^e)^{1-\omega} \right)^{\frac{1}{1-\omega}} \quad (A.9)$$

$$p_{gt} = \left(v_1 (p_t^N)^{1-\omega} + (1-v_1)(p_t^e)^{1-\omega} \right)^{\frac{1}{1-\omega}}. \quad (A.10)$$

Demand functions associated with an individual good i within each category can be expressed as follows:

$$C_{it}^N = n_1 \left(\frac{p_{it}^N}{p_t^N} \right)^{-\lambda} (p_t^N)^{-\omega} C_t ; \; C_{it}^e = n_2 (p_t^e)^{-\omega} C_t ;$$

$$C_{it}^F = n_3 (p_t^e)^{-\omega} C_t ; \; G_{it}^N = v_1 \left(\frac{p_{it}^N}{p_t^N} \right)^{-\lambda} \left(\frac{p_t^N}{p_{gt}} \right)^{-\omega} G_t ;$$

$$G_{it}^e = v_2 \left(\frac{p_t^N}{p_{gt}} \right)^{-\omega} G_t ; \; G_{it}^F = n_3 \left(\frac{p_t^N}{p_{gt}} \right)^{-\omega} G_t.$$

Finally, demands for aggregate sub-baskets are given by:

$$C_t^N = n_1 (p_t^N)^{-\omega} C_t ; \; C_{it}^e = n_2 (p_t^e)^{-\omega} C_t ;$$

$$C_t^F = n_3 (p_t^e)^{-\omega} C_t. \quad (A.11)$$

---

[21]With very few exceptions, "real" denotes variables expressed in units of household consumption baskets.

[22]In the baseline model $\lambda = \omega$.

[23]An asterisk (*) on nominal variables indicates denomination in foreign currency.

$$G_{it}^N = v_1 \left(\frac{p_{it}^N}{p_t^N} \right)^{-\lambda} \left(\frac{p_t^N}{p_{gt}} \right)^{-\omega} G_t \, ;$$

$$G_t^e = v_2 \left(\frac{p_t^e}{p_{gt}} \right)^{-\omega} G_t \, ; \quad G_t^F = v_3 \left(\frac{p_t^e}{p_{gt}} \right)^{-\omega} G_t. \quad \text{(A.12)}$$

Nontraded Goods Sector

The production function of the nontraded goods sector producers depends on labor (capital is assumed to be fixed) and is assumed to exhibit diminishing marginal returns.

$$Y_t^n = Q_n (L_t^n)^\alpha, \quad \text{(A.13)}$$

where Q_n is aggregate productivity in the nontraded sector (held fixed in the baseline model.) Firms follow Calvo pricing; i.e., in each period every firm faces a fixed probability $(1-q)$ of changing its price. By the law of large numbers in equilibrium, q fraction of firms keep their prices fixed, whereas $(1-q)$ fraction of the prices adjust.

Price-Setting Problem

Every individual firm i faces the following demand:

$$Y_{it}^{dN} = \left(p_{it}^N \right)^{-\lambda} \left\{ n_1 C_t + v_1 (p_{gt})^\lambda G_t \right\} \equiv \left(p_{it}^N \right)^{-\lambda} D_t^N \quad \text{(A.14)}$$

Combining the last two equations, the firm's labor demand can be expressed as follows:

$$L_{it}^n = Q_n^{-\frac{1}{\alpha}} \left(p_{it}^N \right)^{-\frac{\lambda}{\alpha}} \left(D_t^n \right)^{\frac{1}{\alpha}}.$$

When provided a chance to re-set its (nominal) price, firm i seeks to maximize expected profits (in real terms):

$$\max_{P_{it}^n} E_t \sum_{j=0}^\infty J_{t+j} q^j \left\{ \left(\frac{P_{it}^N}{P_{ct+j}} \right)^{1-\lambda} D_{t+j}^n \right.$$

$$\left. - w_{t+j} Q_n^{-\frac{1}{\alpha}} \left(\frac{P_{it}^N}{P_{ct+j}} \right)^{-\frac{\lambda}{\alpha}} (D_{t+j}^n)^{\frac{1}{\alpha}} \right\}, \quad \text{(A.15)}$$

where J_{t+j} is the firm's discount factor between dates t and $t+j$.[24] The first order condition, describing the optimal price is given by:

$$(p_{it}^n)^{1-\lambda+\frac{\lambda}{\alpha}} = \frac{\lambda}{\alpha(1-\lambda)} \cdot \frac{E_t \left\{ \sum_{j=0}^\infty J_{t+j} q^j w_{t+j} Q_n^{-\frac{1}{\alpha}} \left(\frac{P_{ct+j}}{P_{ct}} \right)^{\frac{\lambda}{\alpha}} D_{nt+j}^{\frac{1}{\alpha}} \right\}}{E_t \left\{ \sum_{j=0}^\infty J_{t+j} q^j \left(\frac{P_{ct+j}}{P_{ct}} \right)^{\lambda-1} D_{nt+j} \right\}}$$

$$\equiv \frac{\lambda}{\alpha(1-\lambda)} \cdot \frac{V_{1t}}{V_{2t}}. \quad \text{(A.16)}$$

Using V_{1t} and V_{2t} to denote the numerator and the denominator of the right-hand side of the previous equation is useful for the purpose of solving the model. Note that V_{1t} and V_{2t} can be expressed recursively as follows:

$$V_{1t} = w_t Q_n^{-\frac{1}{\alpha}} D_{nt}^{\frac{1}{\alpha}} + E_t \left\{ J_{t+1} q (1+\pi_{ct+1})^{\frac{\lambda}{\alpha}} V_{1t+1} \right\} \quad \text{(A.17)}$$

$$V_{2t} = D_{nt} + E_t \left\{ J_{t+1} q (1+\pi_{ct+1})^{\lambda-1} V_{2t+1} \right\}. \quad \text{(A.18)}$$

Aggregate Prices, Output, and Labor Demand in the Nontraded Sector

Since only a $(1-q)$ fraction of the firms change their prices every period, the nominal price of the nontraded goods sub-basket follows the following law of motion:

$$P_t^n = \left\{ q(P_{t-1}^n)^{1-\lambda} + (1-q)(P_{it}^n)^{1-\lambda} \right\}^{\frac{1}{1-\lambda}},$$

where P_{it}^n is the optimal re-set price. Dividing both sides by P_{ct} yields the real price of the nontraded goods basket:

$$p_t^n = \left\{ q \left(\frac{p_{t-1}^n}{1+\pi_{ct}} \right) + (1-q)(p_{it}^n)^{1-\lambda} \right\}^{\frac{1}{1-\lambda}}. \quad \text{(A.19)}$$

Aggregate output in the nontraded goods sector (in units of the total consumption basket) is given by aggregate demand for nontradables:

$$Y_t^n = (p_t^n)^{1-\lambda} D_{nt}. \quad \text{(A.20)}$$

Finally, aggregate labor demand of the nontraded goods producers can be expressed as follows:

$$L_t^n = \left[(1-q)(p_{it}^n)^{-\frac{\lambda}{\alpha}} + q \left(\frac{p_{t-1}^n}{1+\pi_{ct}} \right)^{-\frac{\lambda}{\alpha}} \right] D_{nt}^{\frac{1}{\alpha}} Q_n^{-\frac{1}{\alpha}}. \quad \text{(A.21)}$$

Exportable Goods Sector

Exportable goods producers have a similar production function: $Y_t^e = Q_e (L_t^e)^\alpha$. Since prices in this sector are flexible, all firms in equilibrium will have the same

---

[24]Because firms are owned by consumers, the discount factor is set to equal the consumers' intertemporal marginal rate of substitution.

price and output. The optimal level of output is chosen by maximizing real profits:[25]

$$\max_{Y_t^e} \left[p_t^e Y_t^e - w_t Q_e^{-\frac{1}{\alpha}} (Y_t^e)^{\frac{1}{\alpha}} \right], \tag{A.22}$$

which implies that optimal output and employment levels are given by

$$Y_t^e = \left(\alpha \frac{p_t^e}{w_t} Q_e^{\frac{1}{\alpha}} \right)^{\frac{\alpha}{1-\alpha}} \tag{A.23}$$

$$L_t^e = \left(\alpha \frac{p_t^e}{w_t} Q_e \right)^{\frac{1}{1-\alpha}}. \tag{A.24}$$

Before exporting, the exportable goods producer must satisfy domestic demand, which from (A.11) and (A.12) can be expressed as

$$Y_t^{de} = \left\{ n_2 (p_t^e)^{-w} C_t + v_2 \left(\frac{p_t^e}{p_{gt}} \right)^{-w} G_t \right\}.$$

Thus, exports are given by

$$Y_t^{ex} = Y_t^e - \left\{ n_2 (p_t^e)^{-w} C_t + v_2 \left(\frac{p_t^e}{p_{gt}} \right)^{-w} G_t \right\}. \tag{A.25}$$

Government and the Central Bank

The government can finance its spending by taxing labor income or by using its aid proceeds:

$$p_{gt} G_t = \tau_t w_t L_t + \gamma s_t A_t^*, \tag{A.26}$$

where γ is the key variable measuring the fraction of aid spent by the government and A_t^* is the current period aid (grants) in foreign currency.[26]

The central bank's budget constraint is given by

$$M_t = M_{t-1} + (\gamma - \theta) S_t A_t^*,$$

where θ is the fraction of aid dollars sold on the market by the central bank. Note that in the absence of alternative sterilization measures, the net effect of aid on the money supply is jointly determined by the government's decision on spending (through γ) and the central bank's decision on absorption (through θ). Dividing both sides by P_{ct} yields the law of motion for the real money supply:

$$m_t = \frac{m_{t-1}}{1+\pi_{ct}} + (\gamma - \theta) s_t A_t^*. \tag{A.27}$$

The unused portion of the aid is added to the forex reserves.

Market Clearing

The labor market clearing condition is

$$L_t = \underbrace{\left[(1-q)(p_{it}^n)^{-\frac{\lambda}{\alpha}} + q \left(\frac{p_{t-1}^n}{1+\pi_{ct}} \right)^{-\frac{\lambda}{\alpha}} \right] D_{nt}^{\frac{1}{\alpha}} Q_n^{-\frac{1}{\alpha}}}_{\equiv L_t^N}$$

$$+ \underbrace{\left(\alpha \frac{p_t^e}{w_t} Q_e \right)}_{\equiv L_t^e}. \tag{A.28}$$

Combining equations (A.2), (A.26), and (A.27), one can obtain the economy-wide resource constraint, or the current account equation:

$$\underbrace{C_t + p_{gt} G_t}_{\text{Aggregate Consumption}} - \underbrace{\left\{ (p_t^n)^{1-\lambda} D_t^n + p_t^e \left(\alpha \frac{p_t^e}{w_t} Q_e^{\frac{1}{\alpha}} \right)^{\frac{\alpha}{1-\alpha}} \right\}}_{\text{Domestic Output}}$$

$$= \underbrace{\theta A_t^* s_t.}_{\text{Sale of Aid Dollars}} \tag{A.29}$$

The equation highlights that in the absence of foreign borrowing, the only way the economy can consume more than it produces is through the central bank's sale of foreign exchange. It can also be interpreted as the foreign exchange market equilibrium. The left-hand side represents net imports (or demand for foreign exchange in excess of export revenues), whereas the right-hand side represents the supply of additional foreign exchange by the central bank.[27]

Equilibrium

For the purpose of convenience it is useful to summarize the system of equations that describes equilibrium at any point in time.

$$u_{ct} = \beta (1+i_t) E_t \left\{ \frac{u_{ct+1}}{1+\pi_{ct+1}} \right\} \tag{A.30}$$

$$u_{mt} = u_{ct} \frac{i_t}{1+i_t}. \tag{A.31}$$

$$-u_{Lt} = (1-\tau_t) w_t u_{ct} \tag{A.32}$$

---

[25]The optimal level of output is well defined as long as there is diminishing marginal product of labor (i.e., $\alpha < 1$).

[26]Recall that the (consumer price index-based) real exchange rate s_t also equals the real price of tradables p_t^e.

[27]If consumers were allowed to hold foreign currency, the supply side would also be affected by the private sector's decisions regarding currency composition of its asset portfolio. This case (dollarization) may be an interesting extension to the present set-up.

$$(p^n_{it})^{1-\lambda+\frac{\lambda}{\alpha}} = \frac{\lambda}{\alpha(1-\lambda)} \frac{V_{1t}}{V_{2t}} \tag{A.33}$$

$$p^n_t = \left\{ q\left(\frac{p^n_{t-1}}{1+\pi_{ct}}\right)^{1-\lambda} + (1-q)(p^n_{it})^{1-\lambda} \right\}^{\frac{1}{1-\lambda}} \tag{A.34}$$

$$1 = \left(n_1\left(p^N_t\right)^{1-\omega} + \left(1-n_1\right)\left(p^e_t\right)^{1-\omega} \right)^{\frac{1}{1-\omega}} \tag{A.35}$$

$$p_{gt} = \left(v_1\left(p^N_t\right)^{1-\omega} + \left(1-v_1\right)\left(p^e_t\right)^{1-\omega} \right)^{\frac{1}{1-\omega}} \tag{A.36}$$

$$p_{gt}G_t = \tau_t w_t L_t + \alpha_t s_t A^*_t + b_t - (1+i_{t-1})\frac{b^c_{t-1}}{1+\pi_{ct}} \tag{A.37}$$

$$m_t = \frac{m_{t-1}}{1+\pi_{ct}} + (\alpha-\theta)s_t A^*_t + b^{cb}_t - \frac{b^{cb}_{t-1}}{1+\pi_{ct}} - \delta^*_t s_t \tag{A.38}$$

$$L_t = \left[(1-q)(p^n_{it})^{-\frac{\lambda}{\alpha}} + q\left(\frac{p^n_{t-1}}{1+\pi_{ct}}\right)^{-\frac{\lambda}{\alpha}} \right]$$

$$D^{\frac{1}{\alpha}}_{nt} Q^{-\frac{1}{\alpha}}_n + \left(\alpha\frac{p^e_t}{w_t}Q_e \right)^{\frac{1}{1-\alpha}} \tag{A.39}$$

$$C_t + p_{gt}G - \left\{ (p^n_t)^{1-\lambda} D_{nt} + p^e_t\left(\alpha\frac{p^e_t}{w_t}Q^{\frac{1}{\alpha}}_e \right)^{\frac{\alpha}{1-\alpha}} \right\}$$

$$= (\theta A^*_t + \delta^*)s_t, \tag{A.40}$$

where

$$V_{1t} = w_t Q^{-\frac{1}{\alpha}}_n D^{\frac{1}{\alpha}}_{nt} + E_t\left\{ J_{t+1}q(1+\pi_{ct+1})^{\frac{\lambda}{\alpha}}V_{1t+1} \right\} \tag{A.41}$$

$$V_{2t} = D_{nt} + E_t\left\{ J_{t+1}q(1+\pi_{ct+1})^{\lambda-1}V_{2t+1} \right\} \tag{A.42}$$

$$D^n_t = \left\{ n_1 C_t + v_1(p_{gt})^\lambda G_t \right\}. \tag{A.43}$$

In the model discussed, the uncertainty comes from aid inflows, which follow an AR(1) process:

$$A^*_t = \overline{A} + \rho(A^*_{t-1} - \overline{A}) + e_t, e_t \sim N(0,\sigma^2), \overline{A} \geq 0. \tag{A.44}$$

Parameter values, used in the experiments are as follows:

α	λ	q	χ	ε	κ	τ	ρ
0.8	5	0.3	0.1	3	2	0.2	0.7

n_1	n_2	v_1	v_2	$\overline{A}$	β	σ	$Q_n=Q_e.$
0.5	0.25	0.9	0.1	0.012	0.96	0.001	1

Appendix 8.2. Solution Method

The system of equations from (A.30) to (A.44) describes a dynamic nonlinear system. The method of collocation is applied to solve the system.[28] Commonly used linearization-based techniques can result in very inaccurate calculations of the solution to a nonlinear model, particularly when shocks are large.[29] The method of collocation helps assess and ensure reasonable accuracy over the desired part of the state space.[30]

Solving the above system is complicated by (1) the nonlinear structure of the model, and (2) uncertainty created by aid shocks. The first step in solving the model is to separate variables into three groups: actions, states, and expectational variables.

The *actions* are the contemporaneous endogenous variables, i.e., agents' decisions and equilibrium outcomes. In our model these include consumption (C_t), interest rate (i_t), prices (p^n_{it}, p_{gt}, p^n_t, p^e_t), money supply (m_t), labor supply (L_t), wage rate (w_t), inflation (π_{ct}), and government spending (G_t):

$$x_t = [C_t \ i_t \ p^n_{it} \ p_{gt} \ p^n_t \ p^e_t \ m_t \ L_t \ w_t \ \pi_{ct} \ Gt]'. \tag{A.45}$$

State variables are those that are predetermined and are therefore taken by agents as given at the beginning of each period. Typically they include all exogenous variables and past values of endogenous variables. In the simplified version of the model, there are three such variables: level of aid, previous period money holding, and past price of nontraded goods:

$$sv_t = [m_{t-1} \ p^n_{t-1} \ A^*_t]'. \tag{A.46}$$

The state vector describes the state of nature that agents face each period and on which they base their actions. It follows a law of motion:[31]

$$sv_{t+1} = g(x_t, sv_t, e_{t+1}). \tag{A.47}$$

The *expectational variables* are expressions under the expectation sign. They appear in three places in the system: the Euler equation (A.30), and the expressions for V_{1t} and V_{2t} which enter the pricing equation (A.33). Thus, the vector of expectational variables is three-dimensional:

$$z_{t+1} = \left[\frac{u_{ct+1}}{1+\pi_{ct+1}} \ J_{t+1}q(1+\pi_{ct+1})^{\frac{\lambda}{\alpha}}V_{1t+1} \right.$$

$$\left. J_{t+1}q(1+\pi_{ct+1})^{\lambda-1}V_{2t+1} \right]'. \tag{A.48}$$

---

[28]Miranda and Fackler (2002) provide an extensive exposition of the method.

[29]Carroll (2001) and Kim and Kim (2003) illustrate the inaccuracies that could result from linearization-based solutions.

[30]See, for example, Gapen and Cosimano (2005).

[31]The law of motion in this case can be represented as

$$sv_{t+1} = \left[\frac{sv_t(1)}{1+x_t(10)} \right] + (\alpha-\theta)\cdot x_t(6)\cdot sv_t(3); \ x_t(5); \ (\overline{A}+\rho(sv_t(3)-\overline{A})+e_{t+1}) \right].$$

Bringing all the variables in equations (A.30) to (A.44) to the left-hand side, the system can be represented as[32]

$$F(x_t, sv_t, E_t z_{t+1}) = 0. \qquad (A.49)$$

The next step is to note that the solution of the model relates actions to states via some nonlinear function:

$$x_t = \tilde{f}(sv_t). \qquad (A.50)$$

Also note that the expectational variables are functions of the next period's states and actions. Hence, the current value of z_t is also a function of the states:

$$z_t = f(sv_t). \qquad (A.51)$$

Then, using the law of motion for sv_t, z_{t+1} must be given by

$$z_{t+1} = f(g(x_t, sv_t, e_{t+1})). \qquad (A.52)$$

Plugging this into (A.49):

$$F(x_t, sv_t, E_t f(g(x_t, sv_t, e_{t+1}))) = 0. \qquad (A.53)$$

The main element of the collocation method is to approximate $E_t f(g(x_t, sv_t, e_{t+1}))$ by discretizing the state space and the stochastic distribution of the shocks. The procedure goes as follows. First, the true continuous distribution of e_t (using Gaussian Quadrature) is approximated with a discrete probability distribution with m realizations $\{e_1,\ldots,e_m\}$ and associated probabilities $\{prob_1,\ldots,prob_m\}$. Second, the function $f(\cdot)$ is approximated with a linear combination of n-degree Chebyshev polynomials:[33]

$$f(sv_t) \approx \sum_{j=1}^{n} c_j \phi_j(sv_t), \qquad (A.54)$$

where $\phi_j(sv_t)$ are polynomial basis functions and c_j are unknown coefficients. Thus, for any the system of equations (A.53) can be written as

$$F\left(x_t, sv_t, \sum_{k=1}^{m}\sum_{j=1}^{n} c_j \phi_j(g(x_t, sv_t, e_k)) prob_k\right) = 0, \qquad (A.55)$$

which is a deterministic system and can be solved for x_t given sv_t given the polynomial coefficients $c_j, j=1,\ldots,n$. The coefficients are solved for by discretizing the state space, i.e., by adopting n values (nodes) of the state vector along the state space, denote $\{sv_1,\ldots,sv_n\}$. Typically the nodes are chosen in the neighborhood of the steady state where the system is expected to evolve. The solution algorithm is as follows:
- First, guess the values of $c_j, j=1,\ldots,n$ and solve the system (A.55) at all nodes $\{sv_1,\ldots,sv_n\}$ given c_j's.
- Second, given the first step solution, record the contemporaneous values of z_t at each of the n nodes.
- Third, update the values of $c_j, j=1,\ldots,n$ by imposing the adopted approximation:

$$z_k = f(sv_k) = \sum_{j=1}^{n} c_j \phi_j(sv_k), \forall k=1,\ldots,n$$

(note that these are n linear equations in n unknown coefficients c_j, so updating c_j's is straightforward.)
- Finally, return to step 1 and iterate until convergence in c_j's is achieved.

[32]Note that if we knew how $E_t z_{t+1}$ is determined, then given the values of the state variables, we could determine agents' actions by solving a deterministic system above. The difficulty presented by the uncertainty is that $E_t z_{t+1}$ and x_t are jointly determined and need to be consistent with rational behavior.

[33]Recall that the Weierstrass theorem tells us that any continuous function can be approximated with a linear combination of polynomials with an arbitrary degree of accuracy.

References

Acemoglu, Daron, Simon Johnson, James Robinson and Yungyung Thaicharoen, 2003, "Institutional Causes, Macroeconomic Symptoms: Volatility, Crises and Growth," *Journal of Monetary Economics*, Vol. 50 (January), pp. 125–31.

Adam, Christopher, 2001, "Uganda: Exchange Rate Management, Monetary Policy and Aid" (unpublished; Bank of Uganda/UK Department for International Development).

———, and David L. Bevan, 2003, "Aid, Public Expenditure and Dutch Disease," Center for the Study of African Economies Working Paper No. 2003–02 (February).

Adam, Christopher, Stephen O'Connell, Edward Buffie, and Catherine Pattillo, 2006, "Monetary Policy Responses to Aid Surges in Africa," paper presented at the UNU-Wider Conference on Aid: Principles, Policies and Performance, Helsinki, June 16–17.

Adenauer, Isabelle, and Laurence Vagassky, 1998, "Aid and the Real Exchange Rate: Dutch Disease Effects in African Countries," *Intereconomics: Review of International Trade and Development*, Vol. 33 (July/August), pp. 177–85.

Adler, John H., 1965, "Absorptive Capacity: The Concept and its Determinants," *Brookings Institute Staff Paper* (Washington: Brookings Institution).

Agenor, Pierre-Richard, Nihal Bayraktar, and Karim El Aynaoui, 2005, "Roads Out of Poverty? Assessing the Links Between Aid, Public Investment, Growth and Poverty Reduction," World Bank Policy Research Working Paper No. 3490 (Washington: World Bank).

Arellano, Cristina, Aleš Bulíř, Timothy Lane, and Leslie Lipschitz, 2005, "The Dynamic Implications of Foreign Aid and Its Variability," IMF Working Paper No. 05/119 (Washington: International Monetary Fund).

Berg, Andrew, and Anne Krueger, 2003, "Trade, Growth and Poverty: A Selective Study," IMF Working Paper No. 03/30 (Washington: International Monetary Fund).

Berg, Andrew, Philippe Karam, and Douglas Laxton, 2006, "Practical Model-Based Monetary Policy Analysis: A How-To Guide," IMF Working Paper No. 06/81 (Washington: International Monetary Fund).

Berg, Elliot, 1961, "Backward Sloping Labor Supply Functions in Dual Economies: The Africa Case," *The Quarterly Journal of Economics,* Vol. 3, pp. 468–92.

———, 1983, "Absorptive Capacity in the Sahel Countries," Report to the Club Du Sahel (Paris: Organization for Economic Cooperation and Development).

Bevan, David L., 2005, "An Analytic Overview of Aid Absorption: Recognizing and Avoiding Macroeconomic Hazards," paper presented at the Seminar on Foreign Aid and Macroeconomic Management, Maputo, Mozambique, March 14–15.

Blanchard, Olivier, and Nobuhiro Kiyotaki, 1987, "Monopolistic Competition and the Effects of Aggregate Demand," *American Economic Review*, Vol. 77, pp. 647–66.

Bourguignon, François, Hans Lofgren, Maurizio Bussolo, Hans Timmer, and Dominique van der Mensbrugghe, 2005, "Building Absorptive Capacity to Meet the MDGs" (unpublished; Washington: World Bank).

Buffie, Edward, Christopher S. Adam, Stephen O'Connell, and Catherine Pattillo, 2004, "Exchange Rate Policy and the Management of Official and Private Capital Flows in Africa," *Staff Papers,* International Monetary Fund, Vol. 51, Special Issue.

Bulíř, Aleš, and Javier Hamann, forthcoming, "Volatility of Development Aid: From the Frying Pan into the Fire?" IMF Working Paper (Washington: International Monetary Fund).

Calvo, Guillermo, 1983, "Staggered Prices in a Utility Maximizing Framework," *Journal of Monetary Economics*, Vol. 12, pp. 383–98.

Carroll, Christopher, 2001, "Death to the Log-Linearized Consumption Euler Equation! And Very Poor Health to the Second-Order Approximation," *Advances in Macroeconomics,* Vol. 1, No. 1.

Celasun, Oya, and Jan Walliser, 2005, "Predictability of Budget Aid: Experiences in Eight African Countries," paper prepared for the World Bank Practitioners' Forum on Budget Support, May, Cape Town, South Africa.

Chowdhury A., and T. Mckinley, 2006, "Gearing Macroeconomic Policies to Manage Large Inflows of ODA: Implications for HIV/AIDS Programmes," International Poverty Center Working Paper No. 17.

Clemens, Michael, Steven Radelet, and Rikhil Bhavnani, 2004, "Counting Chickens When they Hatch: The Short-Term Effect of Aid on Growth," Center for Global Development Working Paper 44 (Washington: Center for Global Development).

Clement, Jean A.P., 2005, *Postconflict Economics in Sub-Saharan Africa, Lessons from the Democratic Republic of the Congo* (Washington: International Monetary Fund).

Deninger, K., and J. Okidi, 2001, "Rural Households: Incomes, Productivity and Nonfarm Enterprises," in *Uganda's Recovery: The Role of Farms, Firms and Government*, ed. by R. Reinikka and P. Collier (Washington: World Bank).

Easterly, William, Ross Levin, and David Roodman, 2003, "New Data, New Doubts: A Comment on Burnside's and Dollar's 'Aid, Policies and Growth'," NBER Working Paper No. 9846 (Cambridge, Massachusetts: National Bureau of Economic Research).

Elbadawi, Ibrahim A., 1999, "External Aid: Help or Hindrance to Export Orientation in Africa?" *Journal of African Economies*, Vol. 8, No. 4, pp. 578–616.

———, 2002, "Real Exchange Rate Policy and Non-Traditional Exports in Developing Countries" in *Non-Traditional Export Promotion in Africa: Experience and Issues*, ed. by Gerald Helleiner (New York: Palgrave).

Fanizza, Domenico, 2001, "Foreign Aid, Macroeconomic Stabilization, and Growth in Malawi," *IMF Seminar Series* No. 07 (January), pp. 1–21 (Washington: International Monetary Fund).

Foster, Mick, and Tony Killick, 2006, "What Would Doubling Aid do for Macroeconomic Management in Africa?" ODI Working Paper 264 (London: Overseas Development Institute).

Gapen, Michael T., and Thomas F. Cosimano, 2005, "Solving Ramsey Problems with Nonlinear Projection Methods," *Studies in Nonlinear Dynamics and Econometrics*, Vol. 9, No. 2.

Guillaumont, Patrick, 1971, *L'absorption du Capital* (Paris: Cujas).

———, and Lisa Chauvet, 2001, "Aid and Performance: A Reassessment," *Journal of Development Studies*, Vol. 37, No. 6 (August), pp. 66–92.

Gupta, Sanjeev, Benedict Clements, Alexander Pivovarsky, Erwin R. Tiongson, 2003, "Foreign Aid and Revenue Response: Does the Composition of Aid Matter?" IMF Working Paper No. 03/176 (Washington: International Monetary Fund).

Gupta, Sanjeev, Robert Powell, and Yongzheng Yang, 2005, "The Macroeconomic Challenges of Scaling Up Aid to Africa," IMF Working Paper No. 05/179 (Washington: International Monetary Fund).

Hausmann, Ricardo, Lant Pritchett, and Dani Rodrik, 2004, "Growth Accelerations," NBER Working Paper No.10566 (Cambridge, Massachusetts: National Bureau of Economic Research).

Heller, Peter, 2005, "Pity the Finance Minister: Issues in Managing a Substantial Scaling Up of Aid Flows," IMF Working Paper No. 05/180 (Washington: International Monetary Fund).

———, and Sanjeev Gupta, 2002, "Challenges in Expanding Development Assistance," IMF Policy Discussion Paper 02/5 (Washington: International Monetary Fund).

International Monetary Fund, 2003a, "Fund Assistance for Countries Facing Exogenous Shocks" (unpublished; Washington: International Monetary Fund).

———, 2003b, "Tanzania—Financial System Stability Assessment" (unpublished; Washington: International Monetary Fund).

———, 2004, "The Federal Democratic Republic of Ethiopia—Ex Post Assessment of Long-Term Fund Engagement" (unpublished; Washington: International Monetary Fund).

———, 2005a, "The Macroeconomics of Managing High Aid Inflows," IMF Policy Paper (August). Available via the Internet: http://www.imf.org/external/np/pp/eng/2005/080805a.pdf.

———, 2005b, "Update on the Assessments and Implementation of Action Plans to Strengthen Capacity of HIPCs to Track Poverty-Reducing Public Spending" (unpublished; Washington: International Monetary Fund).

———, 2006, "United Republic of Tanzania—Ex Post Assessment of Longer-Term Program Engagement" (unpublished; Washington: International Monetary Fund).

International Monetary Fund Independent Evaluation Office, 2004, "Evaluation of the IMF's Role in Poverty Reduction Strategy Papers (PRSPs) and the Poverty Reduction and Growth Facility (PRGF)" (Washington: International Monetary Fund).

Isard, Peter, Leslie Lipschitz, Alexandros Mourmouras, and Boriana Yontcheva, eds., 2006, *The Macroeconomic Management of Foreign Aid: Opportunities and Pitfalls* (Washington: International Monetary Fund).

Kappel, R., J. Lay, and S. Steiner, 2005, "Uganda: No More Pro-Poor Growth?" *Development Policy Review*, Vol. 23, No. 1.

Keynes, John Maynard, 1929, "The German Transfer Problem," *Economic Journal,* Vol. 39 (March), pp. 1–7.

Kim, Jinill, and Sunghyun Henry Kim, 2003, "Spurious Welfare Reversals in International Business Cycle Models," *Journal of International Economics,* Vol. 60, Issue 2 (August), pp. 471–500.

Klein, Michael, and Tim Harford, 2005, *The Market for Aid* (Washington: World Bank).

Leite, Carlos, and Charalambos Tsangarides, forthcoming, "Infrastructure for Developing Countries: The Growth Pill?" IMF Working Paper (Washington: International Monetary Fund).

McGillivray, Mark, and Oliver Morrissey, 2001, "Fiscal Effects of Aid," WIDER Discussion Paper 2001/61(August), (Helsinki: World Institute for Development Economics Research, United Nations University).

Milesi-Ferretti, Gian Maria, and Philip R. Lane, 2004, "The Transfer Problem Revisited: Net Foreign Assets and Real Exchange Rates," *Review of Economics and Statistics,* Vol. 86 (November), No. 4, pp. 841–57.

Miranda, Mario J. and Paul L. Fackler, 2002, *Applied Computational Economics and Finance* (Cambridge, Massachusetts: MIT Press).

Mohanty, M.S., and Philip Turner, 2006, "The Global Economy and Africa: The Challenges of Increased Financial Inflows," paper presented at conference on Central Banks and the Challenge of Development, Bank for International Settlements, Basel, March 14–15. Available via the Internet: http://www.bis.org/events/cbcd06.htm.

Nkusu, Mwanza, 2004a, "Aid and Dutch Disease in Low-Income Countries: Informed Diagnosis for Prudent Prognoses," IMF Working Paper No. 04/49 (Washington: International Monetary Fund).

———, 2004b, "Financing Uganda's Poverty Reduction Strategy: Is Aid Causing More Pain Than Gain?" IMF Working Paper No. 04/170 (Washington: International Monetary Fund).

Nyoni, Timothy S., 1998, "Foreign Aid and Economic Performance in Tanzania," *World Development*, Vol. 26, No. 7, pp. 1235–240.

Obstfeld, Maurice, and Kenneth Rogoff, 1995, "Exchange Rate Dynamics Redux," *Journal of Political Economy,* Vol. 103 (June), pp. 624–60.

O'Connell, Stephen A., Christopher Adam, Edward F. Buffie, and Catherine A. Pattillo, 2006, "Managing External Volatility: Central Bank Options in Low-Income Countries," in *Monetary Policy in Emerging Markets and Other Developing Countries,* ed. by Nicoletta Batini (Hauppauge, New York: Nova Science Publishers).

Ogun, Oluremi, 1995, "Real Exchange Rate Movements and Export Growth: Nigeria, 1960-1990" (unpublished; Nairobi: African Economic Research Consortium).

Ouattara, Bazoumana, and Eric Strobl, 2003, "Do Aid Inflows Cause Dutch Disease? A Case Study of the CFA Franc Countries Using Dynamic Panel Analysis," Manchester University School of Economics Discussion Paper Series No. 0330 (Manchester, UK: Manchester University).

Prati, Alessandro, and Thierry Tressel, 2005, "What Monetary Policy for Aid-Receiving Countries?" Paper presented at the DESAA Development Forum on Integrating Economic and Social Policies to Achieve the United Nations Development Agenda, March 14–15.

Rajan, Raghuram, and Arvind Subramanian, 2005a, "What Undermines Aid's Impact on Growth?" IMF Working Paper No. 05/126 (Washington: International Monetary Fund).

———, 2005b, "Aid and Growth: What Does the Cross-Country Evidence Really Show?" IMF Working Paper No. 05/127 (Washington: International Monetary Fund).

Sackey, Harry A., 2001, "External Aid Inflows and the Real Exchange Rate in Ghana," AERC Paper No. 110 (November) (Nairobi: African Economic Research Consortium).

Sekkat, Khalid, and Aristomene Varoudakis, 2000, "Exchange Rate Management and Manufactured Exports in Sub-Saharan Africa," *Journal of Development Economics*, Vol. 61, No. 1, pp. 237–53.

Selassie, Abebe A., Benedict Clements, Shamsuddin Tareq, Jan Kees Martijn, and Gabriel Di Bella, 2006, *Designing Monetary and Fiscal Policy in Low-Income Countries,* IMF Occasional Paper No. 250 (Washington: International Monetary Fund).

Torvik, Ragnar, 2001, "Learning by Doing and the Dutch Disease," *European Economic Review,* Vol. 45, No. 2, pp. 285–306.

United Nations, 2006, "Dealing with the Macroeconomic Impact of the Scaling up of Aid," background paper for a conference of African ministers of finance entitled "Financing for Development: From Commitment to Action," May 21–22, Abuja, Nigeria. Available via the Internet: http://www.financingmdgsconference. org/session_papers.

United Nations Millennium Project, 2005, *Investing in Development: A Practical Plan to Achieve the Millennium Development Goals* (New York: United Nations Development Program).

White, Howard, and Ganeshan Wignaraja, 1992, "Exchange Rates, Trade Liberalization and Aid: The Sri Lankan Experience," *World Development,* Vol. 20, No. 10 (October), pp. 1471–480.

World Bank and International Monetary Fund, 2005, *Global Monitoring Report—MDGs: From Consensus to Momentum* (Washington: World Bank and International Monetary Fund).

Recent Occasional Papers of the International Monetary Fund

253. The Macroeconomics of Scaling Up Aid: Lessons from Recent Experience, by Andrew Berg, Shekhar Aiyar, Mumtaz Hussain, Shaun Roache, Tokhir Mirzoev, and Amber Mahone. 2007.
252. Growth in the Central and Eastern European Countries of the European Union, by Susan Schadler, Ashoka Mody, Abdul Abiad, and Daniel Leigh. 2006.
251. The Design and Implementation of Deposit Insurance Systems, by David S. Hoelscher, Michael Taylor, and Ulrich H. Klueh. 2006.
250. Designing Monetary and Fiscal Policy in Low-Income Countries, by Abebe Aemro Selassie, Benedict Clements, Shamsuddin Tareq, Jan Kees Martijn, and Gabriel Di Bella. 2006.
249. Official Foreign Exchange Intervention, by Shogo Ishi, Jorge Iván Canales-Kriljenko, Roberto Guimarães, and Cem Karacadag. 2006.
248. Labor Market Performance in Transition: The Experience of Central and Eastern European Countries, by Jerald Schiff, Philippe Egoumé-Bossogo, Miho Ihara, Tetsuya Konuki, and Kornélia Krajnyák. 2006.
247. Rebuilding Fiscal Institutions in Post-Conflict Countries, by Sanjeev Gupta, Shamsuddin Tareq, Benedict Clements, Alex Segura-Ubiergo, Rina Bhattacharya, and Todd Mattina. 2005.
246. Experience with Large Fiscal Adjustments, by George C. Tsibouris, Mark A. Horton, Mark J. Flanagan, and Wojciech S. Maliszewski. 2005.
245. Budget System Reform in Emerging Economies: The Challenges and the Reform Agenda, by Jack Diamond. 2005.
244. Monetary Policy Implementation at Different Stages of Market Development, by a staff team led by Bernard J. Laurens. 2005.
243. Central America: Global Integration and Regional Cooperation, edited by Markus Rodlauer and Alfred Schipke. 2005.
242. Turkey at the Crossroads: From Crisis Resolution to EU Accession, by a staff team led by Reza Moghadam. 2005.
241. The Design of IMF-Supported Programs, by Atish Ghosh, Charis Christofides, Jun Kim, Laura Papi, Uma Ramakrishnan, Alun Thomas, and Juan Zalduendo. 2005.
240. Debt-Related Vulnerabilities and Financial Crises: An Application of the Balance Sheet Approach to Emerging Market Countries, by Christoph Rosenberg, Ioannis Halikias, Brett House, Christian Keller, Jens Nystedt, Alexander Pitt, and Brad Setser. 2005.
239. GEM: A New International Macroeconomic Model, by Tamim Bayoumi, with assistance from Douglas Laxton, Hamid Faruqee, Benjamin Hunt, Philippe Karam, Jaewoo Lee, Alessandro Rebucci, and Ivan Tchakarov. 2004.
238. Stabilization and Reforms in Latin America: A Macroeconomic Perspective on the Experience Since the Early 1990s, by Anoop Singh, Agnès Belaisch, Charles Collyns, Paula De Masi, Reva Krieger, Guy Meredith, and Robert Rennhack. 2005.
237. Sovereign Debt Structure for Crisis Prevention, by Eduardo Borensztein, Marcos Chamon, Olivier Jeanne, Paolo Mauro, and Jeromin Zettelmeyer. 2004.
236. Lessons from the Crisis in Argentina, by Christina Daseking, Atish R. Ghosh, Alun Thomas, and Timothy Lane. 2004.
235. A New Look at Exchange Rate Volatility and Trade Flows, by Peter B. Clark, Natalia Tamirisa, and Shang-Jin Wei, with Azim Sadikov and Li Zeng. 2004.
234. Adopting the Euro in Central Europe: Challenges of the Next Step in European Integration, by Susan M. Schadler, Paulo F. Drummond, Louis Kuijs, Zuzana Murgasova, and Rachel N. van Elkan. 2004.
233. Germany's Three-Pillar Banking System: Cross-Country Perspectives in Europe, by Allan Brunner, Jörg Decressin, Daniel Hardy, and Beata Kudela. 2004.
232. China's Growth and Integration into the World Economy: Prospects and Challenges, edited by Eswar Prasad. 2004.
231. Chile: Policies and Institutions Underpinning Stability and Growth, by Eliot Kalter, Steven Phillips, Marco A. Espinosa-Vega, Rodolfo Luzio, Mauricio Villafuerte, and Manmohan Singh. 2004.
230. Financial Stability in Dollarized Countries, by Anne-Marie Gulde, David Hoelscher, Alain Ize, David Marston, and Gianni De Nicoló. 2004.
229. Evolution and Performance of Exchange Rate Regimes, by Kenneth S. Rogoff, Aasim M. Husain, Ashoka Mody, Robin Brooks, and Nienke Oomes. 2004.
228. Capital Markets and Financial Intermediation in The Baltics, by Alfred Schipke, Christian Beddies, Susan M. George, and Niamh Sheridan. 2004.

227. U.S. Fiscal Policies and Priorities for Long-Run Sustainability, edited by Martin Mühleisen and Christopher Towe. 2004.
226. Hong Kong SAR: Meeting the Challenges of Integration with the Mainland, edited by Eswar Prasad, with contributions from Jorge Chan-Lau, Dora Iakova, William Lee, Hong Liang, Ida Liu, Papa N'Diaye, and Tao Wang. 2004.
225. Rules-Based Fiscal Policy in France, Germany, Italy, and Spain, by Teresa Dában, Enrica Detragiache, Gabriel di Bella, Gian Maria Milesi-Ferretti, and Steven Symansky. 2003.
224. Managing Systemic Banking Crises, by a staff team led by David S. Hoelscher and Marc Quintyn. 2003.
223. Monetary Union Among Member Countries of the Gulf Cooperation Council, by a staff team led by Ugo Fasano. 2003.
222. Informal Funds Transfer Systems: An Analysis of the Informal Hawala System, by Mohammed El Qorchi, Samuel Munzele Maimbo, and John F. Wilson. 2003.
221. Deflation: Determinants, Risks, and Policy Options, by Manmohan S. Kumar. 2003.
220. Effects of Financial Globalization on Developing Countries: Some Empirical Evidence, by Eswar S. Prasad, Kenneth Rogoff, Shang-Jin Wei, and Ayhan Kose. 2003.
219. Economic Policy in a Highly Dollarized Economy: The Case of Cambodia, by Mario de Zamaroczy and Sopanha Sa. 2003.
218. Fiscal Vulnerability and Financial Crises in Emerging Market Economies, by Richard Hemming, Michael Kell, and Axel Schimmelpfennig. 2003.
217. Managing Financial Crises: Recent Experience and Lessons for Latin America, edited by Charles Collyns and G. Russell Kincaid. 2003.
216. Is the PRGF Living Up to Expectations? An Assessment of Program Design, by Sanjeev Gupta, Mark Plant, Benedict Clements, Thomas Dorsey, Emanuele Baldacci, Gabriela Inchauste, Shamsuddin Tareq, and Nita Thacker. 2002.
215. Improving Large Taxpayers' Compliance: A Review of Country Experience, by Katherine Baer. 2002.
214. Advanced Country Experiences with Capital Account Liberalization, by Age Bakker and Bryan Chapple. 2002.
213. The Baltic Countries: Medium-Term Fiscal Issues Related to EU and NATO Accession, by Johannes Mueller, Christian Beddies, Robert Burgess, Vitali Kramarenko, and Joannes Mongardini. 2002.
212. Financial Soundness Indicators: Analytical Aspects and Country Practices, by V. Sundararajan, Charles Enoch, Armida San José, Paul Hilbers, Russell Krueger, Marina Moretti, and Graham Slack. 2002.
211. Capital Account Liberalization and Financial Sector Stability, by a staff team led by Shogo Ishii and Karl Habermeier. 2002.
210. IMF-Supported Programs in Capital Account Crises, by Atish Ghosh, Timothy Lane, Marianne Schulze-Ghattas, Aleš Bulíř, Javier Hamann, and Alex Mourmouras. 2002.
209. Methodology for Current Account and Exchange Rate Assessments, by Peter Isard, Hamid Faruqee, G. Russell Kincaid, and Martin Fetherston. 2001.
208. Yemen in the 1990s: From Unification to Economic Reform, by Klaus Enders, Sherwyn Williams, Nada Choueiri, Yuri Sobolev, and Jan Walliser. 2001.
207. Malaysia: From Crisis to Recovery, by Kanitta Meesook, Il Houng Lee, Olin Liu, Yougesh Khatri, Natalia Tamirisa, Michael Moore, and Mark H. Krysl. 2001.
206. The Dominican Republic: Stabilization, Structural Reform, and Economic Growth, by a staff team led by Philip Young comprising Alessandro Giustiniani, Werner C. Keller, and Randa E. Sab and others. 2001.
205. Stabilization and Savings Funds for Nonrenewable Resources, by Jeffrey Davis, Rolando Ossowski, James Daniel, and Steven Barnett. 2001.

Note: For information on the titles and availability of Occasional Papers not listed, please consult the IMF's *Publications Catalog* or contact IMF Publication Services.